Incommensurability and Its Implications for Practical Reasoning, Ethics and Justice

Values and Identities: Crossing Philosophical Borders

Series Editors:

Paul Crowther, Professor of Philosophy at the National University of Ireland, Galway

Tsarina Doyle, Lecturer in Philosophy at the National University of Ireland, Galway

How do values define human identity and the different activities through which this identity finds expression? *Values and Identities: Crossing Philosophical Borders* publishes research-led monographs and edited collections that face this problem head on. Titles in this series investigate specific forms of value and, in particular, how they interact across societal contexts to form more complex identities.

Titles in the Series:

Virtue as Identity: Emotions and the Moral Personality, Aleksandar Fatić

Human Value, Environmental Ethics and Sustainability: The Precautionary Ecosystem Health Principle, Mark Ryan

Normative Identity, Per Bauhn

The Value of Money: The Metaphysics of Financial Value, Eyja M. Brynjarsdottir (forthcoming)

Incommensurability and Its Implications for Practical Reasoning, Ethics and Justice
Martijn Boot

Incommensurability and Its Implications for Practical Reasoning, Ethics and Justice

Martijn Boot

London · New York

Published by Rowman & Littlefield International Ltd
Unit A, Whitacre Mews, 26–34 Stannary Street, London SE11 4AB
www.rowmaninternational.com

Rowman & Littlefield International Ltd. is an affiliate of Rowman & Littlefield
4501 Forbes Boulevard, Suite 200, Lanham, Maryland 20706, USA
With additional offices in Boulder, New York, Toronto (Canada), and Plymouth (UK)
www.rowman.com

Copyright © 2017 Martijn Boot

All rights reserved. No part of this book may be reproduced in any form or by any electronic or mechanical means, including information storage and retrieval systems, without written permission from the publisher, except by a reviewer who may quote passages in a review.

British Library Cataloguing-in-Publication Data
A catalogue record for this book is available from the British Library

ISBN: HB 978-1-7866-0227-5

Library of Congress Cataloging-in-Publication Data Available
ISBN: 978-1-78660-227-5 (cloth : alk. paper)
ISBN: 978-1-78660-228-2 (paperback)
ISBN: 978-1-78660-229-9 (electronic)

∞™ The paper used in this publication meets the minimum requirements of American National Standard for Information Sciences – Permanence of Paper for Printed Library Materials, ANSI/NISO Z39.48–1992.

Printed in the United States of America

Contents

Acknowledgements		vii
Introduction		1
PART 1: INCOMMENSURABILITY AND ITS IMPLICATIONS FOR PRACTICAL REASONING		**5**
1	Incommensurability and Incomplete Comparability	7
2	Spurious Challenges	31
3	Real Challenges: Imprecise Equality and Parity versus Incomplete Comparability	37
4	Implications of Incomplete Comparability for Practical Reasoning	53
PART 2: IMPLICATIONS OF INCOMMENSURABILITY FOR PUBLIC DECISION-MAKING, ETHICS AND JUSTICE		**69**
5	Conflicts of Justice	71
6	Rival Theories of Justice	89
7	Implications of Incommensurability for John Rawls's Theory of Justice	97
8	Do We Need a Theory of Justice? A Reply to Amartya Sen	149
9	Equity and Efficiency in Health Care	167
10	Legitimacy versus Integrity	175
11	Partial Justice	197

12 Autonomy and Recognition	211
Glossary	219
Bibliography	227
Index	235
About the Author	239

Acknowledgements

This book is the result of long-lasting research on incommensurability of values. I started with a doctoral research at Balliol College, Oxford University, which was supervised by G. A. Cohen and Joseph Raz. The study was funded by an award of the *Arts and Humanities Research Council*. I described the results in my DPhil dissertation entitled *Incommensurability, Incomplete Comparability and the Scales of Justice*. A large part of the present book is based on this dissertation. I continued my research at the University of Chicago, the Erasmus University Rotterdam and the Waseda University in Tokyo. At the Erasmus University I participated in a project named 'Transition from Ideal to Nonideal Theories of Justice', supervised by Ingrid Robeyns. This project was financed by a grant of the Netherlands Organization for Scientific Research (NWO). Chapter 8 of this book is the result of my participation in the Erasmus University project.

I am grateful to the philosophers who constructively commented on (parts of) drafts of earlier texts: Elizabeth Anderson, Monika Betzler, Dan Brock, John Broome, Ruth Chang, G. A. Cohen, Roger Crisp, Norman Daniels, Joshua Gert, John Gray, James Griffin, Daniel Hausman, Frances Kamm, Daniel McDermott, David Miller, Martha Nussbaum, Derek Parfit, Martin Peterson, Wlodek Rabinowicz, Joseph Raz, Henry Richardson, Ingrid Robeyns, Debra Satz, Adam Swift and several anonymous reviewers.

(Parts of) the following articles are reprinted in this book by permission of the publisher:

- 'Problems of Incommensurability', *Social Theory and Practice* 43 (2017): 313–342.
- 'The Right Balance', *The Journal of Value Inquiry* 51 (2017): 13–32.

- 'The Aim of a Theory of Justice', *Ethical Theory and Moral Practice* 15 (2012): 7–21.
- 'Parity, Incomparability and Rationally Justified Choice', *Philosophical Studies* 146 (2009): 75–92.

Introduction

If values conflict and rival human interests clash we often have to weigh them against each other. A central issue of the contemporary philosophical debate on incommensurability concerns the question whether values, if they are incommensurable, can be rationally weighed and whether conflicts between these values can be rationally resolved. Many philosophers believe that this question can be answered affirmatively. One of the aims of this book is to show that this is not always true. Under particular conditions incommensurable values cause problems for comparability of options and rational resolution of value conflicts.

The literature about incommensurability is extensive. Still it has three shortcomings. First, it contains misunderstandings about the nature of the implications of incommensurability for practical reason. The resulting confusion is a cause of continuing disagreement on these implications. Second, there is surprisingly little attention to consequences of incommensurability of values for public decision-making, ethics and justice. Third, the literature on incommensurability is usually written in unnecessarily technical language and difficult to understand for readers who are not fully initiated into the matter. This is a pity because the subject is important and interesting to a wide audience of philosophers, ethicists, political theorists, economists and public policymakers. This book will try to bridge these three gaps. First, I will clarify and continue contemporary debates about incommensurability. One of the central aims is to show the relation between incommensurability of values and what might be called 'incomplete comparability' of options. Second, a large part of the book (part 2) will discuss possible implications of incommensurability for public decision-making, ethics and justice. Third, I have tried to avoid unnecessary technical language so that the book is accessible and comprehensible not only for specialists but also for a large audience of interested theorists and students in the fields of ethics, justice, economics and politics. Besides I have added a glossary in which the key notions are defined and explained.

This book challenges the widespread belief that incommensurability of values does not cause significant problems for comparison of options and practical decision-making.[1] I will show that incommensurability is a central, although not sufficient, condition of 'incomplete comparability'. The theses I defend may be challenged in different ways. I make a distinction between spurious challenges (based on misunderstandings and confusions) and real challenges (based on pertinent and valid arguments). The discussion of these challenges will help to further illuminate the issues and to remove misunderstandings. I will pay due attention to a fundamental but often ignored or unrecognized characteristic of incommensurable values, namely, the absence of any equivalence relation: no amount of one value is equivalent to any, even rough, amount of the other value. This may create problems for impartially weighing incommensurable values and options. As far as I know, implications of incommensurability for public decision-making and especially for justice have never been systematically investigated. This is remarkable because these areas are often concerned with weighing conflicting incommensurable values and rival human interests.

STRUCTURE OF THE BOOK

The book has two parts. Part 1 discusses incommensurability of values, incomplete comparability of options and the implications for practical reasoning. Part 2 is devoted to possible consequences for public decision-making, ethics and justice. Some chapters have small overlaps to avoid the need of going back to earlier explanations. Each chapter is preceded by a summary of its most important claims. The topics of part 1 are the following.

- Relation between incommensurability and incomplete comparability (chapter 1)
- Spurious challenges of the incomplete comparability thesis (chapter 2)
- Real challenges: imprecise equality and parity versus incomplete comparability (chapter 3)
- Implications of incomplete comparability for practical reasoning and rational justification of the choice (chapter 4)

The theoretical conclusions of part 1 are applied to concrete issues of part 2, such as 'conflicts of justice' (chapter 5), comparisons of rival theories of justice (chapter 6), implications of incommensurability for John Rawls's theory of justice (chapter 7), the need of a theory of justice (chapter 8), equity versus efficiency in the allocation of scarce health care resources (chapter 9), legitimacy versus integrity in the public/private split (chapter 10). Chapter 11 discusses the question whether justice and jurisdiction are always capable of weighing competing ethical demands and principles impartially and decisively. The trial against the Dutch politician Geert Wilders is taken as a concrete and topical example. The final chapter (chapter 12) shows that incommensurability and incomplete comparability have not only problematic but also important positive implications. They create room for autonomous choices – choices that are not dictated by but remain within the constraints of reason. I will make a connection with the contemporary free will debate, especially the issue of alternative possibilities as a condition of free will. Another positive aspect of insight into the issue of competing incommensurable values is that it makes us aware of a plurality of weighty human values that cannot be reduced to or traded off against each other without loss of irreducible value. This promotes recognition of different possible rankings of universally valid human values and ethical principles. In contrast with toleration (which has a negative connotation) and value relativism (which makes all human values context-dependent), recognition and value pluralism are positive concepts that generate respect for the differences in weights assigned to human values by different persons, societies and cultures. This may help to promote a peaceful coexistence between people, recognizing each other in their ordering of universally valid but sometimes conflicting human values.

HOW TO READ THIS BOOK?

Because each chapter is preceded by a brief summary, the reader can get a quick survey of the book's line of reasoning by reading the summaries of the twelve chapters. The central ideas are described in chapters 1, 4, 5 and 12. If the reader is mainly interested in these ideas and less in the challenges and specific applications he or she can limit himself or herself to these chapters without losing the thread of the argumentation.

NOTE

1. Philosophers who largely deny significant problems of incommensurability for practical reason are, among others, Ruth Chang, 'Introduction', in *Incommensurability, Incomparability, and Practical Reason*, ed. Ruth Chang (Cambridge, Mass.: Harvard University Press, 1997), 1–34; James Griffin, 'Incommensurability: What's the Problem?' in *Incommensurability, Incomparability, and Practical Reason*, ed.

Chang, 35–51; Nien-hê Hsieh, 'Is Incomparability a Problem for Anyone?' *Economics and Philosophy* 23 (2007): 65–80; Henry Richardson, *Practical Reasoning about Final Ends* (Cambridge: Cambridge University Press, 1997), chapter VI; Amartya Sen, 'Incompleteness and Reasoned Choice', *Synthese* 140 (2004): 43–59; Michael Stocker, *Plural and Conflicting Values* (Oxford: Oxford University Press, 1999). Also Joseph Raz who believes that 'incommensurability of the value of options is a pervasive feature with far-reaching theoretical consequences', nevertheless thinks that incommensurability does not prevent a completely justified and rational choice. See Joseph Raz, 'Incommensurability and Agency', in *Incommensurability, Incomparability, and Practical Reason*, ed. Chang, 128.

Part 1

INCOMMENSURABILITY AND ITS IMPLICATIONS FOR PRACTICAL REASONING

Chapter 1

Incommensurability and Incomplete Comparability

SUMMARY

A central characteristic of two incommensurable values is the absence of any equivalence relation: no amount of one value is equivalent – not even roughly equivalent – to any amount of the other value. Many philosophers deny a relation between incommensurability and incomparability. This is not correct. Incommensurability of values is an important, although not sufficient, cause of what might be called 'incomplete comparability' of alternatives for choice. Two options A and B are incompletely comparable, if it is simultaneously (1) not true that A is better than B, (2) not true that A is worse than B and (3) not true that A is (roughly) equally good as B. I refer to this value relation as '3NT' ('triply not true'). This 3NT value relation may be the cause of significant problems of incommensurability for rational decision making and complete justification of the choice – problems that are discussed in chapter 4.

****

Incommensurability literally means 'inability to be compared by a common standard'. There are different versions of incommensurability, such as semantic, mathematical and value-incommensurability. When I use the notion 'incommensurability' without further specification, I mean 'incommensurability of values', which is the topic of this book. Incommensurability and commensurability of values can be defined as follows.

Incommensurability

Two values are incommensurable if they have different dimensions that cannot be reduced to each other or to a common dimension so that their amounts cannot be measured and compared on a common cardinal scale of units of value.

Commensurability

Two values are commensurable if they can be reduced to each other or to a one-dimensional 'super-value' (e.g., pleasure or monetary value), so that their amounts can be measured and compared on a common cardinal scale of units of value.

These definitions need further explanation. A key notion is 'dimension'. Dimension means a measurable extent. Disparate values differ in dimensions. For instance, a dimension of freedom differs from a dimension of equality, and dimensions of quality of a work of art differ from dimensions of quality of food. The amounts of a value may differ. For instance, the amounts of a particular freedom, say freedom of speech or freedom of movement, may vary from small to large. If we compare two alternatives for choice, for instance, two restaurants, we compare them with respect to the relevant values, for instance, quality of food and quality of decor. These values have different dimensions. This means that the extent of quality of food is expressed in another dimension (unit of value) than the extent of quality of decor, just as the extent of unlike physical measures, such as length and weight, is expressed in disparate dimensions. Just as length cannot be measured in units of weight, and vice versa, so can amounts of unlike human values not be measured on one and the same scale of units of a particular dimension, unless they can be reduced to each other or to a common one-dimensional value (e.g., pleasure or monetary value). In the latter case, the values are commensurable. Otherwise they are incommensurable. Another phrase in the previous definitions is 'cardinal scale'. A cardinal scale measures amounts of values, expressed in quantities of units of value. It should be distinguished from an ordinal scale – a list of rankings in terms of 'more/less value' or 'more/less importance' – terms that do not indicate how much the amounts of value differ in quantities of units of value. As we will see, incommensurability excludes measurements and comparisons on a common cardinal scale, but not necessarily on a common ordinal scale.

Some theorists identify incommensurability with incomparability.[1] Many others deny a relation between these notions.[2] This chapter, and chapters 2 and 3, will show why the latter view is not correct. Also the former view is not entirely correct because many options that bear incommensurable values are comparable. Take, for example, two restaurants: restaurant A, which has excellent food, and restaurant B, which has inferior food but a slightly nicer decor. Although quality of food and quality of decor are incommensurable values, comparison of the options is not difficult: other things being equal, restaurant A is overall better than restaurant B. To give another example, take two societies: A and B. The citizens of society A have basic liberties (e.g., freedom of movement, speech and religion) and amply sufficient economic welfare to live a decent life. The citizens of society B have somewhat more economic welfare but lack basic liberties. Incommensurability of the values 'economic welfare' and 'basic liberties' does not prevent the comparability of the two societies: society A can be ranked higher than society B, assuming that basic liberties are more important than somewhat increased welfare above a level that is already amply sufficient. Because of the many cases in which incommensurable values do not cause any problem for the comparability of options, several theorists tend to trivialize the relation between incommensurability and incomparability. For instance, Michael Stocker points at the omnipresence of unproblematic incommensurability as an indirect argument against difficulties for rational decision making and rational justification of choices.[3] Similarly, Amartya Sen finds it regrettable that in the literature so much attention is paid to something that is so 'omnipresent' and has so 'little discriminating relevance' as incommensurability.[4] He argues:

> Noncommensurability can hardly be a remarkable discovery in the world in which we live. And it need not, by itself, make it very hard to choose sensibly. For example, a fine mango may give us nutrition as well as some palatal or olfactory pleasure, whereas buying the record of a good song may offer a very different reward (not immediately reducible into the dimensions of the other) . . . and yet we may have no great difficulty in opting for the mango when immensely hungry or starved, and going for the song, when well endowed with tasty food but short of melodious entertainment. The choice need not be hard to make in many situations, despite the non-commensurability involved. The distinct dimensions of values may not be reducible into one another, and yet there may be no problem whatsoever in deciding what one should sensibly do when our priorities or weights over these values are clear enough.[5]

Sen's and Stocker's arguments against the significance of incommensurability for practical reasoning and justified choice are based on the misunderstanding that if A is omnipresent and often does not cause B, A cannot be an important cause of B. This fails to recognize that a cause may be important without being sufficient. Many people smoke, but many smokers do not get lung cancer. The explanation is that smoking is an insufficient, instead of unimportant, cause of lung cancer. We shall see that incommensurability is the central, although not sufficient, cause of what I call 'incomplete comparability'. In addition to incommensurability, the satisfaction of additional conditions is required for incomplete comparability. Presently we will discuss these conditions. Ruth Chang gives several examples in support of the view that incommensurability does not pose problems for the comparability of options.[6] However, these examples lack at least one of the two additional conditions of 'incomplete comparability'. In the previous quotation Sen argues that incommensurability can 'hardly be a remarkable discovery' because – although 'the distinct dimensions of values may not be reducible into one another' – 'there may be no problem whatsoever in deciding what one should sensibly do when our priorities or weights over these values are clear enough'. However, assignment of the right priorities and weights is precisely the central problem of incommensurability if the additional conditions are satisfied.

INCOMPLETE COMPARABILITY

If A and B are incomparable, A is neither better than, nor worse than, nor equally good as, B: otherwise A and B would not be incomparable. Conversely, if A is neither better than, nor worse than, nor equally good as, B, it may be a sign – although it does not logically demonstrate – that A and B are incomparable (for reasons that I will mention later, I prefer the notion 'incomplete comparability' to 'incomparability'). In line with this thought, which I will further substantiate, I define 'incomplete comparability' as follows.

Incomplete comparability

Two options A and B are *incompletely comparable* if – all things considered and in an impartial and objective perspective – it is simultaneously

(i) not true that A is (definitely) better than B,
(ii) not true that A is (definitely) worse than B,
(iii) not true that A and B are (roughly) equally good.

Call this threefold denial '3NT' (triply not true).

Some terms in the definition need an explanation. Option A is '(definitely) better' than option B if reason shows that it is better to choose A instead of B (so that it is irrational or less rational to choose B rather than A), and A is 'definitely worse' than B if reason shows that it is better to choose B instead of A (so that it is irrational or less rational to choose A rather than B). 'Impartial and objective' means 'detached from a specific personal belief, intuition or subjective preference'. The three 'not true' statements must be explained in this light: reason as such – that is, reason detached from a specific personal belief, intuition or subjective preference – neither shows that it is better to choose one option rather than the other nor shows that it does not matter which option is chosen. In other words, reason as such 'under-determines the choice'[7] (see also the explanation given in chapter 4).

At first sight 3NT is puzzling and is difficult to understand. Indeed, if A is not better than B and B is not better than A, it seems to follow that A and B are equally good; and if *A* is not equally good as *B*, then it seems to follow that *A* is better than *B* or *B* is better than *A*. The puzzle is due to the tacit assumption that *A* and *B* are (completely) comparable. The puzzle disappears if 3NT is caused by incomparability (or incomplete comparability).

Many theorists recognize the possibility of '3NT' but explain it differently. Raz and Adam Morton interpret 3NT as 'incomparability'.[8] Derek Parfit explains 3NT as 'imprecise equality', John Broome as 'vagueness' and T.K. Seung and Daniel Bonevac as 'indeterminacy'.[9] As indicated earlier, I regard 3NT as a sign of 'incomplete comparability'. The designation '3NT' remains neutral between the different interpretations, but I think the only correct explanation is 'incomplete comparability', as I hope to make plausible in this chapter and the three following ones. In chapter 4 I will show that 3NT as such – that is, irrespective of how it is explained – has important problematic consequences for practical reason, rational decision making and complete justification of the choice. Chang emphatically denies that 3NT means incomparability. She interprets it as a fourth value relation within the domain of (complete) comparability. She calls this fourth value relation 'parity' and explains it as 'imprecise cardinal equality'.[10] In chapter 3 I will show that this interpretation is mistaken and that it conceals important implications of 3NT for practical reasoning. There I will also give reasons why 'incomplete comparability' is an adequate explanation of 3NT. I use the terms '3NT' and 'incomplete comparability' interchangeably.

CONDITIONS OF INCOMPLETE COMPARABILITY (3NT)

We shall see that in addition to incommensurability of the relevant values, two other conditions must be satisfied before 3NT applies and can be spoken of incomplete comparability of the options. One of the reasons why there is much confusion about the possible relation between incommensurability of values and incomplete comparability of options is that many thinkers do not realize that the additional conditions must also be fulfilled.

If we compare two valuable options, we compare them with respect to a particular value. Ruth Chang calls this the 'covering value'.[11] For instance, if we want to compare two persons with respect to their philosophical talent, then 'philosophical talent' is the covering value. Most covering values have multiple 'contributory values' – values that contribute to the content of the covering value. For example, the covering value 'philosophical talent' has, among others, 'originality' and 'analytical skill' as contributory values. Suppose we want to evaluate two options with respect to a covering value that consists of two contributory values. The options are incompletely comparable (in the sense of 3NT), if and only if the contributory values are not only incommensurable but also satisfy the two additional conditions. If one or more of the three conditions are not fulfilled, the options are completely comparable.

Conditions of incomplete comparability (3NT):

1. *Incommensurability*: The contributory values have unlike dimensions that cannot be reduced to each other or to a common dimension so that their amounts cannot be measured and compared on a common cardinal scale of units of value.
2. *Significant bidirectionality*: One option contains a significantly larger amount of one contributory value, while the other option contains a significantly larger amount of another contributory value.
3. *Symmetry*: The contributory values are 'in the same league'; that is, neither contributory value is significantly more important than the other.

Here follows a further explanation of each condition.

INCOMMENSURABILITY

If the covering value has only one dimension (i.e., if the covering value does not contain disparate contributory values), the options are completely comparable. This is the case, for instance, if we compare careers with respect to their salaries, or if we compare different kinds of food with respect to their vitamin C content or if we evaluate a slimming diet and physical exercise with respect to their weight-reducing effect. These examples lack the 'incommensurability condition' because the relevant covering value concerns a one-dimensional common measure: respectively, salary, vitamin C content and weight reduction. Let us consider the example of weight reduction mainly by means of calorie-intake reduction (lifestyle *C*) versus weight reduction mainly by means of increased physical exercise (lifestyle *E*) (see table 1.1).

Compared to lifestyle *E*, lifestyle *C* means a significantly larger reduction of calorie intake, while, conversely, lifestyle *E* means a significantly larger increase of physical exercise. So there is significant bidirectionality – one of the additional conditions of incomplete comparability. Besides, there is

Table 1.1. Comparison of two weight-reducing lifestyles *C* and *E*

	Reduction of calorie intake (calories/day)	Increase of exercise (minutes/day)
Lifestyle C	120	30
Lifestyle E	30	120

multidimensionality: the unit of increased physical exercise (minute) differs from the unit of reduced food intake (calorie). Still the two lifestyles are completely comparable, because the 'incommensurability condition' is not satisfied. The two lifestyles can be reduced to the one-dimensional covering value 'weight reduction'. This shows that 'multidimensionality' is no problem if we can reduce the different dimensions to a single one. Therefore, we can answer the question which lifestyle is overall better with respect to weight reduction. Obviously it would not be correct to add up the reduced calories and increased exercise minutes and to conclude that – given the fact that the total scores of both lifestyles are equal (150) – they are equally good. This would be correct only if the unit of reduced food intake (calorie) is equivalent to the unit of increased exercise (minute), which is not the case. We have to determine the relative importance or comparative effectiveness of the two dimensions with respect to weight reduction in order to be capable of answering the question which lifestyle is better with respect to weight reduction. In other words, we have to determine how many calories of reduced food intake are equivalent to how many minutes of increased physical exercise.

Let us now discuss the difference with another example: the assessment of two philosophers, A and B, with respect to their philosophical talent. Suppose that philosopher A is significantly more original, while philosopher B has a significantly larger analytical skill (satisfaction of the significant bidirectionality condition). Originality and analytical skill have different dimensions that cannot be reduced to a one-dimensional common measure or one-dimensional covering value. That is why their amounts cannot be measured and compared on a single common scale of one-dimensional units of value (satisfaction of the incommensurability condition). In addition, neither value is significantly more important than the other (satisfaction of the symmetry condition). Thus, all the three necessary conditions of incomplete comparability are satisfied. While in the previous example of weight reduction the multidimensionality and significant bidirectionality problem could be resolved by commensuration, this is impossible in the present example due to the incommensurability of the contributory values. Let us give scores to the philosophers for the contributory values (table 1.2).

Philosopher A is better than philosopher B with respect to originality. This is expressed in an originality score of 4 out of 5 for philosopher A versus an

Table 1.2. Comparison of two philosophers with respect to two contributory values of philosophical talent

	Originality (score out of 5)	*Analytical skill* (score out of 5)
Philosopher A	4	1
Philosopher B	1	4

originality score of 1 out of 5 for philosopher *B*. The opposite applies to the scores of analytical skill. Do the equal total scores mean that both philosophers are equally good? As we have seen in the diet/exercise example, the answer is 'no'. We must take into account the relative weights of the contributory values. The existence of an equivalence relation and exchange rate in the weight reduction example makes it possible to arrive at correct total scores. But the problem with the philosophers-example is that a determinate equivalence relation and an exchange rate between the contributory values do not exist. Presently I will further explain and elaborate on this problem, but for the moment it is enough to suspect that a particular difference in the amount of philosophical talent on the originality scale is not (necessarily) interchangeable with a particular difference in the amount of philosophical talent on the scale of analytical skill. Superiority along the 'originality scale' seems not capable of unambiguously compensating for inferiority along the 'scale of analytical skill' (or vice versa) with respect to philosophical talent in a similar way as the differences in lifestyles with respect to weight reduction. So the philosophers-example essentially differs from the example of weight reduction.

SIGNIFICANT BIDIRECTIONALITY

Bidirectionality means that the amount of one contributory value is larger in one option than in the other option while the opposite applies to another contributory value. If bidirectionality is lacking, complete comparability is maintained despite the incommensurability of the contributory values. If one option is better than the other option with respect to all contributory values (the amounts of all contributory values are larger in one option), or if one option is, compared to the other, equally good with respect to one contributory value (the options have an equal amount of this contributory value) and better with respect to the other contributory value(s), there is complete comparability: the relevant option is unambiguously better than the other. For instance, if we want to compare philosopher A and philosopher B with respect to their philosophical talent and we assume for the sake of simplicity that the covering value 'philosophical talent' consists of only two incommensurable contributory values – originality and analytical skill – then philosophers A and B are completely comparable with respect to philosophical talent if A is better than B with respect to both originality and analytical skill (= absence of bidirectionality). However, if philosopher A is better than philosopher B with respect to originality but worse than philosopher B with respect to analytical skill (satisfaction of the bidirectionality condition), it may be the case that they are incompletely comparable (if also the other additional condition of incomplete comparability is fulfilled). This does not mean that in this case nothing could be said about their place on the scale of philosophical talent compared to other philosophers. For instance, it would be unambiguously true that philosopher A is better than philosopher C if C would be worse than A with respect to both originality and analytical skill, and it would be unambiguously true that philosopher B is worse than philosopher D if B is worse than D with respect to both originality and analytical skill. In other words, ranking of philosophers with respect to philosophical talent is possible, but this ranking may be incomplete. This illustrates that incomplete comparability and incomplete ordering are interrelated. It is one of the reasons why 'incomplete comparability' is a better name than 'incomparability'. Another reason is that the relevant incomparability is not complete: although the options may be overall incomparable – that is, incomparable with respect to the covering value (the contributory values taken together) – they are usually comparable with respect to the contributory values separately. Presently I will argue in more detail why the notion 'incomplete comparability' is more appropriate than the notion 'incomparability'.

The condition under consideration in this section is '*significant* bidirectionality'. This means that the amount of each contributory value in one option significantly differs from its amount in the other option.[12] Suppose option A contains a significantly larger amount of one contributory value than option B, while option B contains an amount of another contributory value that is only trivially larger than the amount of this contributory value in A. In that case, there is no problem for the comparability of the options, because, other things being equal, A is better than B. For instance, if philosopher A is significantly better than philosopher B with respect to originality and philosopher B is only trivially better than philosopher A with respect to analytical skill, then (if other things are equal) A and B remain completely comparable: A is better than B. Another example is given by Bernard Williams.[13] If the citizens of society A have much more liberty than the citizens of society B, while the latter have only trivially more equality, then (other things being equal) society A is better than society B.

SYMMETRY

This third condition of incomplete comparability runs as follows: the relevant two contributory values are in the same league; that is, neither contributory value is significantly more important than the other.[14] Incommensurability implies that the amounts of the relevant values cannot be compared on a common *cardinal* scale. This does not exclude that the relevant options can be compared on a common *ordinal* scale – a list of rankings that do not indicate cardinal differences in amounts of value.[15] To take an example, already mentioned before, suppose that the citizens of a society have basic liberties (e.g., freedom of movement, speech and religion) and sufficient economic welfare to live a decent life. The citizens of another society have somewhat more economic welfare but lack basic liberties. Incommensurability of the values 'economic welfare' and 'basic liberties' does not prevent the comparability of the two societies: the former can be ranked higher than the latter (assuming that basic liberties are more important than somewhat increased welfare above a sufficient level). This comparative ranking is possible despite the fact that the amounts of the relevant values cannot be measured and compared on a common cardinal scale. In other words, if two values are incommensurable but asymmetrical (i.e., if one value has a higher ranking on an ordinal scale than the other), comparability of options is often maintained.[16]

ASSIGNMENT OF WEIGHTS

The weights we assign to different contributory values depend on the importance we attach to them, which, in turn, at least partly depends on our aims, interests and predilections. That is why different people with different aims, interests and predilections (or even one and the same person with different or changeable aims and interests) easily assign different weights to the same values. The assignment of weights to incommensurable values may be problematic, precisely because incommensurable values are, by definition, 'not measurable by the same standard' and cannot be weighed on the same cardinal scale. Unlike the determination of amounts, assignment of weights is often based on intuitive and subjective instead of 'impartial and objective' determination. As we will discuss later, different persons often have considerably different intuitions. That is why different people (even if they have similar aims and interests) may easily assign different weights to the same values. Also one and the same person may have great difficulties in assigning determinate weights and may reveal strong intrapersonal variation in the assignment of weights. And personal weightings too may be very incomplete, not always capable of creating determinate relative weights.[17]

Comparison of two options with respect to a multidimensional covering value of which the contributory values are bidirectionally divided is a bipartite procedure, consisting of (1) determination of amounts of contributory values and (2) assignment of weights to contributory values. The first part of the comparison is more or less objective and results in more or less determinate and interpersonally similar conclusions about the relative position of the options with respect to the separate contributory values. The second part is often intuitive and subjective. Incommensurability may prevent the assignment of 'impartial and objective' weights and cause 'objective' incomplete comparability.[18] This objective incomplete comparability may be 'resolved' and changed into subjective comparability by personal weight assignment. Because the intuitions on which the subjective weight assignment is based may significantly differ, the final judgments may significantly differ. The objective incomplete comparability of the relevant options seems to make the conflicting judgements objectively irresolvable. A further justification of this claim will be given in the next section, where we will discuss two concrete examples of plausible incomplete comparability.

THE LARGE IMPROVEMENT ARGUMENT

We have seen that, if the relevant values do not satisfy one or more of the conditions of incomplete comparability (incommensurability, significant bidirectionality and symmetry), the options are completely comparable. However, this does not yet demonstrate that, conversely, if the values do satisfy these conditions, the relation between the relevant options is an instance of incomplete comparability (3NT). I will adduce what might be called the 'large improvement argument' and other arguments (see also a later section 'A second example') to show that this is plausible. As far as I know, the large improvement argument and its implications for practical reason have never been explicitly described. This argument shows similarities in form with, but is fundamentally different from, the 'small improvement argument'. The latter is adduced to demonstrate imprecise equality (see chapter 3). The large improvement argument for incomplete comparability makes use of the 'large improvement phenomenon'. John Broome's so-called standard configuration may help to clarify this.[19] In this configuration a 'standard option' A is, with respect to a particular covering value, compared with a chain of options B that gradually improve. Option A bears two incommensurable contributory values, v_1 and v_2. Options B bear the same contributory values, but the amount of value v_1 is smaller, and the amount of value v_2 is larger, than in option A (satisfaction of the bidirectionality condition of incomplete comparability). In the chain of options B the amount of v_1 is fixed while the amount of v_2 increases. To further clarify this, I will apply the standard configuration to two concrete examples. Here is the first example, which I borrow from John Broome, in an adapted version. We compare career A with a chain of careers B, with respect to the covering value 'goodness as a career'. Career A is adventurous, interesting and challenging, but its salary is moderate. The careers B are boring and not challenging but give more financial security (figure 1.1).

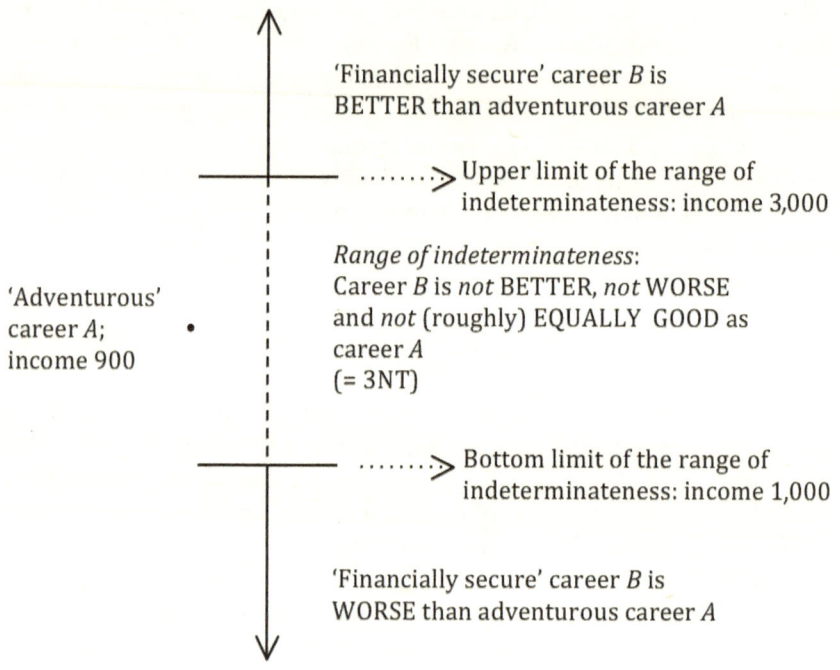

Figure 1.1. 'Adventurous career' A compared with a chain of 'financially more secure' careers B

We assume that all other things relevant to 'goodness of a career' are equal. The income of the careers B gradually increases from the bottom to the top of the chain. Suppose that the B careers at the bottom of the chain are worse than the standard career A, because their income and financial security are only trivially larger than those of career A while the latter is significantly more interesting. Careers B at the top of the chain are supposed to be better than career A, because their incomes are so much larger than career A's income that A's more interesting content pales into insignificance compared to B's considerably better income. Between the bottom and upper extreme, it is plausible that there is a range in which the careers B are neither definitely better nor definitely worse than career A. B is regarded as neither definitely better nor definitely worse than A if it is neither irrational to choose A instead of B nor irrational to choose B instead of A. It is plausible that this range is wide. Indeed, the lower limit of the range will be low because careers B will not become definitely worse than standard career A until the difference in income between A and B has become small. Similarly, the upper limit of the range will be high because careers B will not become definitely better than career A until the difference in income between A and B has become large. (It might even be questioned whether there is an upper limit at all above which B becomes definitely better than A.) Suppose the income of career A is 900, while the incomes of careers B at the bottom limit and the upper limit of the range are 1,000 and 3,000, respectively (see figure 1.1). Let us take a career B between these two limits with an income of 1,200; call it career $B_{1,200}$. Improve this career by doubling the income so that we get career $B_{2,400}$. The latter career is still always between the two limits. This means that, although career $B_{1,200}$ is not worse than career A, the considerably improved career $B_{2,400}$ is not (definitely) better than career A. This means that $B_{1,200}$ cannot be equally good, not even roughly equally good as A. If $B_{1,200}$ were (roughly) equally good as A, then $B_{2,400}$, which is considerably better than $B_{1,200}$, were also considerably better than A. This argument for A and $B_{1,200}$ not being roughly equally good, although neither is better than the other, I call the large improvement argument. It makes plausible that in the relevant range the B careers are *not* better, *not* worse and *not* equally good – *not even roughly equally good* – as career A. If so, this means that in this range the relations between careers B and career A are instances of 3NT value relations (incomplete comparability). I call the 3NT zone the range of indeterminateness: the range in which an impartial/objective and determinate comparative worth of two options *does not exist*. Unlike inconclusiveness, indeterminateness does not mean that we do not (yet) know the comparative worth of the options, due to the complexity of the issue and insufficient knowledge. Instead, it means that, even in principle, such a comparative worth cannot be determined because it does not exist, due to incomplete comparability of the options. (I prefer the term 'indeterminateness' to 'indeterminacy' because the latter is often identified with 'vagueness' or 'impreciseness', which is a different phenomenon; see chapter 3.)

At first sight the large improvement phenomenon is puzzling. How is it possible that, if A is not worse than B, a considerable improvement of A does not make A better than B? A plausible explanation is that the relevant items are to some extent incomparable. If the relevant options are incompletely comparable, the large improvement phenomenon is not surprising anymore. Explanation of 3NT in terms of incomplete comparability, instead of explanations in terms of (complete) comparability, is further supported by the *non-existence* of an equivalence relation between the relevant items. One of the characteristics of incomparable items is the impossibility to equate them in value or extent.[20] The fact that a level of (even rough) equivalence is absent in the whole chain of items in the standard configuration shown in figure 1.1 is consistent with this characteristic of incomparability. None of the B careers in the chain is (roughly) equally good as career A. There is a zone where B is worse than A (the zone below the lower limit of the range of indeterminateness); there is a zone where B is neither better than, nor worse than, nor roughly equally good as, A (the range of indeterminateness); and there is a zone where B is better than A (the zone above the upper limit of the range of indeterminateness). Thus a level of equivalence is lacking in the whole chain. This means that B is incapable of being (roughly) *equated* with A by increasing or decreasing the financial security. Note that the upper and lower limits of the range of indeterminateness do not represent levels of (rough) equivalence either.

'INCOMPLETE COMPARABILITY' INSTEAD OF 'INCOMPARABILITY'

As I pointed out earlier, the notion 'incomplete comparability' is more appropriate than 'incomparability'. There are four reasons. First, the relevant options are usually comparable with respect to the separate contributory values (e.g., adventure and financial security separately) of the covering value (e.g., goodness as a career). Second, other contributory values of the relevant covering value may lack bidirectionality so that one option may be definitely better than, or equally good as, the other option with respect to the combination of these other contributory values. Third, incompletely comparable options belong to a set of options that are incompletely orderable. For instance, while career A is incompletely comparable with careers B (at least in the range of indeterminateness), it may be completely comparable with other careers (e.g., where there is no bidirectionality or symmetry of the relevant values). Fourth, the relevant 'incomparability' does not exclude the possibility to determine, on an ordinal scale, that neither of the relevant competing values is more important than the other.

A SECOND EXAMPLE

Let us now apply the large improvement argument to a second example. Suppose a budget is made available for a newly developed and expensive treatment of patients suffering from a relatively rare disease. The disease has two forms, a serious and less serious one. There are 1,000 patients: 500 suffer from the serious type and 500 from the less serious one. Suppose that patients who suffer from the serious type have significantly less benefit from treatment (addition of

0.5 QALY [= Quality Adjusted Life Year]) than patients who suffer from the less serious form (addition of 4 QALYs). There are no other differences between the two groups, and the cost of the treatment of a seriously ill patient is the same as the cost of the treatment of a moderately ill patient. The available budget is sufficient for the treatment of not more than 500 patients, and we assume that we have to make a choice between treating either the seriously ill or the moderately ill patients. What is better: treatment of the patients who are worst-off (policy A) or the patients who have more benefit (policy B)?[21] See table 1.3.

Table 1.3. Two rival policies A and B with respect to allocation of scarce health care resources

Policy	Allocation criterion	Type of patients selected for treatment	Health benefit (gain in QALYs)	
			Per patient	Total
A	Priority to worst-off patients ('equity')	Seriously ill (n = 500)	0.5	250
B	Maximization of health benefit ('efficiency')	Moderately ill (n = 500)	4	2,000

This question is difficult to answer because of the incommensurability of the rival values – priority to the worst-off versus maximization of health benefit.[22] Also this second example may be an instance of incompletely comparable (3NT) options because the competing values satisfy the conditions incommensurability, significant bidirectionality and symmetry. To further clarify this, let us again apply Broome's standard configuration to this example. Let health care policy A be the 'standard option', which is compared with a chain of health care policies B. Policy A has more concern for the worst-off patients while policy B yields more health benefit. The larger health benefit produced by policy B further increases upwardly along the chain. Let us assume that the policies B in the lower part of the chain are worse than the standard, because there the health benefit is only trivially larger than that of policy A while it has no concern for the worst-off. Let us further assume that in the upper part of the chain B is better than A, because there B produces vastly more health benefits than A. Between the upper and lower parts of the chain there is a zone in which we assume that B is neither definitely better nor definitely worse than A. In this zone, let us consider a policy B_1 that yields a significantly larger total health benefit than policy A (1,000 versus 250 QALYs); see table 1.4.

A is superior with respect to concern for the worst-off patients, while B_1 is superior with respect to health benefit. Which policy is overall superior?

Table 1.4. Three policies with respect to allocation of scarce health resources

Policy	Allocation criterion	Total health benefit (QALYs)
A	Priority to the worst-off patients	250
B_1	Maximization of health benefit	1,000
B_2 (improved B_1)	Maximization of health benefit	3,000

It seems justified to conclude that B_1 is (impartially/objectively, rationally determinably or definitely) neither better nor worse than A. If so, this seems to mean that both policies are (roughly) equally good. But this need not be the case. Take a considerably improved policy B_2, which yields a much larger total health benefit than policy B_1: 3,000 instead of 1,000 QALYs. Other things being equal, B_2 is considerably better than B_1. However, it is possible and not irrational to conclude that B_2 is again not (impartially/objectively and definitely) better than A. If this is true, then B_1 is not equally good – not even roughly equally good – as A. Indeed, if B_1 would be (roughly) equally good as A, B_2 would be considerably better not only than B_1 but also than A. However, this 'transitivity' does not occur because we have concluded that B_2 is not better than A. In the relevant range, health benefit of B considerably increases, without making B definitely or impartially better than A. In those cases Raz speaks of the 'failure of transitivity'.[23] The conclusion that, after a considerable improvement of B_1 to B_2, B is still always not better than A implies that B_1 and A are not (roughly) equally good. This is the large improvement argument. People who disagree with the large improvement argument must assume the existence of a (rough) level of equivalence between the fundamentally disparate values 'concern for the worst-off' ('need') and 'efficiency'. This would mean that there is an amount of value of giving priority to the worst-off patients that is equivalent to a particular amount of health benefit ('efficiency'): for instance, the treatment of one seriously ill patient, which yields a health benefit of, say, 0.5 QALY, is overall equivalent to the treatment of one less seriously ill patient, which yields a health benefit of, say, 4 QALYs (relative weight of 'need' versus 'efficiency' is then 8). Given the fundamental disparity and incommensurability of these values, the existence of such a level of equivalence is implausible. Let us call this the 'incommensurability argument'. W. D. Ross similarly argues that it is unintelligible how any amount of a particular value could be equal in value to any amount of a fundamentally different and incommensurable value.[24] Aristotle succinctly summarizes the problem: 'Without commensurability, no equality'.[25] Only strict trichotomists assume the existence of a level of equivalence between disparate values. In the anthology *Incommensurability, Incomparability and Practical Reason*, edited by Ruth Chang, only one of the thirteen contributors, Donald Regan, adheres to the trichotomy thesis (the thesis that there are only three positive value relations: 'better than', 'worse than' and 'equally good as'). It is true that, although the other twelve contributors do not believe in the existence of a *precise* level of equivalence, this does not necessarily mean that they do not believe in *rough* equivalence either. However, Derek Parfit and Ruth Chang, who explain 3NT as imprecise equality, recognize that what they call 'impreciseness' may be 'very large',[26] which entails the absence of even rough equality and the presence of the large improvement phenomenon. One might argue that reducing disparate values to the common measure 'intrinsic value' – as proposed by Fred Feldman[27] – could resolve the relevant problem because it could assume the existence of equivalence in intrinsic value. However, this approach does not resolve the problem of measuring and comparing amounts of conflicting incommensurable values if we cannot make use of a single one-dimensional cardinal scale. Unlike the common measure 'pleasure' of classical utilitarianism, the common measure 'intrinsic value' is complex and multifaceted instead of simple and one-dimensional. This creates a problem if the relevant disparate contributory values of intrinsic value clash.

If the large improvement argument and the incommensurability argument are valid, it is plausible that there is a wide range of rational indeterminateness in which the assignment of determinate and impartial relative weights is impossible, given the absence of any level of (rough) equivalence. While the 'large improvement argument' shows that it is quite well possible and not irrational to conclude that B_1 and A are not (roughly) equally good, the 'incommensurability argument' renders this conclusion still more plausible. In addition to the 'large improvement argument' and the 'incommensurability argument', there are still two other arguments that support the view that, in the relevant cases, an (rough) equivalence relation does not exist. I will successively adduce these arguments. In Erik Nord's empirical study, medical professionals and other well-informed people were asked how much treatment efficiency (aggregated benefit from treatment) they would want to sacrifice in order to give (some or complete) priority to the worst-off.[28] The answers made it possible to deduce the relative weights the respondents assigned to concern for the worst-off (need) compared to efficiency. They assigned considerably divergent relative weights to these competing values: the relative weights varied by a multiplicative factor of 10–100. Dan Brock, who refers to Nord's research and to similar studies, draws the following conclusion:

> Most people and many theories of distributive justice have a concern both for maximising overall benefits with scarce health care resources *and* for helping the worst off or sickest, but there is a large range of indeterminacy regarding the proper tradeoff between these two concerns when they are in conflict.[29]

The considerably divergent relative weights and the connected 'large range of indeterminacy' are in line with the large improvement phenomenon. They are difficult to explain in terms of 'the *small* improvement phenomenon' or 'unavoidable precision'. The same applies to other examples, for instance, the empirical study by Daniels and Sabin in which medical students applied considerably different relative weights to conflicting values related to the distribution of scarce health care resources.[30] We might call this line of reasoning (pointing at the empirical fact that equally rational and well-informed persons assign considerably different relative weights to the relevant incommensurable values) the 'empirical argument'.[31] Joseph Raz would give the following explanation.[32] In the relevant cases reason 'under-determines' the choice. In other words, within the wide range of different relative weights (assigned by equally rational and well-informed persons), reason does not show that there is a (single) right relative weight (still less what the right relative weight could be). We might call this argument – against the existence of a determinate relative weight between incommensurable values – the 'argument from rational under-determination'.

In sum, there are four interrelated arguments that support the existence of 3NT or incomplete comparability: the large improvement argument, the incommensurability argument, the empirical argument and the argument from rational under-determination. Neither argument conclusively demonstrates the non-existence of a (rough) equivalence relation between the relevant values, but (especially taken together) they make it plausible. If so, it means that, over a large range of increasing value (in the present example: increasing health benefit), the relation between A and B is an instance of 'incomplete comparability' in the defined sense: A is neither better than, nor worse than, nor equally good – not even roughly equally good – as B. This is the range of indeterminateness. In this range 'reason under-determines the choice', because a (impartial and determinate) comparative worth of the relevant options does not exist.

THE 'PARADOX OF ABSENT EQUIVALENCE'

It is worth emphasizing that in figure 1.1 there is a range where B is worse and a range where B is better than A, but nowhere there is a level or range where A and B are (roughly) equally good. In other words, starting from the bottom part of the chain and gradually increasing the value of B, B changes from being worse into being better than A, *without passing a level or range where A and B are equally good – not even roughly equally good*. This surprising, unexpected and enigmatic phenomenon might be called the 'Paradox of Absent Equivalence'. This paradox can be explained by the fact that A and B are (to some extent) incomparable: a level of (rough) equivalence exists only if the relevant options are comparable. As far as I know, the paradox of absent equivalence and its problematic implications for the rational assignment of relative weights have never been explicitly noticed and analysed. One of the causes of this gap is that, as we will discuss in chapter 3, some leading theorists explain the absence of equivalence in terms of 'imprecise equality'. This notion conceals what is the case: the absence of any, even imprecise, equality.

PREVALENCE OF INCOMPLETE COMPARABILITY

Most theorists agree that many values are incommensurable. But, as we have seen, incommensurability is not sufficient to render options incompletely comparable: the relevant values must also satisfy the additional conditions 'significant bidirectionality' and 'symmetry'. Therefore, incomplete comparability is less prevalent than incommensurability. Still many human values and interests are not only incommensurable but may also often satisfy the other conditions that cause incomplete comparability of the relevant options. That is why many other examples of incompletely comparable options can be added to the examples discussed earlier: for instance, options that embody conflicting prudential, political or ethical values, such as a policy that is better for economic growth versus one that is better for the environment; a larger increase of total welfare versus a more equal distribution of welfare; more liberty versus more equality of opportunity in school education; a policy that produces greater public security versus one that better protects personal privacy (compare the debate about the practices of the American National Security Agency [NSA], revealed by Edward Snowden). The previous standard configuration can be applied to all relevant competing options and values. For instance, standard option A may represent a particular amount of personal privacy that is compared with a chain of options B that represent less personal privacy but increasing public security. I have worked out this example in another publication.[33]

TENTATIVE CONCLUSIONS

We can draw the following tentative conclusions about the relation between incommensurability and incomplete comparability:

- Incommensurability is a central but not sufficient cause of incomplete comparability. Incomplete comparability is a 'multiconditional' concept: it occurs if and only if the contributory values of the covering value satisfy all the following three conditions: (1) incommensurability, (2) significant bidirectionality and (3) symmetry.

- If one or more of these conditions are not satisfied, complete comparability is maintained.
- If all three conditions are satisfied, there is incomplete comparability in the sense that it is neither true that one option is (impartially/objectively) better than the other nor true that the options are (roughly) equally good.

From these conclusions we can infer that unproblematic comparability is maintained if at least one of the following conditions applies:

1. The covering value is one-dimensional.
2. Multidimensional contributory values of the covering value can be reduced to a one-dimensional super-value.
3. There is no significant bidirectionality of the contributory values.
4. The contributory values can be lexically ranked.
5. The contributory values are not symmetrical.

Here follows a further explanation of the previous cases in which comparability of options is maintained. With respect to the first case: the amounts of a one-dimensional value are more or less objectively determinable and comparable. The same applies to cases 2 and 3. Because they concern measurements and comparisons of one-dimensional amounts of values or comparisons of separate one-dimensional values, the result of the judgment can be more or less objective in the sense of being independent of the evaluating person and independent of weighing disparate values. Assigning lexical priority (case 4) means that one value gets absolute weight and always receives priority in cases of conflicts with another value. For instance, if equal distribution of welfare has lexical priority to maximization of total welfare, the option/policy that produces more equal distribution always gets priority, independent of the amounts of total welfare produced by another option/policy. The 'lexical priority approach' avoids the problem of determining equivalence relations between, and relative weights of, multidimensional values, because a lexically prior value (however small its amount) always gets priority to another value (however large its amount). Suppose we want to compare options A and B with respect to a covering value consisting of two contributory values v_1 and v_2. If v_1 has lexical priority to v_2, option P is better than option Q even if P, compared to Q, contains only a little bit more of value v_1 and much less of value v_2. So lexical priority of one value over another does not only mean that the former has more weight but that it has, as it were, an infinitely larger weight than the latter, entailing that the smallest amount of the lexically prior value has a larger weight than the largest amount of the other value. Something similar may, but does not always, apply to asymmetrical values (case 5). Suppose that v_1 is more important than v_2, and option P bears a moderately larger amount of v_1 while option Q bears a moderately larger amount of v_2, then P is better than Q. However, if P bears a moderately larger amount of v_1 and Q bears a considerably larger amount of v_2, then it may remain unclear whether P is better than Q. In that case we need to know the relative weight of v_1 compared to v_2 in order to know which option is overall better. Lexical priority, by contrast, is always capable of resolving conflicts between incommensurable values because it always avoids the need of assigning relative weights.

NOTES

1. See, for example, Joseph Raz, *The Morality of Freedom* (Oxford: Oxford University Press, 1986); Raz, 'Incommensurability and Agency', in *Incommensurability, Incomparability, and Practical Reason*, ed. Ruth Chang (Cambridge, Mass.: Harvard University Press, 1997).

2. See, for example, Chang, 'Introduction', in *Incommensurability, Incomparability, and Practical Reason*, ed. Chang; and James Griffin 'Incommensurability, What's the Problem', ed. Chang; and Amartya Sen, 'Incompleteness and Reasoned Choice', *Synthese* 140 (2004): 43–59.

3. Michael Stocker, *Plural and Conflicting Values* (Oxford: Oxford University Press, 1999), 153, 155, 168, 207. See also Chang, 'Introduction'; Griffin 'Incommensurability, What's the Problem'.

4. Sen, 'Incompleteness and Reasoned Choice', 45.

5. Ibid., 44.

6. Chang, 'Introduction'.

7. Raz, *The Morality of Freedom*, chapter 13.

8. Ibid.; Adam Morton, *Disasters and Dilemmas, Strategies for Real-Life Decision Making* (Oxford: Basil Blackwell), chapter 3.

9. Derek Parfit, *Reasons and Persons* (Oxford: Clarendon Press, 1984), 431; John Broome, *Ethics out of Economics* (Cambridge: Cambridge University Press, 1999), 123–144; T.K. Seung and Daniel Bonevac, 'Plural Values and Indeterminate Rankings', *Ethics* 102 (1992): 799–813.

10. Ruth Chang, *Making Comparisons Count* (New York: Routledge, 2002), 145.

11. Chang, 'Introduction', 5.

12. Of course, 'significance' is a rather vague and subjective notion. I use it in the sense that the difference in amounts of the relevant value cannot be rationally ignored or disregarded in the comparative judgment. Conversely, a difference in amount is insignificant if it can be rationally ignored or disregarded.

13. Bernard Williams, *Moral Luck* (Cambridge: Cambridge University Press, 1981), 77.

14. One might raise the following objection. How can we maintain that two options are incompletely comparable if we are able to conclude that neither of the values borne by the options is more important than the other? The answer is as follows. The conclusion 'not less important' is the result of a comparison on an ordinal instead

of a cardinal scale. If the value borne by one option is not less important than the value borne by the other, this does not necessarily mean that the options are equally good, not even roughly equally good. This has been discussed earlier and will be demonstrated later in the chapter (see the section 'The large improvement argument'). If the relevant options appear to be not (roughly) equally good, while neither is better than the other, they are incompletely comparable. Unawareness of the distinction between symmetrical values and equally good options has confused several thinkers; see, for instance, Michael Stocker, 'Abstract and Concrete Value: Plurality, Conflict, and Maximization', in *Incommensurability, Incomparability, and Practical Reason*, ed. Chang, 203; Paul-Erik Veel, 'Incommensurability, Proportionality and Rational Legal Decision-Making', *Law & Ethics of Human Rights* 4 (2010): 177–228. Veel indirectly conflates and confuses 'equal standing' with 'equivalence'.

15. Steven Lukes, 'Comparing the Incomparable: Trade-Offs and Sacrifices', ed. Chang, 281, note 14, argues that 'To the extent that it is claimed that X is better than Y, there is some answer, however imprecise, to the question "how much better?"' Chang rightly disagrees: '[A]n answer to Luke's quantitative question "How much better?" is not required by comparison. . . . Comparability does not require that comparison be a matter of quantities of value, let alone quantities of some unit of value. To think that comparability requires a single quantitative unit of value according to which items can be measured is to mistake commensurability for comparability.' Chang, 'Introduction', 18–19.

16. Sometimes also options that bear asymmetrical values may be incompletely comparable, namely, if the amount of the more important value is small and the amount of the less important value is large, and if, in addition, the former value has no lexical priority to the latter.

17. See Adam Morton, *Disasters and Dilemma, Strategies for Real-Life Decision Making* (Oxford: Basil Blackwell, 1991), especially chapter 3, 'Incomparabilities'; John Broome, *Weighing Goods: Equality, Uncertainty and Time* (Oxford: Blackwell Publishers, 1995), 93; Ruth Chang, 'The Possibility of Parity', *Ethics* 112: 666.

18. Compare the discussion of the phrase 'objective incommensurability' in Broome, *Ethics Out of Economics*, 158–161; and compare Joseph Raz, *Engaging Reason: On the Theory of Value and Action* (Oxford: Oxford University Press, 2001), 243. He argues that 'impersonally' the conflicting considerations may be incomparable, while this does not exclude comparability for the relevant person.

19. John Broome, 'Is Incommensurability Vagueness?', ed. Chang, 67–89.

20. Compare the *Oxford English Dictionary* definition of 'incomparability': '*without an equal* in quality or extent'.

21. There are several other concrete examples of conflicts between need of treatment and benefit from treatment or between 'equity' and 'efficiency' as selection criterion for treatment; see, for instance, Dan Brock, 'Ethical Issues in the Use of Cost Effectiveness Analysis for the Prioritisation of Health Care Resources', in *Public Health, Ethics, and Equity*, ed. Sudhir Anand, Fabienne Peter, and Amartya Sen (Oxford: Oxford University Press, 2006).

22. This example is analogous to the one discussed by Rawls: the aggregative-distributive dichotomy concerning *maximization* of welfare versus *fair*

distribution of welfare. John Rawls, *A Theory of Justice*, revised edition (Cambridge, Mass.: Belknap Press of Harvard University Press, 1999), 32–33.

23. Raz, *The Morality of Freedom*, chapter 13.

24. W. D. Ross, *The Right and the Good* (Oxford: Oxford University Press, 1950), 154.

25. Aristotle, *Ethics* (Penguin Books, 1978) [ISBN 0 14 044.055 0], 185.

26. Derek Parfit, *On What Matters* (Oxford: Oxford University Press, 2011); Ruth Chang, personal communication.

27. Fred Feldman, 'Adjusting Utility for Justice: A Consequentialist Reply to the Objection from Justice', *Philosophy and Phenomenological Research* 60 (1995): 567–585.

28. Erik Nord, 'The Trade-Off between Severity of Illness and Treatment Effect in Cost-Value Analysis of Health Care', *Health Policy* 24 (1993): 227–38.

29. Brock, 'Ethical Issues in the Use of Cost Effectiveness Analysis for the Prioritisation of Health Care Resources', 213.

30. Norman Daniels and James Sabin, 'Limits to Health Care: Fair Procedures, Democratic Deliberation, and the Legitimacy Problem for Insurers', *Philosophy & Public Affairs* 26 (1997): 303–350.

31. Cf. also Rawls (*A Theory of Justice*, 34) about weighing the two competing values of the 'aggregative-distributive dichotomy' – efficiency versus equity – in the distribution of welfare: '[V]ery different weightings are consistent with these principles.' Of course, interpersonal differences in the assignment of weights and disagreement about the right weights are not a demonstration of the absence of an impartially or objectively right answer, but, conversely, if it is true that such an answer does not exist or that reason under-determines the answer, it is not surprising that equally rational and well-informed people assign different relative weights.

32. Raz, *The Morality of Freedom*, chapter 13.

33. Martijn Boot, 'The Right Balance', *The Journal of Value Inquiry* 51 (2017): 13–32.

Chapter 2

Spurious Challenges

SUMMARY

The thesis that incommensurability of values may cause incomplete comparability of options can be challenged in different ways. This chapter is devoted to spurious challenges – challenges that originate from misunderstandings, confusions and spurious arguments. The next chapter discusses real challenges, which are based on valid arguments. Many spurious challenges originate from being unaware that incommensurability is not a sufficient but important cause of incomplete comparability.

NOTE FOR THE READER

This chapter and the following one are not essential for understanding the ideas developed in this book. The reader who is less interested in the challenges may continue at chapter 4.

****

The incomplete comparability thesis – the claim that, if two additional conditions are satisfied, incommensurability entails incomplete comparability – seems plausible, given the four arguments in support of it, which we discussed in the previous chapter. However, there is still much disagreement about the implications of incommensurability of values for the comparability of options and for rational decision-making, and there are several possible challenges to the incomplete comparability thesis. I make a distinction between spurious challenges (based on misunderstandings, confusions and spurious arguments) and real challenges (based on pertinent and valid arguments). This chapter is devoted to spurious challenges, while the next chapter discusses and replies to real challenges. In 2007 I completed my first research project on incommensurability with a DPhil dissertation. My supervisor was the late professor of social and political theory at the University of Oxford, G. A. Cohen. Initially Cohen raised some objections to the validity of the conditions for incomplete comparability discussed in chapter 1. In the end he recognized that his objections were incorrect. The reason that I still discuss them is that they are based on widespread misunderstandings and confusions.

CHALLENGE 1: 'EASY CHOICE'

Cohen argued that there are numerous examples of easy rational choices between incommensurable options. He gave the following example (already mentioned in chapter 1). Suppose we want to make a choice between two restaurants, A and B, based on a comparison with respect to the covering value 'quality as a restaurant', assuming, for the sake of simplicity, that this covering value contains only two contributory values: 'quality of the food' and 'quality of the decor'. Restaurant A has very good food. Restaurant B has lousy food but a nicer decor. So the incommensurable contributory values are bidirectional (i.e., one restaurant is better with respect to one contributory value, the alternative restaurant with respect to another). Still we can compare the restaurants. The comparison shows that restaurant A is definitely better than restaurant B. However, this example does not refute the 'incomplete comparability thesis', because one condition of incomplete comparability is not satisfied: 'symmetry' – the condition that neither contributory value is more important than the other. With respect to the quality of a restaurant, the quality of the food is more important than the quality of the decor. But also if the values would be symmetrical (quality of the decor not less important than the quality of the food), the example is inadequate. A minimum quality of food is required to make a restaurant a relevant alternative for choice. Lousy food lacks this minimum. Cohen's restaurant example is a version of what I call the 'insignificant amount fallacy', which we will discuss in more detail in chapter 3.

CHALLENGE 2: 'SIGNIFICANT AMOUNT'

Cohen thought that the adjective 'significant' in the condition 'significant bidirectionality' is inconsistent with the incommensurability condition. Remember that the significant bidirectionality condition runs as follows: the amount of one contributory value is significantly larger in option 1 than in option

2, while the amount of the other contributory value is significantly larger in option 2 than in option 1. Cohen asked: How can one speak about significantly different amounts in the absence of a common metric? The answer is, of course, that there is no absence of a common metric in the different amounts of one and the same contributory value. The judgment that the amount of Peter's analytical skill significantly differs from John's analytical skill is unproblematic because it does not concern disparate values that lack a common metric. Similarly, the judgment that Peter has a significant amount of analytical skill and an insignificant amount of originality is not based on a comparison or commensuration of analytical skill and originality. Therefore, these judgments are not inconsistent with the belief that originality and analytical skill are incommensurable values. In a similar way the judgment that John is good in mathematics and Peter is good in literature and the judgment that John is significantly better than Peter in mathematics while Peter is significantly better than John in literature are not based on a comparison of mathematics and literature and can therefore not be inconsistent with the belief that mathematics and literature lack a common metric. This shows the importance of making a distinction between the difference in amounts of the same value and the difference in amounts of disparate values. The first difference is obviously not any problem for comparability because it concerns one and the same value: there is no incommensurability between different amounts of the same dimension.

CHALLENGE 3: 'EQUAL VALUE'

Cohen adduced another example to challenge the conditions of incomplete comparability. Take a career as a development aid worker and a career as a scientist, which contain the relevant contributory values in such a way that all conditions of incomplete comparability are satisfied. According to Cohen the options are 'nevertheless comparable because the person might be clear that, to take an extreme case, if he had to pay money to get one rather than the other, then he would pay the same for each'. My reply is as follows. It is obviously permitted to put equal or different price tags to the alternatives. It concerns personal intuitive weight assignment and personal intuitive balancing of the different relevant contributory values. However, reason does not show that these, and not other, price tags should be put to the options: reason 'under-determines' the choice, in the sense we discussed in chapter 1. Unless one believes in one right, or single rational, answer, other agents are not mistaken or less rational if they have other intuitions or preferences and put different price tags to the same options. Precisely the incomplete comparability of the options renders assigning different weights rationally permissible, while none of these weights is rationally required (the difference between rational permissibility and rational requirement will be further discussed in chapter 4). As shown in chapter 1, options that are incompletely comparable in an impartial perspective may become comparable in a personal perspective. In the end Cohen admitted that his objection 'failed to distinguish appropriately between the personal and the objective context'. Still another point is worth being stressed. Many daily decisions do not require rational deliberations and overall rational justification. Therefore, we usually experience no difficulties in making these daily decisions, whether there is complete comparability or not. Elizabeth Anderson:

> Many acts are based on the free play of moods, interests, whims, impulses, appetites, mere tastes, likings, and other non-rational motivations. It is not irrational to follow the lead of these motivations wherever practical reason permits it. . . . It would be a dull and rigid vision of human life if all of life's choices must be tied to rational comparisons according to a common criterion leaving no room for the free play of these other motivations. Our need to make space for the free play of non-rational motivations could thus be seen as a rational ground for not seeking to make comparative value judgments at every turn. . . . Practical reason makes space available for other motivations by taking no interest in the construction of comparative value judgments.[1]

To prevent misunderstandings it is important to note that the absence of complete comparability does not mean that the final choice is irrational. In cases of incompletely comparable options reason is able to select the options that are rationally eligible but unable to guide the choice between these eligible options and to prescribe the choice of one option *rather than* the other (again 'reason under-determines the choice' and does not show which option *should* be chosen). Each choice is rationally permissible, but neither is rationally required.

CHALLENGE 4: 'AMOUNT AND IMPORTANCE'

Another criticism by Cohen concerns the notion 'importance of a value', which plays a role in the 'symmetry condition' of incomplete comparability, and runs as follows: 'Neither contributory value is more important than the other.' Cohen objects that the importance of a value is already present in the amount of a value and *vice versa*. He argues as follows. One 'just discernable difference' of an important value contains a greater amount of value than one 'just discernable difference' of a less important value. This creates a bridge from importance to comparability. To explain it differently, there is a definitional connection between amount and importance. One value is more important than another if the least discriminable amount of one value has more value (e.g., twice as much value) than the least discriminable amount of the other value. All we need to know for making a comparison is the number of units of each value. On this interpretation of importance, commensurability of values is universal. Cohen called this comment his 'inconsistency objection', which he summarized as follows: If one exercises the concept of importance in terms of commensurability of the relevant values, one cannot also affirm the incommensurability of those values.

Here is my reply. The concept of importance need not, and usually cannot, be exercised in terms of commensurability of the relevant values. Take the following example. People usually consider a life with superficial pleasures but without basic liberties less good than a life with basic liberties (e.g., freedom of speech and conscience) but without the relevant pleasures. The reason is evident: basic liberties are (considered) more important than superficial pleasures. It is not necessary to commensurate these values in order to be able to conclude that basic liberties are more important than superficial pleasures. If so, there is no inconsistency between recognizing the incommensurability of some values and recognizing a difference in importance of these values. Although a more important value may be regarded as containing more value per just discernable unit than a less important value, this does not entail that these values must be commensurable. As Chang rightly argues, we can rank options or values with respect to their importance or weight in an *ordinal* way, not requiring commensuration.[2] In cases of incommensurable values we have to rely on comparisons in ordinal terms (e.g., 'less important', 'more important' and 'much more important'), instead of cardinal terms (e.g., 'twice as important'). Unlike cardinal weights, ordinal weights (e.g., 'more weighty' and 'much less weighty') can be assigned without commensuration.

CHALLENGE 5: 'INSIGNIFICANT AMOUNT'

Suppose philosopher A has a great analytical skill but a moderate originality; philosopher B has hardly any analytical skill and trivially more originality than philosopher A. Then, given the non-fulfilment of the significant bidirectionality condition, philosophers A and B are comparable (A is better than B). According to Cohen, this is a contradiction, because originality and analytical skill are assumed to be incommensurable and incomparable. However, Cohen's objection omits to make a distinction between the incommensurability of *values* and the comparability or incomplete comparability of *options* that bear these values. Incommensurability of values does not always lead to incomplete comparability of the options that bear these values; it only does if all conditions are satisfied. The values (originality and analytical skill) are incommensurable, but the options (the philosophers *A* and *B*), which bear these values, become comparable if at least one condition of incomplete comparability is not satisfied – as in the example under consideration, where the '*significant* bidirectionality condition' is not fulfilled: if the amount of one of the contributory values, or the difference in the amount of the same contributory value (in this case 'originality') in the bearers of value is so insignificant that it may be 'virtually' disregarded, then the other contributory value (in this case 'analytical skill') becomes the single significant – and therefore the single relevant – contributory value with respect to which the philosophers can be compared and with respect to which philosopher *A* is the unambiguously better one. There is no contradiction here: the *values* (originality and analytical skill) remain incommensurable, but the *options* (the bearers of values) become comparable, because the problem of weighing the amounts of disparate values is avoided.

The above challenges could be refuted easily because they are based on misunderstandings and confusions. The next chapter is devoted to real challenges, based on pertinent and valid arguments.

NOTES

1. Elizabeth Anderson, 'Practical Reason and Incommensurable Goods', in *Incommensurability, Incomparability, and Practical Reason*, ed. Ruth Chang (Cambridge, Mass.: Harvard University Press, 1997), 100.

2. Ruth Chang, 'Introduction', in *Incommensurability, Incomparability, and Practical Reason*, ed. Chang, 2.

Chapter 3

Real Challenges
Imprecise Equality and Parity versus Incomplete Comparability

SUMMARY

Some leading philosophers explain a 3NT value relation between options as 'imprecise equality' or 'parity'. However, these explanations are inadequate and conceal possible problems of 3NT for the comparability of the options and for a complete rational justification of the choice. The notions 'imprecise equality' and 'parity' conflate two fundamentally different phenomena: 'real imprecise equality' and 'incomplete comparability'. The latter has nothing to do with impreciseness and entails the absence of any equality, including imprecise equality. In the appendix of this chapter I refute Ruth Chang's argumentation for the possibility of parity as a fourth value relation within the domain of complete comparability.

(*Note*: This chapter is rather technical. Like the previous chapter it is not essential for understanding the ideas developed in this book. The reader who is less interested in the challenges may continue at chapter 4.)

****

The trichotomy thesis states that there are not more than three possible positive value relations between two valuable items, A and B: A is better than B, A is worse than B or A is equally good as B. In chapter 1 we have seen that this thesis is implausible and that there is a fourth possibility in which it is (i) not true that A is better than B, (ii) not true that A is worse than B *and* (iii) not true that A and B are (roughly) equally good. I call this fourth value relation '3NT' ('triply not true') and explain it as 'incomplete comparability' of A and B. There are two important and influential challenges of the claim that 3NT entails incomplete comparability:

1. 3NT means 'imprecise equality' instead of incomplete comparability.
2. 3NT means 'parity' instead of incomplete comparability.

The two challenges have connections with each other, because parity is also explained as a kind of imprecise equality. 'Incomplete comparability', by contrast, entails the absence of any equality, including imprecise equality. The challenges are important because they suggest that 3NT is no significant problem for the comparability of options and for a complete rational justification of the choice. This chapter discusses imprecise equality, followed by a discussion of parity. The conclusion will be that neither imprecise equality nor parity is an adequate explanation of 3NT. More important, they conceal problems of 3NT for a complete rational justification of the choice (see chapter 4, especially the appendix).

IMPRECISE EQUALITY

Derek Parfit puts the following question about the literary talent of novelist Proust and poet Keats: 'Must it be true, of Proust and Keats, either that one was the greater writer, or that both were *exactly equally* as great?' He answers: 'There could not be, even in principle, such precision.'[1] Parfit bases his argument on what is usually called the

Small improvement phenomenon

Although A is not worse than B, a small improvement of A does not make A better than B.

If two items are precisely equally good, the smallest improvement of one item makes it already better than the other. But if two items are roughly equally good, this need not be the case. I use 'rough equality' and 'imprecise equality' interchangeably. I follow Parfit in believing that the relevant imprecision does not mean that one item is a little bit better than the other or that, as a consequence of insufficient information or insight, we do not exactly know which option is better than the other. The relevant imprecision is supposed to be fundamental and to be related to vagueness in the sense of imprecise definability and measurability of the relevant values. Applied to comparing the literary talents of two writers, a poet P and a novelist N, this means the following. For the sake of simplicity, let us assume that the covering value – literary talent – is made up of not more than two contributory values: expressivity and originality. Suppose P and N are roughly equally expressive and roughly equally original, then they are roughly equally good with respect to literary talent. Let us slightly improve P's literary talent by slightly improving his expressivity. Call this slightly better poet '$P+$'. It may be the case that $P+$, although he is better than P, is not better than N. This is the small improvement phenomenon. Suppose we now considerably (instead of slightly) improve P's literary talent by considerably improving his expressivity. Call this considerably better poet '$P{++}$'. Then $P{++}$ is not only better than P, but (unlike $P{+}$) also better than N. If $P{++}$ would not be better than N, N and original P could not be roughly equally good.

LARGE VERSUS SMALL IMPROVEMENT PHENOMENON

Let us now compare writer O, who is very original but has little expressivity, to writer E, who is very expressive but has little originality. Suppose we conclude that neither is better than the other. A large increase in O's originality need not render him better than E, because the latter remains much better than O with respect to expressivity. I call this the large improvement phenomenon.

Large improvement phenomenon
Although A is not worse than B, a large improvement of A does not make A better than B.

If this applies to writers O and E, it means that O is not only not equally good but also not roughly equally good as E. Indeed, if O would be roughly equally good as E, a large improvement of O would make him better than E. Let us assume that Proust and Keats are the above-mentioned novelist N and poet P. Then their comparative relation fundamentally differs from the comparative relation between writer O and E. While Proust and Keats have roughly equal originality and roughly equal expressivity, O has significantly more originality than E, and E has significantly more expressivity than O. Keats and Proust are 'imprecisely equal' with respect to literary talent, given the *small* improvement phenomenon, while O and E are not, given the *large* improvement phenomenon. The difference between the two relations is caused by the presence of significant bidirectionality of the relevant contributory values in the relation between O and E and the absence of explicit significant bidirectionality in the relation between Proust and Keats. Imprecise equality is caused by the vagueness of human values (e.g., originality and expressivity) and the imprecise measurability of their amounts, so that even if we compare two items or persons with respect to a single contributory value (e.g., originality) of the covering value (e.g., literary talent), the small improvement phenomenon will apply if this single contributory value is vague and its amounts are imprecisely measurable. Below I will further explain that the 'rough equality' relation between N and P (and between Proust and Keats) fundamentally differs from the value relation between O and E. As we will see, the latter is an instance of 'incomplete comparability', which, unlike the former relation, does not depend on vagueness and imprecise measurability of amounts of values.

INCOMPLETE COMPARABILITY

To further clarify, and make plausible, the difference between imprecise equality (which underlies the small improvement phenomenon) on the one hand, and 'incomplete comparability' (which underlies the large improvement phenomenon) on the other hand, let us again take John Broome's insightful example of two careers, which we already discussed in chapter 1. Compare an adventurous and interesting but moderately paying career ('career A') with a chain of boring but better-paying and financially more secure careers ('careers B'). We saw that there is a range of indeterminateness in which the B careers are not better, not worse and not equally good – not even roughly equally good – as career A (see figure 1.1 in chapter 1). The cause of indeterminateness is the *non-existence* of determinate comparative value relations in the relevant range. Imprecise/rough equality is different. Examples have been discussed above. Another example is shown

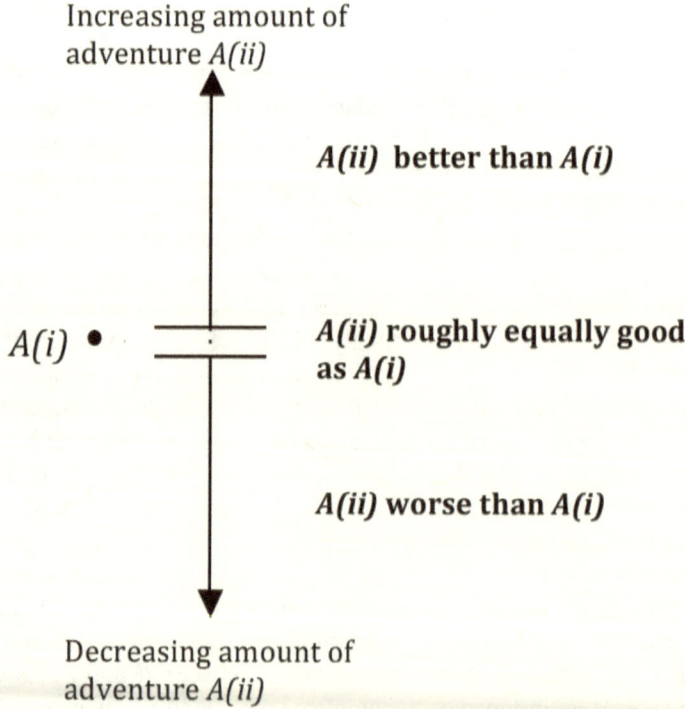

Figure 3.1. Adventurous career $A(i)$ compared with a chain of adventurous careers $A(ii)$

in figure 3.1, which further illustrates the difference with figure 1.1 in chapter 1.

In figure 3.1 adventurous careers are compared with respect to a single value, 'adventure'. Adventurous career $A(i)$ is imprecisely equally good as a *narrow* range of adventurous careers $A(ii)$. There applies a *small* improvement phenomenon, due to the vagueness and imprecise measurability of the amounts of the relevant value ('adventure'). The large improvement phenomenon, by contrast, cannot be explained by 'rough/imprecise equality'. Indeed, how is it possible that, if A and B are roughly equally good, a considerable improvement of A does not make A better than B? A more plausible explanation is that the relevant items are to some extent incomparable. If the relevant items are incomparable, the large improvement phenomenon and 3NT necessarily apply. Explanation in terms of incomplete comparability is further supported by the *non-existence* of a determinate comparative value relation. One of the characteristics of incomparable items is the impossibility to equate them in value. The fact that a level of (even rough) equivalence is absent in the whole chain of items in the standard configuration shown in figure 1.1 of chapter 1 is consistent with this characteristic. None of the B careers in the chain is (roughly) equally good as career A: there is a zone where B is worse than A, a zone of 3NT (where B is neither better than, nor worse than, nor roughly equally good as A) and a zone where B is better than A. This means that B is even incapable of being (roughly) *equated* with A by increasing or decreasing the financial security. Note that the upper and lower limits of the range of indeterminateness (3NT) do not represent levels of (rough) equivalence either.

In contrast to the large improvement phenomenon, the small improvement phenomenon, shown in figure 3.1 is no proof of incomparability. It is a sign of rough instead of precise equality, and rough equality is a form of comparability.[2] Parfit's approach – and Ruth Chang's approach, see the following discussion – conflate the two distinct phenomena 'incomplete comparability' (as illustrated in figure 1.1 of chapter 1) and 'imprecise equality' (as illustrated in figure 3.1). Parfit distinguishes degrees of imprecise equality and occasionally uses the notion 'very imprecise equality', for instance, in his discussion of Sidgwick's 'dualism'.[3] Sidgwick believes that impartial reasons for action are incomparable with self-interested ones. Parfit disagrees and explains why. Suppose we have to compare and choose between 'saving ourselves from one minute of discomfort' and 'saving a million people from death or agony'. The latter option is definitely better than the former. If so, there is comparability between self-interested and impartial reasons. (I think Parfit's argument is invalid and an instance of what I call the 'insignificant amount fallacy' [see the appendix of this chapter]: 'saving ourselves from one minute of discomfort' is so insignificant, especially compared to the extremely significant alternative ('saving a million people from death or agony'), that we can safely disregard the former option without the need to weigh it against the latter.)

Parfit admits that Sidgwick's view is partly right because the comparability of self-interested and impartial reasons may be 'very imprecise'. To show this, he gives the following example.

> I could save either my own life or the lives of several distant strangers. . . . And I might have such reasons whether the number of these strangers would be two or two thousand. . . . If these claims are true, the relative strength of these two kinds of reason is very imprecise.[4]

Parfit regards the two options as 'imprecisely equally good'. He recognizes that in this example 'the impreciseness is very large'. If we can rationally choose between saving two strangers (A) and saving my own life (B), then – assuming that it would be irrational to choose a worse option – neither option is worse than the other. If we considerably improve A by a factor of 1,000 (saving 2,000 strangers instead of 2) and we can again rationally choose B, then B is apparently again not worse than A. If so, this means that the original (not-improved) A is not only not better and not worse than B but also not equally good, not even imprecisely equally good, as B (given the large improvement phenomenon). Nevertheless Parfit believes that A and B are (imprecisely) comparable and (imprecisely) equal. However, if not-improved A is not definitely worse than B and a 1,000-fold improvement of A makes it not better than B, an explanation of the relation between A and B in terms of 'imprecise equality' seems impossible. Indeed, how can we reconcile this large improvement phenomenon with the existence of (rough) equivalence? If A and B would have (roughly) equal amounts of (overall) value, then a considerable (manifold) increase in B's amount of value would imply that B's amount of value becomes considerably larger than A's amount of value. There is a more comprehensible and plausible explanation for the relevant 'large improvement phenomenon': A and B are incompletely comparable (instead of imprecisely comparable) and lack any equivalence (instead of being imprecisely equal). In sum, Parfit (like Chang) regards two options, neither of which is worse than the other, as being 'imprecisely equally good' not only if a small but also if a large improvement of one item does not make it better than the other. The latter is difficult to understand. It resembles the unintelligible claim that, although the size of A is roughly equal to the size of B, a considerable increase of A's size does not make it larger than the size of B. This odd result shows that a distinction should be made between '(real) imprecise equality', due to the vagueness or imprecise measurability of the amount of values, and 'incomplete comparability', which has to do neither with impreciseness nor with equality.

SIGNIFICANCE

Chang thinks that a comparison of the alternatives is necessary to the justification of a choice and that incomparability of alternatives may pose a significant problem for practical reason.[5] Indeed, if alternatives cannot be compared, what reason can there be for choosing the one *rather than* the other? If (in)comparability of options has consequences for practical reason, it is important to have insight into the distinction between incomplete comparability and rough/imprecise equality. The two conditions have significantly different theoretical and practical implications for the rational justification of the choice and for the possibility to make trade-offs. This will be discussed in more detail in chapter 4.

CONCLUSION

The notion 'imprecise equality' used by some leading theorists conflate two distinct phenomena:

1. 'Real imprecise equality', due to imprecise measurability of amounts of the relevant values
2. 'Incomplete comparability', due to incommensurability of the relevant values

Imprecise equality is an imprecise version of equality – one of the three current value relations, within the domain of (complete) comparability. Incomplete comparability, by contrast, concerns neither impreciseness nor equality. Unlike imprecise equality, incomplete comparability may cause significant problems for the rational justification of the choice and is incompatible with trade-offs between the amounts of the relevant values, because any equivalence, even rough equivalence, is lacking.

APPENDIX: RUTH CHANG'S PARITY [I]

(*Notes*: For my comment on Chang's claim that parity gives practical reasons a 'voice' and avoids the problem of incompletely justified choice, see the appendix of chapter 4: 'Ruth Chang's parity [II]'.

The following text is nearly a complete copy of part 1 of 'Parity, Incomparability and Rationally Justified Choice', *Philosophical Studies* 146 (2009): 75–92. The reader may skip this appendix, because it is not essential for understanding the line of reasoning.)

Let us now discuss Chang's notion 'parity'. Suppose we are confronted with a choice between two alternatives, one of which is better in one respect, while the other is better in another respect. If we cannot say that one respect is less important than the other, the decision may be hard. Suppose, for instance, we hesitate between two moral requirements such as a duty to tell the truth and a requirement to avoid causing harm, or we have to decide between a policy that promotes economic growth and one that is more favourable for the environment. Before we decide, we shall want to compare and weigh the alternatives carefully. However, suppose that the options are incomparable, how can we make a rationally justified choice? The possibility to make such a choice seems to depend on the possibility to compare the options. Indeed, if they are incomparable, what reason could there be for choosing one option rather than the other?

Joseph Raz thinks that the alternatives mentioned here are incomparable, due to the incommensurability of the relevant values.[6] He does not believe, however, that the choice between incomparable options is beyond the scope of reason. Reason checks whether the alternatives for choice are 'rationally eligible', but it cannot guide the choice between the rationally eligible but incomparable options. The final choice depends on the agent's will. The decisive role of the will renders the choice to some extent arbitrary, but the rational eligibility of the options entails that the choice is still rationally justified.

Chang, by contrast, endorses the view that incomparability of options precludes a rationally justified choice.[7] She tries to show, however, that in many putative cases of incomparability, like those mentioned above, the relevant options are 'on a par' instead of 'incomparable'. Chang regards parity as a fourth value relation within the domain of complete comparability, in addition to the standard value relations, 'better than', 'worse than' and 'equally good as'. She suggests that the preservation of comparability in the case of parity secures the possibility of a completely rationally justified choice.

AIM

I will challenge Chang's argument for the possibility of parity. Chang's demonstration of parity is based on the 'small improvement argument' and the 'chaining argument'. The small improvement argument shows that with respect to alternatives for choice it may be the case that none of the three standard value relations applies. Raz regards this as a sign that the relevant options are incomparable.[8] Chang, by contrast, adduces the 'chaining argument' to show that the relevant options are comparable.[9] This would demonstrate the existence of a fourth positive value relation, parity: a value relation that does not belong to the three standard value relations but still entails comparability. I shall challenge the chaining argument by demonstrating that the premise on which it is based – the so-called difference principle – is mistaken. This undermines Chang's argument for the possibility of parity as a fourth value relation within the domain of complete comparability.

CHALLENGE OF THE ARGUMENT FOR PARITY

Let us consider one of Chang's putative examples of parity. It concerns the comparison of two careers A and B with respect to the value 'goodness as a career', containing two contributory values: 'salary' (S) and 'pleasant working environment' (E). Career A has a very good salary (10S) and an average working environment (5E) while career B has an average salary (5S) and a very pleasant working environment (10E). Now the question is whether careers A and B are comparable (figure 3.2). Raz thinks they are incomparable due to the incommensurability of salary and quality of working environment. Chang, by contrast, thinks that the chaining argument can demonstrate that they are comparable.

The chaining argument consists of two parts. The first one, which Chang calls a 'nominal/notable comparison', runs as follows:

> If we slightly decrease the salary of notable career A (10S, 5E) we are left with a career identical to this career but slightly worse in salary, e.g. career (9S, 5E). In this way we can create a continuum of careers starting with notable career A (10S, 5E) and ending with nominal career C (1S, 5E), a career with a very bad salary and an average working environment (see figure above). It is clear that nominal career C (1S, 5E) is definitely comparable with notable career B (5S, 10E): it is worse.

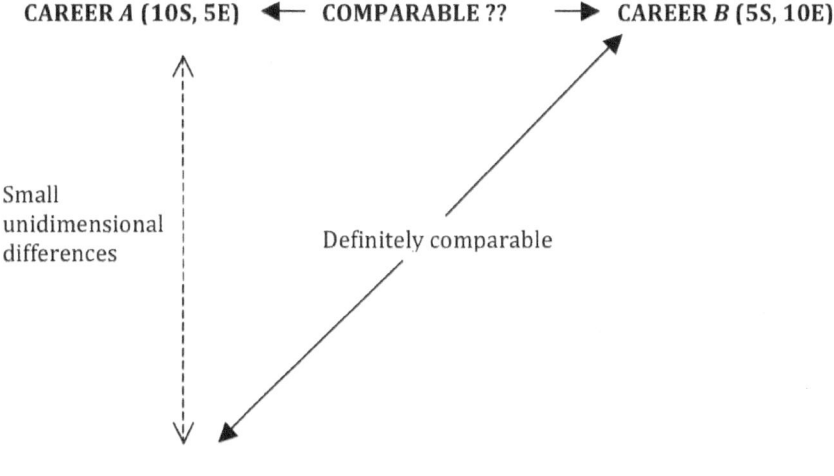

Figure 3.2. Is career A comparable with career B?

The second part of the 'chaining argument' is meant to show that if career C (1S, 5E) is comparable with career B (5S, 10E), career A (10S, 5E) too is comparable with career B (5S, 10E). This part crucially depends on the 'difference principle', which states that 'a small uni-dimensional difference in value cannot trigger incomparability where before there was comparability':

> If career B (5S, 10E) is comparable with career C (1S, 5E), then it is also comparable with a career $C+$ [say, career (2S, 5E)] of which the salary is only slightly higher than that of career C, for the difference between the two careers is a small unidimensional one, and by hypothesis, such a difference can't trigger incomparability between different items where before they were comparable. And if career B is comparable with career $C+$, then applying the principle anew, it follows that career B is comparable with career $C++$ [say, career (3S, 5E)], and so on. Comparability with career B is preserved through the continuum of small uni-dimensional differences, and thus we arrive at the conclusion that career B (5S, 10E) is comparable with career A (10S, 5E).

We shall see that the difference principle is the weak link of the chaining argument. On the face of it the principle seems plausible. Indeed, how could merely unidimensional changes in the amount of value render comparable options incomparable? However, such changes may trigger other changes that may be relevant for (in)comparability. That is why Chang recognizes that the difference principle is not universally applicable. In her book *Making Comparisons Count* she formulates two provisos.[10] The first ('Aristotelian') proviso requires that every small improvement of a respect makes the item indeed better than its unimproved counterpart.[11] The second ('Hegelian') proviso is that the small improvement does not 'trigger' a new value in the improved item that is lacking in its predecessors.[12] The Aristotelian and Hegelian changes, correlated with increases in amounts of value, only occur in specific cases. However, I will show that small unidimensional increases in amounts of value trigger at least three relevant changes that are independent of specific values or cases. This entails that the difference principle is not only 'not universally applicable' but not applicable altogether (i.e., even if the provisos are satisfied). In order to demonstrate this we shall again consider our example of the two careers which Chang herself regards as satisfying the conditions.[13]

CHANGE I: FROM UNI- TO BIDIRECTIONALITY

The first part of the chaining argument – the notable/nominal comparison – poses no problems. There is demonstrable comparability of nominal career C (1S, 5E) and notable career B (5S, 10E): the former is definitely worse than the latter because it is worse in both salary and working environment. However, the second part of the chaining argument is the weak link. Small unidimensional increments of value (small increases in salary), starting from career C (1S, 5E), trigger a change from 'unidirectionality' to 'bidirectionality'[14]: if the salary becomes larger than 5S, the career becomes better than career B (5S, 10E) with respect to salary, while career B is better with respect to working environment. Paradoxically, a one-dimensional change creates a two-dimensional problem of comparison. While before the unidimensional increments, there is no need of a trade-off between different dimensions, the new situation cannot avoid such a trade-off. The controversy with respect to comparability of the relevant options A and B concerns precisely the question whether such a trade-off is possible. So, although it is demonstrably true that career B is comparable with career C (the *diagonal* in figure 3.2) and although career C is connected with career A by merely small unidimensional differences (the *vertical* line), this does not demonstrate the comparability of career B and career A (the *horizontal* line).

After a similar 'penetrating comment' on the difference principle, raised by an anonymous referee, Chang added the following condition to the Aristotelian and Hegelian provisos:

[The Difference Principle] presupposes that the comparability of two evaluatively very different items is a matter of balancing or trading off the way one relevant respect is borne against the way another relevant respect is borne. In determining how two evaluatively very different careers compare, we balance the high salary of one career, for example, against the pleasant working environment of the other; the ways in which respects relevant to the comparison are borne can be traded off against one another.[15]

In other words, the difference principle supposes that neither option is Pareto-superior/inferior (i.e., better or worse in all respects). The next section will take this additional condition into account.

CHANGE II: FROM INSIGNIFICANCE INTO SIGNIFICANCE

Let us adapt our career example in such a way that the *nominal* career C is worse than the *notable* career B without being 'Pareto-inferior'. We can take career (6S, 5E) as the *nominal* career C. Then there is bidirectionality between career C (which is better with respect to salary) and career B (which is better with respect to working environment), while C seems to be worse than B, because C is considerably ('5 points') worse with respect to working environment and only slightly ('1 point') better with respect to salary. In that case the difference principle could be applied to show that notable A too must be comparable with B without being undermined by the objection of absent 'bidirectionality'. However, in order to be capable of concluding that '5-point better-working environment' represents definitely more value than '1-point better salary', we must assume comparability between these heterogeneous values while this is precisely what has to be demonstrated.

One could reply that a career with an only trivially higher salary (say, a few cents) is definitely worse than (and therefore comparable to) a career with a much better-working environment. In that case, one could argue, the difference principle shows that notable career A too is comparable with notable career B. However, a negligible difference (like a difference in salary of a few cents) can be virtually disregarded. Indeed, it is not rationally required – even not rational – to assign significant weight to insignificant differences. That is why, in this case (in which the condition of significant bidirectionality is not satisfied), we can conclude that career B is definitely better than career C without trading off the difference in the quality of working environment and the difference in salary. Indeed, the difference in salary can be ignored because the extent to which C's salary is better than that of B is negligible. So we have to consider only the difference in the quality of working environment in order to determine which career is the better one. If, by contrast, the difference in salary is significant, it cannot be disregarded. Then weighing the difference in salary against the difference in the quality of working environment becomes unavoidable. In the relevant example small unidimensional differences gradually trigger significant differences where before the difference was insignificant. Consequently, small unidimensional differences trigger the need of a trade-off between heterogeneous values – a trade-off that could be avoided before.

The inference of comparability *after* the 'insignificance/significance turn' from comparability *before* this turn is a specious way of reasoning, which I call the 'insignificant amount fallacy'.

Insignificant amount fallacy

The inference from 'P and q are comparable' to 'P and Q are comparable'.

P, Q and q represent different options (e.g., different careers) that have the following characteristics:

- P contains a *significantly* larger amount of value $V1$ (e.g., 'quality of working environment') than Q and q.
- Q contains a *significantly* larger amount of value $V2$ (e.g., 'salary') than P.
- q has an *insignificantly* larger amount of value $V2$ than P.

The inference of comparability of P and Q from the comparability of P and q is a *non-sequitur* because P and q can be compared without weighing the difference in amounts of *V1* against the difference in amounts of *V2*, while a comparison of *P* and *Q* cannot avoid such a weighing. That is why 'incomparabilists' may, without being inconsistent, confirm the comparability of *P* and *q* and deny the comparability of *P* and *Q*.[16] Therefore, although the turn from insignificance into significance results from small unidimensional increases, it cannot demonstrate that comparability is preserved.

Although Chang's nominal-notable comparison is not a manifest instance of the 'insignificant amount fallacy', it may be a latent one. This becomes clear when we analyse Chang's description of the 'nominal-notable test':

> Call a bearer 'notable' with respect to a value if it is an exceptionally fine exemplar of that value and 'nominal' if it is an exceptionally poor one. Mozart and Michelangelo, for instance, are notable bearers of creativity and Talentlessi, a very bad painter, a nominal one. Now suppose that Talentlessi bears the same contributory values of creativity as Michelangelo – only in a nominal way . . . [W]e know that Mozart is better than Talentlessi with respect to creativity. . . . Consider, now, Talentlessi +, just a bit better than Talentlessi with respect to creativity and bearing exactly the same contributory values, but a bit more notably. . . . Thus we can construct a 'continuum' of painters including Talentlessi and Michelangelo. . . . Therefore, given that Mozart is comparable with Talentlessi, he is comparable with Michelangelo.[17]

The nominal/notable test infers, via the difference principle, comparability of two excellent alternatives from the comparability of an excellent alternative and a 'very bad'/'exceptionally poor' one. The first objection we can make is that Chang does not show that Talentlessi is not Pareto-inferior to Mozart. Pareto-inferiority would render the relevant nominal-notable test invalid according to the argument given above. But even if we assume that Talentlessi is better than Mozart in a relevant and important aspect of creativity, the phrases 'very bad' and 'exceptionally poor' do not differ much from the term 'insignificant' of the 'insignificant amount fallacy'. That is why the nominal/notable comparison is vulnerable to a similar objection. The difference principle cannot take away the doubt whether comparability of an excellent composer (Mozart) and an excellent painter (Michelangelo) can be inferred from the comparability of an excellent composer (Mozart) and a very bad painter (Talentlessi). The betterness of an option representing a perfect and 'complete' value (excellent composing) compared to an option representing a 'deficient', 'incomplete' and 'eroded' value (bad painting) does not say much about the comparability of two alternatives, both representing 'full' and 'intact' values, in spite of the fact that an 'incomplete value' is connected with a complete instance of the same value by a series of small unidimensional differences. These differences trigger a change from an incomplete and deficient value into a complete and perfect value – a change that may be relevant for the (in)comparability of the alternatives.

To avoid misunderstandings I want to emphasize that my aim is to challenge Chang's argument for comparability rather than to defend the incomparability of Mozart and Michelangelo. I think it is perfectly possible to compare Mozart and Michelangelo with respect to their creative talent if there is no significant bidirectionality of relevant contributory values of creativity between the two artists. This is, for instance, the case if both artists are (roughly) equally good with respect to all contributory values of creativity, or if one of the artists is better with respect to all these contributory values. Genres (painting or composing) need not be different contributory values with respect to creativity. They may be different forms in which the same contributory values are expressed. We do not want to compare Mozart and Michelangelo with respect to their skill in composing or painting but with respect to their creativity. This makes it less relevant that Mozart is a composer (and is better in composing) and Michelangelo a painter (and is better in painting). The Mozart/Michelangelo example would be more relevant for the issue under consideration (comparability of heterogeneous alternatives) if Mozart and Michelangelo (instead of merely differing in genres of creativity) would 'bidirectionally' differ in distinct and important contributory values of creativity, for instance, originality and technical skill: for example, if Mozart would have a greater originality and less technical skill than Michelangelo, while the latter would have a greater technical skill and less originality. If there is no bidirectionality there is no need of showing comparability because, in that case, comparability is evident. The absence of explicit bidirectionality between Mozart and Michelangelo makes Chang's example less adequate than the career example in which the bidirectionality of the contributory values is explicitly shown. Besides, the absence of explicit and unambiguous bidirectionality between Mozart and Talentlessi (Talentlessi seems Pareto-inferior to Mozart) makes the relevant nominal-notable test vulnerable to the objection described in the above section 'Change I: from uni- to bi-directionality'.

CHANGE III: FROM RATIONAL DETERMINATION INTO RATIONAL UNDER-DETERMINATION OF THE CHOICE

Let us return to our career example. Chang will reply that we can take a notable option B that is very much better with respect to working environment, while nominal option C is only somewhat – but not insignificantly – better with respect to salary. She could argue that in that case, if other things are equal, career *B* is definitely better than and therefore comparable to career *C* (after which the difference principle can do the rest to show that *A* and *B* are equally comparable). Still the definite betterness of *B* compared to *C* cannot be taken for granted. It would entail that we could rationally prefer only *B* (the career with the much better-working environment) and not *C* (the career with the not-insignificantly higher salary). However, there is no reason to believe that it is irrational to choose the latter career. And if both *B* and *C* can be rationally chosen, this may be a sign of their incomparability.[18]

But let us suppose it *would* be irrational to choose nominal career *C* instead of notable career *B*. It would mean that notable *B* and nominal *C* are comparable. In that case the difference principle seems to be capable of showing comparability between notable *A* (career with a very high salary) and notable *B* (career with a very good working environment) without being undermined by the bidirectionality and significance objections. However, if notable *B* is better than (and therefore comparable to) nominal *C*, this does not show that notable *B* and notable *A* are comparable. While in the case of nominal *C* and notable *B* only the latter option is rationally eligible (which may be regarded as a sign of comparability between these two options), reason cannot guide the choice between notable *A* and notable *B*. As said above, the 'rational under-determination' of the choice or the rational permissibility of either choice (while the options are not equally good) is, according to several thinkers, a sign that the relevant options are incomparable. Therefore, Chang cannot maintain that the difference principle demonstrates that these thinkers are mistaken without making this principle a *petitio principii*. In the relevant case small unidimensional differences trigger a change that may be relevant for the comparability of the options: a change from rational determination into rational under-determination of the choice. This change undermines the difference principle because this principle requires that, apart from the unidimensional differences, everything else that may be relevant to (in)comparability remains the same.

CONCLUSION

The previous sections have shown that Chang's difference principle is incapable of demonstrating comparability in hard cases of comparison without becoming a begging the question. Because the three changes I, II and III, which are triggered by unidimensional changes in amounts of value, are independent of specific values and examples under consideration, they take the edge off the difference principle, not only in cases that do not satisfy the Aristotelian and Hegelian provisos, but in all hard cases of comparison. This undermines the chaining argument for the possibility of parity because it crucially depends on the difference principle.

NOTES

1. Derek Parfit, *Reasons and Persons* (Oxford: Clarendon Press, 1984), 431.
2. Cf. James Griffin, 'Incommensurability: What's the Problem?' in *Incommensurability, Incomparability, and Practical Reason*, ed. Ruth Chang (Cambridge, Mass.: Harvard University Press, 1997), 262–263, fn. 12.
3. Derek Parfit, *On What Matters* (Oxford: Oxford University Press, 2011), chap. 6, section 19.
4. Ibid., p. 138.
5. Ruth Chang, 'Introduction', in *Incommensurability, Incomparability, and Practical Reason*, ed. Chang, 13.
6. Joseph Raz, *The Morality of Freedom* (Oxford: Oxford University Press, 1986), chap. 13.
7. Chang, 'Introduction'.
8. Raz, *The Morality of Freedom*, chap. 13.
9. Ruth Chang, 'The Possibility of Parity', *Ethics* 112 (2002): 673–679.
10. Ruth Chang, *Making Comparisons Count* (New York: Routledge, 2002).
11. Chang argues that this is not always the case, because '[t]o paraphrase Aristotle, you can have too much of a good thing'. Ibid., 132.
12. Chang: 'To paraphrase Hegel, with enough of a change of one kind, a change of another kind kicks in.' See Chang, *Making Comparisons Count*, 132. In response to a 'penetrating comment of an anonymous referee', Chang adds later on a third condition. See the next section.
13. Chang, 'The Possibility of Parity', 676.
14. 'Unidirectionality' means that one option is better or worse than the other option in all aspects, so it has the same meaning as 'Pareto-superior', respectively, 'Pareto-inferior'. 'Bidirectionality' means that one option is better with respect to one aspect while the other option is better with respect to another aspect.
15. Chang, 'The Possibility of Parity', 676.
16. Cf. Bernard Williams, *Moral Luck* (Cambridge: Cambridge University Press, 1981), 77. Williams regards options representing significant differences in amounts of incommensurable values as incomparable but regards them as comparable if the amount of one value in one option only trivially differs from the amount of the same value in the other option.
17. Chang, 'Introduction', 14–16.
18. Several theorists regard two not-equally-good options as 'comparable' if we can rationally choose only one of them and as 'incomparable' if we can rationally choose either. Cf. Raz, *The Morality of Freedom*, chap. 13; Parfit, *On What Matters* (section 'Sidgwick's Dualism'); Walter Sinnott-Armstrong, 'Moral Dilemmas and Incomparability', *American Philosophical Quarterly* 22 (1985): 321–329.

Chapter 4

Implications of Incomplete Comparability for Practical Reasoning

SUMMARY

Incomplete comparability of options (3NT) may have important interrelated implications for practical reasoning, such as ambivalence, rational undecidability, incomplete ordering of options, impossibility to assign objective relative weights, indeterminateness and incomplete rational justification of the choice. These implications are due to 3NT *as such* (the fact that neither option outweighs the other, while they have also not roughly equal weight) irrespective of how 3NT is explained (as 'incomplete comparability', 'imprecise equality' or 'parity'). In the appendix of this chapter I refute Ruth Chang's claim that her interpretation of 3NT in terms of parity gives practical reason a 'voice' and avoids incomplete justification of the choice.

****

In this chapter I will show that incomplete comparability of two options entails rational under-determination of the choice. This makes the choice incompletely rationally justified, because the reasons for choosing one option do not outweigh the reasons for choosing the other option. This conclusion has far-reaching consequences for the scope of practical reason. Incomplete comparability of options may have the following interrelated consequences for practical reasoning:

(1) Ambivalence
(2) Rational undecidability
(3) Incomplete ordering of options
(4) Impossibility to assign objective relative weights

(5) Indeterminateness instead of inconclusiveness
(6) Incomplete rational justification of the choice

In this chapter I will elaborate on these consequences.

AMBIVALENCE

The possibility of 3NT refutes the widespread belief that if neither of two options is better than the other, they are (roughly) equivalent. 'Better', 'worse' and 'equally good' are not exhaustive value relations: it is also possible that neither of two options is better than the other, while they are also not equally good. As a corollary, 'preference' and 'indifference' are not exhaustive attitudes towards valuable options. Absence of preference does not necessarily mean indifference: there is also ambivalence. When confronted with the need to make a choice between two options that have a 3NT value relation, the agent may be ambivalent, instead of being indifferent or having a preference. This shows the weakness of the 'revealed preference theory' – the theory that a choice between two options reveals the agent's preference. The possibility of ambivalence is often ignored or not recognized although it has far-reaching problematic consequences for utilitarian and economic analyses. For instance, if there is ambivalence instead of indifference, it is impossible to construct determinate 'indifference curves'. Indeed, indifference curves consist of points of (subjective) equivalence of the relevant options, while ambivalence concerns 3NT options – options that are (at least impartially/objectively) not equivalent, not even roughly equivalent (see chapter 1). 3NT is actually incompatible with 'indifference curves'. It is true that the impartial/objective non-existence of equivalence need not mean that the person in question may not assign equal value to the relevant options (see chapter 2, section 'Challenge 3: "Equal value"'), but if the agent is ambivalent, it means that also for her there is no point of equivalence. It is often assumed that individuals are always capable of making complete preference orderings, but this is not true if it concerns 3NT options. Especially with respect to the important human values under consideration, personal preferences too may be incomplete.[1] If two values are incommensurable, individuals may be incapable of indicating what amount of one value is (roughly) equivalent to what amount of the other value. If they nevertheless make a choice, their decision need not reveal a preference. Because incomplete preferences are incompatible with indifference curves, it is clear that 3NT has far-reaching consequences for economic and utilitarian analyses that depend on the assumption that there is either preference or indifference.

RATIONAL UNDECIDABILITY

If option A is better than option B, we have sufficient reason to choose A rather than B. If B is better than A we have sufficient reason to choose B rather than A. If A and B are equally good in the sense that they are identical with respect to what is relevant to the choice, we may be indifferent. But if A is not better than B, *and* B is not better than A, *and* A and B are not equally or roughly equally good – what should we choose then? In that case we have no overriding reason to choose one option *rather than* the other, nor reason to be indifferent. This is the case if A and B are 3NT options. This may lead to 'rational undecidability'.

Rational undecidability

The inability to decide between two options on the basis of an overriding reason that justifies the choice of one option rather than the other (while indifference is inappropriate because the options are neither equally nor roughly equally good and have important differences in consequences).

The last part of the definition between the brackets is a necessary addition because in the case of (roughly) equally good options (i.e., options that are more or less interchangeable with respect to what is relevant to the choice) it is true as well that there is no reason to choose one option rather than the other. But in those cases there is no rational undecidability because it does not matter which option is chosen. Indecisiveness in those cases would be tantamount to Buridan's ass's irrational paralysis. The donkey died of hunger due to his own irrationality. He was confronted with two roughly equal haystacks and, having no reason to choose the one rather than the other, he could not make a choice. But his indecisiveness was ungrounded because he could have rationally chosen either. After all, if options are equally good in the sense of identical with respect to what is relevant to the choice, it does not matter which one is chosen. By contrast, if options significantly differ, it does matter. Still, why would a lack of an overriding reason to choose one option rather than the other be a problem? Taking for granted that A and B are incompletely comparable, why should we be worried? Why do we need a reason to choose the one rather than the other if we have a reason for choosing either so that either choice is rational? However, the problem is not constituted by the question whether the choice is supported by reasons; either choice *is*. The problem is that each option is supported by significantly different reasons (neither of which outweighs the other) and that the consequences of the choice are significantly different. That is why we cannot be indifferent. Our concern is not that we threaten to make an irrational choice: our rationality is guaranteed because both options are 'rationally eligible'. Our concern is the question which option we should choose. While in cases of better, worse or equally good options this 'should' is no further question, it is a further question in cases of incompletely comparable options. Our problem is that reason is unable to solve our 'dilemma' and that we have to decide between the rationally eligible options without the further guidance of reason. Tossing a coin – appropriate in cases of options that appear to be equally good – would not be appropriate in this case. It is appropriate if we are indifferent between the options. Indifference entails that it does not matter which option is chosen. But how could it not matter if the options lead to significantly different consequences? Therefore, rational undecidability may be a real problem, especially if it concerns public and ethical decisions and decisions between competing demands of justice that lead to significantly different consequences for persons and society. In part 2 we will work out the consequences of rational undecidability for public decision-making, ethics and justice.

INCOMPLETE ORDERING

A set of options can be completely ordered if each option of the set can be completely compared to each other option of the set. Options can be ordered only incompletely if some of the options are incompletely comparable, that is, if some options are neither better than, nor worse than, nor equally good as some other options of the set (= 3NT). In part 2 we shall see that incomplete ordering of ethical values and principles and of competing claims may have important consequences for ethics in general and justice in particular. In *A Theory of Justice* John Rawls writes:

> [A] conception of right must impose an ordering on conflicting claims. This requirement springs directly from the role of its principles in adjusting competing demands. . . . It is clearly desirable that a conception of justice be complete, that is, able to order all the claims that can arise.[2]

If conflicting claims and competing demands of justice are incompletely comparable, they belong to a set that cannot be completely ordered.[3] We shall discuss this problem in part 2.

IMPOSSIBILITY TO ASSIGN OBJECTIVE RELATIVE WEIGHTS

Many theorists regard relative weight assignment as the solution to conflicts of values, rival human interests and rival demands of justice. For instance, with respect to two competing ways of allocation of scarce health care resources, Frances Kamm argues that the right decision depends on the relative weight to be assigned to the relevant values.[4] Kamm does not explain how the required weights can be assigned. In an empirical study about equity versus efficiency as criteria of selecting patients for medical treatment, equally rational and well-informed people intuitively assigned interpersonally considerably differing relative weights to the relevant values (e.g., concern for worst-off patients versus benefit from treatment; see health care example in chapter 1): the relative weights varied by a multiplicative factor of 10–100.[5] This is not surprising because, as discussed above, rationally determinable and impartial/objective relative weights do not exist if the relevant options are incompletely comparable. The problem of weighing equity against efficiency in health care has been discussed in chapter 1 and will be worked out in chapter 9.

Amartya Sen thinks that incommensurability is 'no problem whatsoever in deciding what one should sensibly do when our priorities or weights over values are clear enough'.[6] However, if the relevant options are incompletely comparable, the problem is precisely that it is not clear what the priorities or weights should be. Still many theorists maintain that the solution should be found in the assignment of weights, but, like Kamm, they do not indicate how. G. A. Cohen has commented on this omission as follows:

> [P]hilosophers . . . do not know how to compute, in general terms, the comparative weights of the values all of which deserve consideration . . . [They] sometimes end their articles by saying this sort of thing: 'It is a task for future work to determine the weight of the consideration that I have exposed'. But nobody ever gets around to that further work. They wish they could, but they can't. . . . Nobody knows how to balance different values against one another .[7]

In chapter 1 we have seen that it is often impossible to assign objective and determinate relative weights to incommensurable values and incompletely comparable options. In part 2 we will see that this impossibility constitutes the central problem of incommensurable values for theories of justice and judicial decision-making.

INDETERMINATENESS

Indeterminateness is the impossibility of determining the relative worth of one option compared to another because a determinate relative worth does not exist. This differs from 'inconclusiveness', which means that a right answer exists but is not yet known or agreed upon. Indeterminateness, by contrast, is not due to insufficient knowledge or another human shortcoming but to the non-existence of a determinate relative worth given the incomplete comparability of the alternatives. Unlike what is often supposed, this does not necessarily mean that the relevant options are roughly equally good. The large improvement argument and the wide zone of indeterminateness (see chapter 1) make this implausible. The crucial problem of indeterminateness is that a determinate equivalence relation (even a rough one) does not exist.

INCOMPLETE RATIONAL JUSTIFICATION OF THE CHOICE

I shall first define some ambiguous notions. A choice may be 'rationally justified' in at least three different cases: (1) the chosen option is neither better than, nor worse than, nor equally good as the non-chosen one (3NT); (2) the chosen option is better than the non-chosen one; or (3) the chosen option is equally good as the non-chosen one. Let us call the first choice 'rationally permissible' or 'rationally eligible', the second choice 'rationally required' and the third one 'rationally indifferent'. 'Rationally permissible/eligible' means that reason permits either choice but remains silent with respect to which option *should* be chosen: reason under-determines the choice. 'Rationally required' means that reason shows which option should be chosen ('reason guides the choice'). 'Rationally indifferent' means that reason shows that it does not matter which option is chosen. Commenting on an earlier draft of this section, Joshua Gert argued that it may be odd to assert that in cases of equal goodness it does not matter which option is chosen, because it suggests that mattering is (merely) a matter of difference in (total amount of) value. But, Gert continues, it could matter a great deal which one chooses of two equally valuable things: not because one would get more value from one than from the other, but simply because of the important differences in kind between the items. I agree. However, I follow Chang's definition of 'equal goodness', namely, 'the state of being identical with respect to what is relevant to the choice'. In that case one can be indifferent between the options. 'If alternatives are equally good, practical reason tells us that it does not matter which alternative is chosen, for the alternatives are, with respect to whatever matters to the choice, exactly the same.'[8] So 'equal goodness' is an ambiguous phrase. Options A and B may be 'equally good' in the following two senses: (1) A and B are identical with respect to what is relevant to the choice: they contain the same relevant values in the same amounts; (2) A and B contain disparate values, but A's overall amount of value is equal to B's overall amount of value. For the reader it is important to know that I use the phrase 'equally good' in the first sense.

A rationally indifferent and a rationally required choice are completely rationally justified because the chosen option is at least as good as the non-chosen one. Rational undecidability, defined in a previous section, is associated with insufficient rational justification of the choice rather than lack of rational permissibility. A choice is rationally permissible or partially rationally justified if the chosen option is not worse than the non-chosen one. Because incomplete comparability implies that neither option is worse than the other, the choice of either of two incompletely comparable options is automatically rationally permissible but only partially/incompletely rationally justified. A choice is completely rationally justified if the chosen option is at least as good as the non-chosen one. Because 'at least as good' means 'equally good or better' and because incomplete comparability implies that the options are neither equally good nor that one is better than the other, neither of incompletely comparable options is at least as good as the other. Therefore, a choice between incompletely comparable options is, although rationally permissible and partially rationally justified, not completely rationally justified, at least in the sense of the above definition. Obviously this does not exclude the possibility of other kinds of (interpersonal) justification such as agreement on decision procedures (e.g., majority rule and decision by lot).

We need not exaggerate the problem of incomplete rational justification with respect to *intra*personal decisions (e.g., career choice, as discussed in chapter 1) instead of *inter*personal decisions or if it concerns trivial instead of important (especially moral) issues. Usually a person experiences no insurmountable problems in making the final choice. Besides, from a particular point of view, 'incomplete comparability' may be considered in a more favourable light. It creates room for free and autonomous choices not dictated by reason and still remaining within the constraints of reason (see chapter 12). This is a kind of freedom different from the freedom to choose between two comparable options that are equally good and interchangeable.

However, the situation becomes different in cases of public or ethical decisions. When it concerns inter- rather than intrapersonal decisions (as in politics, justice and adjudication between conflicting parties), then the 'absence of a reason for choosing one alternative rather than the other' is more problematic: one would hope that reason could guide the decision and could show which alternative should be chosen. Incomplete comparability implies that public and ethical decisions concerning conflicting human interests sometimes have to be taken on the basis of incomplete or partial justification. The argument that a partial justification is at least a justification does not resolve the predicament, because it means that we cannot give a justifying reason for choosing one alternative *rather than* the other. The reasons for choosing one option are not stronger than, and do not defeat, the reasons that can be given for choosing the alternative. This is especially problematic if it concerns public decisions between important but incompatible human interests or choices between competing moral claims or principles of justice. Particularly in those cases it is important to avoid arbitrariness, personal preferences and partiality. Thomas Nagel summarizes this problem as follows:

> [When each of two decisions] seems right for reasons that appear decisive and sufficient, arbitrariness means the lack of reasons where reasons are needed, since either choice will mean acting against some reasons without being able to claim that they are *outweighed*.[9]

In other words, incomplete comparability of options that embody competing weighty interests, ethical principles or demands of justice may lead to incomplete rational and ethical justification of the final choice, because the reasons for the chosen option do not outweigh the reasons for the non-chosen one. This causes an *ethical deficit* 'since either choice will mean acting against some reasons without being able to claim that they are outweighed'.

APPENDIX: RUTH CHANG'S PARITY (II)

(The following text is largely a copy of part 2 of the article 'Parity, incomparability and rationally justified choice', *Philosophical Studies* 146 (2009): 75–92. The reader may skip this appendix, which is not essential for understanding the book's line of reasoning.)

Ruth Chang thinks that 'parity' avoids or resolves the problem of rational justification of the choice. The aim of this appendix is to show that even if 'parity' would be a real possibility within the domain of complete comparability (as we have challenged in the appendix of the previous chapter), its implications for practical reason would not differ from those described earlier. Parity would not avoid 'rational undecidability' and 'incomplete justification of the choice' in the sense described earlier. It makes the final choice not less arbitrary – in the sense of decisively dependent on the agent's will. As Chang argues, '[H]ard cases of comparison are ubiquitous . . . and are plausibly at the root of moral dilemmas and the most intractable sorts of practical conflict generally'.[10] While she believes that, in those cases, parity gives practical reason a 'voice',[11] I will show that reason remains as incapable of guiding the final decision as in the case of incomplete comparability. The underlying cause of hard cases of comparison is the fact that none of the three standard value relations applies (= '3NT'), indicating that it is neither true that one of the options is better or worse than the other nor true that the options are equally good. The problematic implications for the rational justification of the choice are due to 3NT itself, irrespective of whether 3NT is explained as incomplete comparability or parity. Chang believes that parity enables a completely rationally justified choice in hard cases of comparison. She argues as follows:

> Parity expands the range of cases in which justified choice is possible; choices between items about which practical reason might otherwise appear to be silent are in fact choices between comparable items and thus within the scope of practical reason. Parity, it might be said, is what gives practical reason a 'voice' in hard cases.[12]

Chapter 3 has falsified Chang's argument for the possibility of parity. Now I will show that even if parity would be a real possibility, it would – contrary to what Chang suggests in the previous quotation – fail to determine the choice in hard cases, because its practical implications would not differ from those of incomplete comparability. Let us examine whether parity expands the scope of practical reason and whether its implications for a rationally justified choice favourably differ from those of incomplete comparability or Raz's incomparability. I will limit myself to Raz's incomparability, but what follows equally applies to incomplete comparability. Neither of two incomparable options can be worse than the other because 'being worse' requires comparability. Therefore, either choice between incomparable but rationally eligible options is 'rationally permissible'. Raz's incomparability further implies that none of the options is overall better than the other. This means that neither choice is 'rationally required'. Finally, incomparable options are not equally good, which means that the choice is not 'rationally indifferent'. The same implications for practical reason apply to parity, because – like incomparability – it excludes the three traditional value relations.

(1) Because neither option is better than the other, neither choice is 'rationally required'.
(2) Because the options are not equally good, the choice is not 'rationally indifferent'.
(3) Because neither option is worse than the other, either choice is 'rationally permissible'.

Chang writes: 'There are three different cases in which a choice between either alternative is rationally permissible: when the alternatives are (1) equally good, (2) incomparable, or (3) on a par.'[13] However, later she argues that in the case of incomparability reason 'fails to give an answer as to . . . whether it is rationally permissible to choose either'. This turn is not entirely transparent and contradicts the previous quotation. 'Rationally permissible' means 'permissible from the view point of reason'. It is not easy to understand how something can be 'permissible from the view point of reason' and at the same time beyond the reach of reason. If neither option is worse than the other (which is the case if the options are incomparable), either choice is permissible from the view point of reason, as Chang recognizes in the above quotation. In any case, the distinction between two kinds of rational permissibility seems irrelevant with respect to the implications for practical reason. Not only in the case of parity but also in the case of overall incomparability, the agent is capable of concluding that (i) option A is better with respect to 'value $V1$' and option B is better with respect to 'value $V2$' and that (ii) neither option is overall worse than the other. Suppose that, after careful considerations, the agent decides to choose A. Because (ii) prevents a rationally impermissible choice in both cases, it is unclear why the considered choice would be '*not* rationally permissible' if A and B are 'overall incomparable', while the same choice, based on the same considerations, would be 'rationally permissible' if the options are 'on a par'. In sum, both incomparability and parity entail that either choice is rationally permissible and neither choice is rationally required, while the choice is not 'rationally indifferent' either. And in both cases reason under-determines the choice. In other words, not less than Raz's incomparability, parity results in 'rational irresolvability' in the sense defined above. Chang is right that in the case of incomparability the rational choice function fails to give an answer to whether one should rationally choose one alternative:

> [I]f two alternatives are incomparable, no consideration will be able to justify choosing one over the other in that choice situation. For if they are incomparable, it seems that there is no fact concerning everything that matters that could provide grounds for choosing one *over* the other.[14]

But it is clear that the same applies to parity. An 'all things considered' reason for choosing one option *over* the other exists if the relevant option is 'all things considered' better than the other. Not only incomparability but also parity excludes the overall betterness of one option. That is why reason under-determines the choice in both cases. Reason permits either choice (because neither option is *worse* than the other) but fails to guide the choice with respect to which option should be chosen (because neither option is better than the other). In other words, parity and incomparability entail the same 'rational undecidability'.

'VALUE-PUMP' AND RATIONALLY JUSTIFIED CHOICE

Chang adduces the so-called value-pump problem to challenge the possibility of a rationally justified choice between incomparable options. The value-pump means that, in a series of choices, one ends up with less value than one started with. Suppose A is incomparable with B, B is incomparable with $A+$ and $A+$ is better than A. If one is faced with a choice between $A+$ and B, it is rationally permissible to choose either since they are incomparable. Suppose one chooses B. Now suppose that one is offered a choice between B and A. Since they are incomparable, again it is rationally permissible to choose either. Suppose one chooses A. But now one is left with A where before one might have had $A+$, which is better than A. Chang:

> All those who think that there can be justified choice among incomparables, then, must provide a well-motivated, non-ad hoc account of how practical reason prohibits agents from becoming 'merit pumps'.[15]

But parity is not less than incomparability susceptible to the value-pump problem. If the value-pump challenges the possibility of a rationally justified choice between incomparable options, it equally challenges the possibility of a rationally justified choice between options on a par. Chang admits this now, but she tries to adduce the value-pump to demonstrate 'the distinctive role parity plays in reason'. She argues as follows. If alternatives are equally good, it is rationally permissible to choose either, regardless of one's other choices (because there is no value-pump problem). If, by contrast, alternatives are *on a par*, it is rationally permissible to make a particular choice only if it is consistent with previous choices (in order to avoid the value-pump). Chang concludes that

> [i]f we think that there are choices in which whether it is rationally permissible to choose either alternative depends on our other choices, then there is a distinctive role for parity to play in practical reason.[16]

However, not only either choice between options on a par but also either choice between incomplete comparable options is rationally permissible, as Chang recognizes elsewhere, and, in order to circumvent a value-pump, not only parity but also incomparability renders the rational permissibility of a choice dependent on previous choices. Chang admits this. She continues:

> But we can distinguish two sorts of value pump puzzles: those in which the value pump is created by choices delivered by a choice function, and those in which it is created by the failure of a choice function to deliver a correct choice. My focus here is on the puzzle arising when the choice function is not silent.[17]

I wonder whether this distinction between the two sorts of value-pump puzzles is correct and relevant. In both cases reason remains silent, under-determines the choice and does not show which option should be chosen. Besides, the theoretical distinction does not change the fact that in both cases either choice is rationally permissible and that in both cases the value-pump problem has to be avoided. So all implications of parity relevant to practical reason are identical to those of Raz's incomparability and my 'incomplete comparability'.

DECISION BY 'THE WILL'

Chang criticizes Joseph Raz's solution of 'the will' as justifying the ultimate decision in cases of incomparable options. If 'the will' would refer to a special reason already belonging to all that matters to the choice, this would mean double counting. Raz's 'will' as 'brute want' (not motivated by a special reason) does not work either, because, according to Chang, a decision based on a 'brute desire' is only rationally justified if it does not much matter which alternative one chooses, that is, in cases of (roughly) equal goodness or trivial importance.[18] However, Chang too cannot avoid making the choice between options on a par dependent on the will. Now she admits that the consideration relevant to determining what one should do, faced with items on a par, is 'the will': when items are on a par, there is a new kind of reason that comes into play – 'personal' reasons – or 'will-based reasons' – that have to do with one's normative identity. When things are on a par, we have rational space to 'create' reasons for ourselves through an active attitude involving the will that constitute our normative identities, Chang argues.[19] Nothing in this formulation differs from what Raz says about the will with respect to a choice between incomparable but rationally eligible options. This makes the choice between options on a par not less arbitrary than the choice between Raz's incomparable but rationally eligible options. Chang argues that parity creates room for free and autonomous choices not dictated by reason and still remaining within the constraints of reason. This, she continues, is a kind of freedom different from the freedom to choose between equally good options. This is the same autonomy, within the limits of rational permissibility, described by Raz with respect to the choice between incomparable but rationally eligible options:

> Where the considerations for and against two alternatives are incommensurate, reason is indeterminate. It provides no better case for one alternative than for the other. Since it follows that there is no reason to shun one of the alternatives in favour of the other, we are in a sense free to choose which course to follow. That sense of freedom is special, and may be misleading. It is unlike the situation where one course of action is as good as the other. It is indifferent which action we take. They are equally good and equally bad. Incomparability does not ensure equality of merit and demerit. It does not mean indifference. It marks the inability of reason to guide our action, not the insignificance of our choice.[20]

In sum, all implications of parity for practical reason are identical to those of 'incomplete comparability' (3NT):

- In both cases reason under-determines the choice.
- In both cases either choice is 'rationally eligible' and neither choice is 'rationally required' or 'rationally indifferent'.
- Whether we regard hard cases of comparison as instances of incomplete comparability (3NT) or Chang's parity, the resulting practical problem is the same: how to take a final decision if we lack an overriding reason to choose one option *rather than* the other, while the respective choices have significantly different consequences.
- In both cases the absence of an overriding reason makes it impossible to give a complete rational justification of the choice, that is, a justification for choosing one option *rather than* the other.
- Parity is not less than incomplete comparability vulnerable to the value-pump.
- Both parity and incomplete comparability create room for *free and autonomous* choices not dictated by reason and still remaining within the constraints of reason (see also chapter 12).
- Like incomplete comparability, parity renders the final decision arbitrary, that is, dependent on the will of the agent.

These identical implications undermine Chang's belief that 'parity plays a distinctive role in practical reason'. Besides, they corroborate the conclusion of the previous chapter that the argument for the possibility of parity as a distinct positive value relation is unfounded.

CONCLUSIONS

Hard cases of comparison concern the fourth value relation '3NT' in which neither of two options is better than the other while they are not equally good either. Chang interprets many cases of 3NT as 'parity', while Raz explains 3NT as 'incomparability'. Other theorists, who equally recognize the existence of 3NT, give still other names and explanations of this value relation (e.g., 'imprecise equality', 'vagueness' or 'indeterminacy'). The controversy about the correct interpretation of 3NT tends to obscure the more important question of its implications for the rational resolvability of value conflicts. The problem of a rationally justified choice in cases of 3NT is caused by 3NT itself, irrespective of how it is explained. It is not difficult to see why. Practical reason is capable of guiding the choice if one of the trichotomy value relations applies, that is, if (i) A is better than B, or (ii) B is better than A, or (iii) A and B are equally good. In the first case, to be rational, A should be chosen; in the second case B should be chosen; and in the third case it does not matter. But what does practical reason prescribe if 3NT applies, that is, if it is neither true that A and B are equally good, nor true that A is better than B or B is better than A? Unlike in cases (i) and (ii), practical reason under-determines the choice. And unlike in case (iii), reason cannot conclude that it does not matter which option is chosen. This entails 'rational irresolvability' or 'rational undecidability', in the defined sense, and makes the final choice dependent on the will. This shows that the implications for practical reason are related to 3NT itself and not to the explanation of it. Just as an untreatable disease does not become curable by explaining it differently, so does a rationally irresolvable conflict not become rationally resolvable if the explanation of 3NT in terms of overall incomparability is replaced by an explanation in terms of parity. That is why the question of interpretation may easily become a red herring if we are interested in practical implications. Explanation in terms of 'comparability', as happens in Chang's parity approach, misguidedly suggests that 3NT does not pose significant problems for practical reason. The question 'If options are incomparable, what reason could there be for choosing one alternative rather than the other?' is not resolved and not easier to answer if we replace 'incomparable' by 'on a par': the practical problem of knowing how to choose is just as difficult.

NOTES

1. See Adam Morton, *Disasters and Dilemma, Strategies for Real-Life Decision Making* (Oxford: Basil Blackwell, 1991), especially chapter 3, 'Incomparabilities'; John Broome, *Weighing Goods: Equality, Uncertainty and Time* (Oxford: Blackwell Publishers, 1995), 93; Ruth Chang, 'The Possibility of Parity', *Ethics* 112 (2002), 666.
2. John Rawls, *A Theory of Justice*, revised edition (Cambridge, Mass: The Belknap Press of Harvard University Press, 1999), 115–116.
3. Compare Amartya Sen, 'Incompleteness and Reasoned Choice', *Synthese* 140 (2004), 55, 56, and fn 28 and 29, 59.
4. Frances Kamm, 'Deciding Whom to Help, Health-Adjusted Life Years and Disabilities', in *Public Health, Ethics, and Equity*, eds. Anand, Peter and Sen (Oxford: Oxford University Press).
5. Erik Nord, 'The Trade-Off between Severity of Illness and Treatment Effect in Cost-Value Analysis of Health Care', *Health Policy* (1993).
6. Sen, 'Incompleteness and Reasoned Choice', 44.
7. G. A. Cohen, 'Rescuing Conservatism: A Defence of Existing Value', unpublished manuscript, lecture presented at the Centre for Ethics at the University of Toronto, 16 October 2008.

8. Ruth Chang, *Making Comparisons Count* (New York: Routledge, 2002), 171.

9. Thomas Nagel, *Mortal Questions* (Cambridge: Cambridge University Press, 1979), 129, emphasis in original.

10. Chang, 'The Possibility of Parity', 659.

11. Ruth Chang, 'Parity, Interval Value, and Choice', *Ethics* 114 (2005), 333.

12. Ibid.

13. Ibid., 345.

14. Ruth Chang, *Making Comparisons Count* (New York: Routledge, 2002); Chang 2001, 56, emphasis added.

15. Chang, *Making Comparisons Count*, 58.

16. Chang, 'Parity, Interval Value, and Choice', 345.

17. Ibid., 346, fn 18.

18. Chang, *Making Comparisons Count*, 57, 63.

19. Ruth Chang, 'Voluntarist Reasons and the Sources of Normativity', in *Reasons for Action*, eds. David Sobel and Steven Wall (Cambridge: Cambridge University Press, 2009), 243–271.

20. Joseph Raz, *The Morality of Freedom* (Oxford: Oxford University Press, 1986), 333–334.

Part 2

IMPLICATIONS OF INCOMMENSURABILITY FOR PUBLIC DECISION-MAKING, ETHICS AND JUSTICE

Chapter 5

Conflicts of Justice

SUMMARY

This chapter analyses two kinds of possible conflicts of justice: (1) internal conflicts: between competing demands of justice itself and (2) external conflicts: between requirements of justice on the one side and other important values on the other side. The analysis starts from the premise that justice is a multifaceted concept of which the aspects are related to fundamental human values ('values of justice'). Some values of justice may conflict mutually or with other human values. As a corollary, demands of justice may conflict mutually or with other human interests. This may require us to weigh them against each other. Under particular conditions, incommensurability prevents the assignment of impartial weights. In those cases neither option determinately and impartially outweighs the other, so that each decision will act against reasons that are not outweighed by the reasons in favour of which the decision is made. This may cause ethical dilemmas in which neither decision can avoid an element of injustice or ethical deficit.

INTRODUCTION

This chapter concerns conflicts *of* justice – conflicts between distinct requirements of justice itself and between justice and other human interests – rather than conflicts (disputes) *on* justice. Justice is generally regarded as a multifaceted concept of which the aspects are related to important human values such as basic liberties, fair distribution of advantages, equal opportunities, concern for the worst-off, mutual respect and personal privacy. One of the theses to be investigated is that some of these values may clash with each other and with other important human values and that, as a corollary, requirements of justice may conflict mutually and with other human interests. On the face of it the idea that requirements of justice may mutually conflict is perplexing. Justice is usually conceived as a virtue that resolves rather than creates conflicts. Still the idea of conflicting justice is not new. The pre-Socratic philosopher Heraclitus claimed that 'δίκη ἔρις' – 'justice is conflict'.[1] Heraclitus's writings are incompletely passed down and difficult to fathom, but his remarkable statement seems to mean not merely that elements of justice may contingently conflict but that the very essence of justice is conflict, that is, justice is constituted by a tension between competing and conflicting elements, which are in a continuous interaction and strife. Also more recent thinkers have pointed out possible tensions within justice itself. John Stuart Mill argued that 'justice is not some one rule, principle, or maxim, but many, which do not always coincide in their dictates'.[2] Henry Sidgwick arrived at a similar conclusion: 'The different elements included in the notion of Justice . . . are continually liable to conflict with each other.'[3] In addition to possible conflicts between competing requirements of justice itself ('internal conflicts of justice'), this chapter will discuss possible conflicts between justice and other weighty human interests ('external conflicts of justice'). In *The Concept of Law* Herbert Hart argues that justice is not the only thing that matters and that it competes with other virtues.[4] Similarly, political theorists of different directions of thought, such as William Galston and G. A. Cohen, argue that justice may conflict with other human interests.[5] Utilitarian philosophers like Mill and Sidgwick have tried to resolve conflicts of values and conflicting aspects of justice by adopting a single criterion or principle for the assessment of the comparative worth of competing goods and rival claims. According to them, the acceptance of several principles would fail to resolve the conflict, if one side is superior according to one principle and the other according to another principle. Mill:

> There must be some standard, by which to determine the goodness or badness, absolute and comparative [of competing claims]. And whatever that standard is, there can be but one for if there were several ultimate principles, the same decision might be approved by one of these principles and condemned by another; and there would be needed some more general principle as umpire between them.[6]

Mill regards utility as the ultimate criterion for all our decisions with respect to human goods and moral values, including justice. Sidgwick arrives at the same conclusion:

> Utilitarianism furnishes us with a common standard to which the different elements included in the notion of Justice may be reduced. Such a standard is

imperatively required: as these different elements are continually liable to conflict with each other.[7]

However, most contemporary philosophers believe that we cannot appropriately reduce elements of justice to the single criterion 'utility'.[8] If so, we need another way to resolve the internal and external conflicts of justice. It seems plausible that the kind of conflicts under consideration should be resolved by assignment or determination of comparative weights and that the justification of choosing one side rather than the other should be based on which side of the conflict outweighs the other. According to Dworkin, in law and justice one 'has to take into account the relative weight' of principles.[9] Rawls emphasizes the role of assignment of weights as 'an essential part of a conception of justice'.[10] He points out the importance of a complete conception of justice, which is able to order all important conflicting claims and yields determinate and decisive conclusions: '[A] conception of right must impose an ordering on conflicting claims. This requirement springs directly from the role of its principles in adjusting competing demands.' Griffin argues that if the resolution of conflicting rights 'is not to be arbitrary, one must know how to attach weight to them'.[11] Thus, weighing competing principles seems to be an essential characteristic of justice and the solution to conflicts of values and interests. This is symbolized by the attributes of the goddess Justitia – scales, blindfold and sword: they indicate that justice concerns an impartial and decisive weighing procedure resulting in a well-considered and balanced judgment. The key question is how impartial and determinate weights can be assigned to competing values if they are incommensurable, that is, if they have unlike dimensions and their amounts cannot be measured and compared on a common scale. Mill's and Sidgwick's utilitarian approach is supposed to resolve the problem of incommensurability because it reduces all values to the (putatively) one-dimensional value 'utility'. By contrast, the alternative approach, which aims at weighing principles and values of different dimensions, may be susceptible to the incommensurability problem. This chapter investigates whether incommensurability of competing principles and values may prevent the proper function of the scales of justice. I will argue that, under particular conditions, incommensurability may prevent the assignment of impartial and determinate weights to rival demands. This may mean that, in the relevant cases, the justification of either decision between two rival claims can only be partial in the double sense of incomplete and biased: either decision acts against reasons of justice and ethics which are not determinately or impartially outweighed by the reasons in favour of which the decision is taken. I will argue that the consequence may be that the relevant decision contains an injustice or 'ethical deficit' that is not outweighed by the requirement of justice or ethical consideration in favour of which the decision is taken.

Because this chapter largely focuses on conflicts of justice, it may create the impression that it tries to show that unambiguous cases of justice or injustice, without internal or external conflicts, do not exist, as Heraclitus suggests. This is not true. Many requirements of justice are clear and unambiguous. It is evident that many violations of important human values concern serious, unambiguous and reprehensible injustices. Besides, we will discuss that also incomplete rankings of justice do not always prevent unanimous and determinate conclusions about what is the right thing to do.

EXAMPLES

A. Possible internal conflicts of justice

A1. Equality, concern for the worst-off, desert, merit and legitimate entitlement are widely regarded as elements of justice.[12] These elements may clash. For instance, distribution of welfare and resources according to equality and need may conflict with distribution according to desert, merit and legitimate entitlement.[13] This tension parallels rival theories of distributive justice, such as G. A. Cohen's egalitarian theory, John Rawls's justice as fairness and Robert Nozick's libertarian theory.[14] Such disputes *on* justice may reflect conflicts *of* justice – tensions between requirements of justice itself. As Raphael argues, incompatibility between two claims 'is no reason to deny the validity of either as a species of justice'.[15]

A2. Because there are several human rights, it is conceivable that, in particular circumstances, they may conflict.[16] For instance, freedom of expression may clash with the right to privacy;[17] and the right to free speech may clash with the right to protection against discrimination, stigmatization, humiliation and psychological oppression. The latter 'conflict of justice' will be discussed in detail in chapter 11.

B. Possible external conflicts of justice

B1. Efficient distribution of resources may clash with fair distribution. An egalitarian policy may generate a fairer distribution of welfare at the expense of less aggregate welfare; conversely, a utilitarian/efficient policy may yield larger total welfare at the cost of fair distribution.[18] Something similar applies to the distribution of health care resources. Because of the relative scarcity of health care resources,[19] it is important to allocate them in a cost-effective way, maximizing health benefits. However, another ethical criterion of allocation is 'need', determined by the seriousness of the disease and the urgency of treatment. Allocation according to cost-effectiveness and allocation according to need may clash.[20] This example will be discussed in detail in chapter 9.

B2. Rights versus economic interests: Rights may clash with each other (A2) but also with other weighty interests. Here is an example, derived from Clapham:[21]

> Residents near Heathrow Airport made a claim against the Government that the flights and noise levels at night were an unjustifiable interference with their private lives. The judges had to weigh the right to privacy against significant economic interests related to the night flights.

I will work out this example in the next section. Also other human interests may clash with the right to privacy, for instance, public security (cf. Edward Snowden's revelations of possible violations of American citizens' right to privacy by the National Security Agency).

WEIGHING PRINCIPLES, VALUES AND REASONS

The previous examples show that elements of justice may conflict with each other or with other important human values and interests. The solution to these conflicts seems to be the weighing of the relevant conflicting values and interests against each other. However, the metaphor of weighing physical objects on a pair of scales conceals an important but often unnoticed difference with the weighing of values, reasons, interests or principles. If we weigh a physical object A against a physical object B on a material pair of scales, there are not more than three possible outcomes: (1) A outweighs B, (2) B outweighs A, (3) A and B have equal weights. This entails that if neither object outweighs the other, they have equal weights. By contrast, if we weigh valuable options, human interests, reasons or ethical principles, this need not be the case. As we have shown in chapter 1, there is a fourth possibility: neither option outweighs the other, while they have also not equal weight. Applied to options A and B the fourth value relation means that

1. It is not true that A is weightier than B.
2. It is not true that B is weightier than A.
3. It is not true that A and B have (roughly) equal weights.

As discussed in chapter 1 I call this value relation '3NT' ('triply not-true'). The fourth value relation is paradoxical because we usually assume that if A is not weightier than B and B is not weightier than A, A and B have equal weight and that if they have not equal weight, one of them is weightier than the other. This assumption is implicitly based on the supposed truth of the trichotomy thesis, which states that there are only three possible positive value relations ('better/weightier', 'worse/less weighty' and 'equally good/equally weighty'). To show again that the trichotomy thesis need not be true and to illustrate the possibility of the paradoxical fourth value relation and the problematic consequences for the possibility to weigh, let us return to the example of Heathrow Airport (example B2 in the previous section). The judges had to weigh privacy ('option P') against economic interests ('option E'). The key question seems to be 'How much (increased) economic advantage outweighs how much (decreased) privacy?' In answering this question it is important to make a distinction between amounts and relative weights of the competing values at stake. A significant increase of the amount of one value outweighs a trivial decrease of the amount of the other value; and a lexically prior value (a value that has absolute weight) outweighs a less important value, whatever their amounts may be. But what is the right answer if the gain in the amount of one value and the loss of the amount of the other value are both significant, and if the two values are 'symmetrical' – that is, if neither value is lexically prior to, or definitely more important than, the other? The question can be answered if we can determine the relative weights of the relevant competing values, or put differently, if we (at least roughly) know which amount of one value is equivalent to which amount of the competing value. In that case we can substitute for a particular amount of one value the equivalent amount of the other so that we can determine which option contains the largest amount of overall value. However, in the cases under consideration no amount of one value is equal to any amount of the rival value, due to the incommensurability of the values. This can again be illustrated by the large improvement phenomenon. Take an economic option E_1 that, compared to privacy option P, represents a significant economic advantage (e.g., a regional economic growth and increase of employment by 3%, other things being equal). Suppose we conclude that E_1 does not outweigh P and vice versa. This does not necessarily mean that E_1 and P have (roughly) equal weight, which can be shown as follows. Take an option E_2 in which the economic benefit of the night flights is considerably improved compared to option E_1 (e.g., a regional economic growth and increase of employment by 6% instead of 3%, other things being equal). Suppose we conclude again that this considerably improved option E_2 does still always not (definitely) outweigh P. In that case it is not true that option E_1 is roughly equally good or has roughly equal weight, as P. Indeed, if this would be the case, and we largely increase the economic benefit of option E, option E_2 must be significantly better/weightier not only than E_1 but also than P. However, this 'transitivity' does not occur. This large improvement phenomenon makes it plausible that it is not true that E_1 and P are (roughly) equally good or have (roughly) equal weight. Because it is also not true that E_1 has more weight or less weight than P, the value relation between E_1 and P

is characterized by 3NT and is, therefore, an example of the fourth value relation as defined earlier. If the large improvement argument is cogent, there is a wide range of different amounts of value (in the case under consideration, a large range of different amounts of economic benefits) where the fourth value relation applies; this is the range of indeterminateness – the range where we cannot determine that one option outweighs the other (see chapter 1, section 'The large improvement argument'). Above the upper limit of this range option E outweighs option P. Below the bottom limit of the range of indeterminateness option P outweighs option E. Within the range neither option outweighs the other, while they have not roughly equal weights. Thus, nowhere within, above or below the range of indeterminateness there is a level where E and P have roughly equal weight. In other words, rough equivalence relations, substitution rates and trade-offs between the relevant competing values or options appear to be lacking. This means that, within the range of indeterminateness, there is no determinately right answer to the conflict under consideration. In cases of 3NT the final choice runs the risk of becoming more or less dependent on arbitrariness and the discretion of the relevant judge(s) or decision maker(s). Chang similarly argues that the final decision between options on a par is to some extent arbitrary and does not depend on the conclusion that one option is impartially better or weightier than the other, because this is not the case.[22] This may be mirrored in the rival decisions that courts of justice sometimes make in one and the same human rights conflict or other value conflicts (see also chapter 11). In this context Clapham writes: 'There is plenty of room for different people, different judges even, to come to different conclusions.' In our 'Heathrow example' the Chamber of the European Court of Human Rights was internally divided but the majority of judges favoured the privacy of the residents near the airport (five judges voted for the residents, two for the government; see table 5.1).

However, on appeal, the Grand Chamber, which was in turn divided, put the government in the right because of the putatively weightier economic interests (twelve judges voted for the government, five for the residents; table 5.1).[23] These conflicting legal judgments are to be expected with respect to weighing incommensurable rival interests. Where the law and reason do not

Table 5.1. Conflicting legal judgments about the comparative weights of privacy and economic interests in the Heathrow Airport trial (n = number of judges)

	'Privacy outweighs economic interests' (n)	'Economic interest outweighs privacy' (n)	Decision of the chamber
Chamber ($n = 7$)	5	2	In favour of residents
Grand Chamber ($n = 17$)	5	12	In favour of government

give unambiguous guidance and under-determine the decision – thus, where 3NT applies and where rationally determinable relative weights do not exist – personal intuitions and beliefs may significantly influence the outcomes of the judges' assessments. This is not only suggested by this trial but also confirmed by a large-scale empirical study among US judges: in the relevant cases their legal judgments and assessments of comparative weights 'may considerably differ and strongly depend on their political and ideological backgrounds'.[24] We will discuss this in more detail in chapter 11.

Incommensurability of the values 'privacy' and 'economic benefit' is an important reason why the Heathrow Airport trial posed a problem for weighing the conflicting interests. The same applies to many other rival claims that concern 3NT value relations. If the three conditions of incomplete comparability apply, there is a wide range of indeterminateness in which the relevant claims have no determinate position with respect to their comparative worth or weight (see chapter 1).

If this analysis is correct, it refutes the widely spread assumption that if two values, interests, ethical demands or requirements of justice, A and B, conflict, there are only three possible value relations: (i) A outweighs B, (ii) B outweighs A or (iii) A and B have equal weights. An interesting example of this mistaken assumption is Ronald Dworkin's belief that, at least in principle, there is a single correct answer to every legal question or question of justice.[25] Dworkin recognizes that justice concerns weighing principles. A principle provides a reason for deciding the case in a particular way, but it is not a conclusive reason: it will have to be weighed against other principles in the system. Dworkin rejects the idea of indeterminability, because, according to him, this would mean that all hard cases have exactly equal weights which 'is so implausible that it can be set aside at once'. This shows that Dworkin assumes that, if neither of two options is weightier than the other, they have equal weights. However, he overlooks the possibility of 3NT, which means that neither option is weightier than the other, without having equal weight. Dworkin's approach is discussed in more detail in chapter 11.

POSSIBLE SOLUTIONS TO VALUE CONFLICTS

In the philosophical literature we can find at least five putative solutions to value conflicts. They are summarized in table 5.2.

a. Weight assignment

As we discussed earlier, many philosophers regard weight assignment (solution *a* of table 5.2) as the right solution to many conflicts of values. However, we have seen that impartial and determinate weight assignment is

Table 5.2. Putative solutions to conflicts of values

Putative solutions to conflicts of values	What does it mean?	Which option is the right one to choose?
a. Weight assignment	Attaching comparative weights to the values.	The option with the largest overall weight.
b. Commensuration	Reducing the values to a super-value, V (e.g., monetary value or utility).	The option with the largest amount of V. Example: utilitarianism.
c. Reconciliation	Pursuing a balance or integration between the values (e.g., by reinterpretation of the values in the light of each other or in the light of one's ends). 'The Aristotelian approach'.	The option that represents the best integration or comes closest to a 'mutual fit' or right balance.
d. Prioritization	Lexical ordering of values or principles.	The option that contains (the largest amount of) the lexically prior value or satisfies the lexically prior principle. Example: Rawls's lexical ordering of principles of justice.
e. Rational deliberation	Interpersonal deliberation about what is the most rational and reasonable thing to do.	The option that is seen as the most rational and reasonable alternative according to the deliberators.
f. Social choice	Collective decision, democratic choice, majority rule.	The option that is selected by the community as a whole or the majority.

problematic in the cases under consideration. But it is perhaps not excluded that some value conflicts can be resolved in ways that avoid the need of weight assignment, for instance, the utilitarian approach, reconciliation, prioritization, rational deliberation or social choice (solutions b–f of table 5.2). I will briefly discuss these possible 'solutions'. The conclusion will be that they are often incapable of adequately and sufficiently resolving the ethical value conflicts under consideration.

b. Commensuration

As we discussed earlier, Mill writes with respect to competing elements of justice:

> Who shall decide between . . . appeals to conflicting principles of justice? Justice has . . . different sides, which it is impossible to bring into harmony, and the disputants have chosen opposite sides. Any choice between them, on grounds of justice, must be perfectly arbitrary.[26]

The central problem for the scales of justice is that the 'scale' of one aspect of justice (e.g., liberty or merit) has a dimension that differs from the 'scale' of another aspect (e.g., equality or need). How to unite various scales of disparate values to a single scale? This would be possible if there would exist an overarching standard of comparison. The emphasis Mill and Sidgwick put on the importance of a common standard and a single decisive criterion originates from their awareness that incommensurability of the relevant values often leads to indeterminateness between competing claims and principles as we have seen earlier. A central characteristic of incommensurable values is their unlike dimensions and their 'unitary scale resistance'.[27] Utilitarianism seems capable of replacing intuitive and subjective weight assignment by objective measurement. Still, some of the previous examples have shown that utility and fairness are two distinct values, and it seems implausible that fairness can be adequately reduced to utility. Nowadays most political theorists reject utilitarianism as unsatisfying, inadequate and inappropriate, especially with respect to issues of justice. One of them is Rawls, who argues that the utilitarian approach does not do justice to the separateness of persons.[28] He has found alternatives for the utilitarian solution. Before we discuss them, we shall consider another approach that avoids the need of weight assignment: reconciliation of putative clashing values.

c. Reconciliation

Until now we have assumed that the relevant values and demands of justice may really conflict. But what is the evidence for this? Perhaps the values can be reconciled if we try. As Dworkin argues with respect to the putative tension between some fundamental human values:

> Nothing is easier than composing definitions of liberty, equality . . . and justice that conflict with one another. But not much, in philosophy, is harder than showing why these are the definitions that we should accept. Perhaps, after all, the most attractive conceptions of the leading liberal values do hang together in the right way.[29]

Inspired by the Aristotelian idea of 'complete virtue' Richardson proposes an approach that replaces searching for commensurability by searching for compatibility and reconciliation ('mutual fit'):[30]

> The divergence that arises from differently weighting incommensurable cognitive ends may be addressed by deliberation that specifies the ends in terms of their mutual fit rather than by looking in vain for a supervalue in terms of which to commensurate them all.

Richardson shows that it is possible to combine apparently incompatible options and reconcile seemingly conflicting values by specifying one's ends and reinterpreting the relevant values in the light of these ends. As a 'sovereign deliberator' the individual may revise rival principles and values so that they become mutually fitting, or even mutually supporting.[31] In the same vein Dworkin argues that pursuing integrity among our concepts is itself a very important value: 'We don't find the right conception of our values in nature: we construct them and integrity seems a reasonable aim . . . of that process of construction.' 'We have to try and see our values in the light of each other. . . . Values may be regulated without being restricted.'[32] For instance, while unlimited freedom of speech may easily clash with protection against blasphemy and hate speech, free speech as a 'balanced' virtue avoids conflicts. Integration of seemingly conflicting values raises these values to a higher level, analogously to Hegel's *Aufhebung* of apparently opposing theses to a higher synthesis.[33] Regulated free speech, integrated with other values like respect and deference to privacy, is higher-minded and more valuable than unlimited free speech. Similarly, we can often specify different values (e.g., liberty and equality) in such a sense that they do not compromise each other.[34] Another interesting example concerns Rawls's attempt to reconcile concern for the worst-off and welfare maximization by means of his difference principle. This principle avoids relative weight assignment to maximization of welfare and need by allowing inequality-based increase of welfare only if it is to the advantage of the worst-off.[35] These examples show that there is no reason to believe in advance that we cannot find conceptions of values that do not clash. According to Richardson no aspect of an ultimate end is immune in principle from deliberative revision.[36]

However, not all values can be revised, reinterpreted and made compatible without violating their meaning and distorting their integrity. Of course, conflicts based on misconceptions of values may disappear if the values are correctly interpreted. Conflicts based on properly conceived values, by contrast, do not easily lend themselves to a conceptual revision without distorting their meaning. The problem under consideration in this chapter is the question how to rationally resolve conflicts between incommensurable alternatives that do not mutually fit. It is implausible that a single society would be capable of incorporating all possible values in an optimal and harmonious way. As Nagel argues, there are alternative good societies that realize to different degrees the different values of freedom, equality, individualism, economic growth, social coherence, care for the poor and the needy, preservation of nature, development aid and so forth. These values often clash with one another, not just because of the limitations of resources, but because their optimal realizations are to some degree incompatible.[37] Rawls expresses a similar view: The full range of values is too extensive to fit in any one social world, and there is no social world without loss. He argues that the basic error is to think that because values are objective and hence truly values, they must be compatible: in the realm of values, as opposed to the world of fact, not all truths can fit into one social world.[38]

d. Prioritization

Rawls is one of the few political theorists who explicitly recognize the problem of incommensurability and indeterminateness. A large part of his approach consists of attempts to resolve this problem.[39] Rawls shows that people in a pluralistic society adhere to divergent conceptions of the good and moral doctrines that are not only conflicting but 'even incommensurable'. These different conceptions of the good are associated with different conceptions of justice, which are in turn conflicting and incommensurable. Rawls has tried to construct principles of justice that are neutral with respect to conceptions of the good and that may be affirmed by all reasonable and rational people in an overlapping consensus.

We have discussed different criteria – for example, liberty, equality, need and utility – according to which welfare, health care and other advantages can be distributed. We have seen that combining these values in order to create an integrated measure of distributive justice is sometimes problematic due to their incommensurability. Rawls, in whose theory of justice liberty, equality, need and efficiency play a significant role, has tried to overcome this problem of incommensurability by avoiding, rather than resolving, it.[40] He has tried to circumvent trade-offs between these incommensurable values not only by means of reconciliation (especially the difference principle, as discussed earlier), but also and especially by prioritization (lexically ordered principles). Rawls puts (equal basic) liberty at the top of the scheme of lexical priorities, followed by equality (of opportunity). After that, need and utility (maximization of welfare) are integrated in the difference principle. This scheme of lexical priorities avoids the need of *weighing* liberty, equality and concern for the worst-off against each other. The strategy of prioritization is meant to arrive at a complete ordering of principles and values for the basic structure of society, avoiding intuitive and unstructured trade-offs. Can it be applied to the conflicts of justice discussed in this chapter? Although prioritization avoids the need of weighing, it does not prevent reasonable disagreement on the relevant prioritization, if values may be ordered in more than one rational and reasonable way. Because people adhere to different incommensurable conceptions of the good and rank values in line with these conceptions, they will easily arrive at different rankings. In that case the question how to weigh incommensurable values is replaced by the question how to arrive at an agreed-upon prioritization. One of the functions of Rawls's 'original position' and 'veil of ignorance' is to achieve consensus on ranking.[41] Behind the veil of ignorance, where everybody is ignorant about his conception of the good, each party is supposed to choose the same complete and transitive ranking of values and principles. It is questionable whether Rawls's approach is entirely successful (see chapter 7). Amartya Sen points out:

> Even after vested interests and personal priorities have been somehow 'taken out' of consideration through such devices as the 'veil of ignorance', there may remain possibly conflicting views on social priorities, for example in weighing the claims of need over entitlement to the fruits of one's labour.[42]

Besides, the values in the examples of internal and external conflicts of justice discussed earlier do not easily lend themselves for a lexical ordering in the sense that one of the values, however small in amount, gets priority to other values, however large in amount. Some of these examples show that justice cannot always be regarded as the 'first virtue': not every kind of injustice – however small – should always get priority to other values, however large in amount.[43] Besides, because conceptions of the good are sources of weight assignment and priorities and because the veil of ignorance makes us ignorant about our conceptions of the good, it is questionable whether, behind the veil, we are capable of arriving at a determinate ranking. Rawls's approach is discussed in more detail in chapter 7.

e. Rational deliberation

The belief that rational deliberation is capable of significantly and sufficiently narrowing down the wide range of weights assigned to competing values is based on the assumption that the differences in weight assignment are, at least partially, due to inconclusiveness and lack of knowledge or rationality rather than to indeterminateness. This would mean that increase in knowledge and rationality, and exchange of insights, could, at least in principle, promote convergence to consensus about the weights to be assigned. However, as Daniels and Sabin argue, the large interpersonal differences in weights which people assign to different moral concerns 'probably depend on how these moral concerns fit within wider conceptions of the good. . . . If so, there is good reason to think these disagreements will be a persistent feature of the situation'.[44] This is one of the reasons why it is implausible that deliberation will sufficiently narrow down the width of the range of divergent weights to avoid the problem under consideration.[45] However, the main cause by which rational deliberation does not lead to determinate answers is that reason is silent with respect to ranking of, and choices between, the relevant incommensurable options ('reason under-determines the choice').

Incomplete rankings do not always cause indeterminate conclusions. Some options belonging to the set of incompletely ordered alternatives are definitely better than some other options, namely, if the former are better than the latter with respect to at least one relevant value without being worse with respect to any relevant value. This 'dominance partial ordering' shows that some options of the set can be determinately ranked without assigning relative weights. The problem of incomplete ordering can still further be reduced by what is called 'intersection partial ordering'. Although incommensurability prevents objective and determinate relative weight assignment, it does not prevent subjective and intuitive weight assignment. Even if, as is to be expected, different people subjectively assign different relative weights, an agreed-upon ranking is possible with respect to options which may turn out to be superior to other ones according to all interpersonally different weight assignments.[46] But not all problems of incompleteness are resolved by 'dominance' or 'intersection'. Options representing bidirectionally divided values – like those in the previous examples – exclude, by definition, a dominance partial ordering. And disagreement on the ranking of these options means that intersection partial ordering is lacking.

f. Social choice

One might argue that persistent disagreements may be resolved by social choice and the majority rule, which take into account a persistent diversity of perspectives and priorities.[47] However, aggregation of opinions and the majority rule are not always capable of resolving the conflicts of justice under consideration in the right way. Justice based on changing opinions and fluctuating majorities lacks stability, predictability and equal treatment of equal cases. And minorities that have legitimate claims will be disadvantaged by the power of the majority. Besides, democratic decisions and social choices cannot always avoid incomplete rankings of incommensurable principles. This will be further discussed in chapter 8.

ETHICAL DEFICIT

As mentioned earlier, this chapter may wrongly create the impression that it defends the thesis that justice without conflict does not exist. This is not the aim. Sen rightly emphasizes that 'much can be fruitfully said about inequality, poverty and deprivation without requiring anything like a complete ordering of competing claims'. Besides, some incomplete rankings of justice may be the result of inconclusiveness ('tentative incompleteness' waiting for resolution) rather than indeterminateness ('assertive incompleteness').[48]

Even assertively incomplete rankings do not necessarily imply that determinate conclusions cannot be attained. However, we have seen that several internal and external conflicts of justice lack an unambiguous resolution. The utilitarian method, which makes the relevant values commensurable, is inadequate and inappropriate with respect to questions of justice and ethics. An alternative approach consists in trying to reconcile competing values and interests instead of making them commensurable. However, making incompatible options compatible may be as problematic as making incommensurable values commensurable. In several cases competing claims of justice and other ethical demands cannot be adequately and optimally reconciled. In those cases the assignment of weights seems unavoidable. We have seen that if the relevant values are simultaneously incommensurable and symmetrical, the options under consideration cannot be determinately and impartially weighed. This may lead to rational and ethical undecidability and to a more or less arbitrary or subjective final decision. Incomplete rankings of principles challenge the requirements of justice formulated by Rawls, such as decisiveness, consistency, transitivity, stability and non-arbitrariness. The consequence of incompletely rankable demands of justice and ethics is that, in the relevant cases, there seems to be 'no right answer' or 'no single right answer'.[49] In other words, with respect to the relevant options, there is no overall reason for choosing one alternative *rather than* the other, so that the justification of the final choice is necessarily 'partial' in the double sense of 'incomplete' and 'biased'. With respect to internal conflicts of justice this entails that either choice results in a moral deficit, because either decision acts against an undefeated reason of justice and because neither decision can be justified by the fact that the requirement of justice in favour of which the decision is taken outweighs the rival requirement of justice. In those cases we are confronted with an impasse due to rational and moral undecidability,[50] because either choice entails a deficit with respect to one aspect of justice, which cannot be justified by the argument that the decision in favour of the other aspect of justice is overall more just. A similar ethical deficit applies to the relevant external conflicts of justice, if the weight of justice does not outweigh the weight of rival human values and interests and vice versa.

NOTES

1. Heraclitus, fragment 80. Richard D. McKirahan Jr., *Philosophy before Socrates* (Indianapolis/Cambridge: Hackett Publishing Company, 1994).

2. John Stuart Mill, *Utilitarianism* (Indianapolis/Cambridge: Hackett Publishing Company, 1979, 1861), 54.

3. Henry Sidgwick, *The Methods of Ethics* (Indianapolis/Cambridge: Hackett Publishing Company, 1981), 447.

4. H.L.A. Hart, *The Concept of Law* (Oxford: Oxford University Press, 1997), 166–167.

5. William A. Galston, *Liberal Pluralism: The Implications of Value Pluralism for Political Theory and Practice* (Cambridge: Cambridge University Press, 2002), 5; G. A. Cohen, *Rescuing Justice and Equality* (Cambridge, Mass.: Harvard University Press, 2008), 304.

6. John Stuart Mill, *A System of Logic* (London: Longmans, 1949), 620–621.

7. Sidgwick, *The Methods of Ethics*, 447.

8. For instance, Rawls powerfully rejects utility as an appropriate criterion of justice. See John Rawls, *A Theory of Justice*, rev. ed. (Cambridge, Mass.: Belknap Press of Harvard University Press, 1999).

9. Ronald Dworkin, *Taking Rights Seriously* (Cambridge, Mass.: Harvard University Press, 1978), 26.

10. Rawls, *A Theory of Justice*, 37, 115.

11. James Griffin, *On Human Rights* (Oxford: Oxford University Press, 2008), 66.

12. David Daiches Raphael, *Concepts of Justice* (Oxford: Oxford University Press, 2001).

13. See, for instance, Alasdair MacIntyre, *After Virtue*, 2nd ed. (Notre Dame, Ind.: University of Notre Dame Press, 1984), 244–245; and Ibid., 185, 195, 218, 241.

14. Cohen, *Rescuing Justice and Equality*; Rawls, *A Theory of Justice*; Robert Nozick, *Anarchy, State, and Utopia* (New York: Basic Books, 1974).

15. Raphael, *Concepts of Justice*, 218.

16. Andrew Clapham, *Human Rights: A Very Short Introduction* (Oxford: Oxford University Press, 2007); Griffin, *On Human Rights*.

17. Clapham, *Human Rights*, 114–115.

18. Cf. Derek Parfit, 'Equality and Priority', Ratio 10 (1997): 205; Rawls, *A Theory of Justice*, 32–34.

19. Dan Brock, 'Ethical Issues in the Use of Cost Effectiveness Analysis for the Prioritisation of Health Care Resources', in *Public Health, Ethics, and Equity*, eds. Sudhir Anand, Fabienne Peter and Amartya Sen (Oxford: Oxford University Press, 2006), 201–203.

20. Ibid.; Frances Kamm, 'Deciding Whom to Help, Health-Adjusted Life Years and Disabilities', in *Public Health, Ethics, and Equity*, eds. Anand, Peter and Sen; Michael Lockwood, 'Quality of Life and Resource Allocation', in *Bioethics, an Anthology*, eds. Helga Kuhse and Peter Singer (Oxford: Blackwell Publishers Ltd., 2006).

21. Clapham, *Human Rights*, chap. 6.

22. Ruth Chang, *Making Comparisons Count* (New York: Routledge, 2002), 171–172.

23. Clapham, *Human Rights*, 114–115.

24. Cass R. Sunstein, David Schkade, Lisa M. Ellman, Andres Sawicki, *Are Judges Political? An Empirical Analysis of the Federal Judiciary* (Washington, D.C.: Brookings Institution Press, 2006).

25. Ronald Dworkin, *Taking Rights Seriously* (Cambridge, Mass.: Harvard University Press, 1978), 279–290; Ronald Dworkin, *A Matter of Principle* (Cambridge, Mass.: Harvard University Press, 1985), 119–145; Ronald Dworkin, 'Indeterminacy in Law', in *The Oxford Companion to Philosophy*, ed. Ted Honderich (Oxford:

Oxford University Press, 1995), 399; Ronald Dworkin, 'Do Liberal Values Conflict?', in *The Legacy of Isaiah Berlin*, eds. Ronald Dworkin, Mark Lilla and Robert B. Silvers (New York: NYRB, 2001).

26. John Stuart Mill, *Utilitarianism*, ed. Roger Crisp (Oxford: Oxford University Press, 2002), 100–102.

27. I owe this phrase to Sunstein. See Cass R. Sunstein, 'Incommensurability and Kinds of Valuation: Some Applications in Law', in *Incommensurability, Incomparability, and Practical Reason*, ed. Ruth Chang (Cambridge, Mass.: Harvard University Press, 1997).

28. Rawls, *A Theory of Justice*.

29. Dworkin, 'Do Liberal Values Conflict?' 90.

30. Henry S. Richardson, *Practical Reasoning about Final Ends* (Cambridge: Cambridge University Press, 1997), 304. Stocker proposes a similar Aristotelian approach. See Michael Stocker, *Plural and Conflicting Values* (Oxford: Oxford University Press, 1999).

31. Richardson, *Practical Reasoning about Final Ends*, 212–218.

32. The Legacy of Isaiah Berlin, 132, 135.

33. Martha C. Nussbaum, *Frontiers of Justice: Disability, Nationality, Species Membership* (Cambridge, Mass.: Belknap Press of Harvard University Press, 2006), 401.

34. Dworkin, 'Do Liberal Values Conflict?' 81–90.

35. Rawls, *A Theory of Justice*, 280.

36. Richardson, *Practical Reasoning about Final Ends*, 218.

37. Thomas Nagel, 'Pluralism and Coherence', in *The Legacy of Isaiah Berlin*, 106.

38. John Rawls, *Political Liberalism* (New York: Columbia University Press, 1996), 197, fn. 32.

39. See, for instance, Rawls, *A Theory of Justice*, 56, 65. As Hardin argues, 'Making his own theory overcome indeterminacy is a central, driving concern that has largely been neglected in the voluminous literature responding to Rawls's theory.' See Russell Hardin, *Indeterminacy and Society* (Princeton/Oxford: Princeton University Press, 2003), 105.

40. Rawls, *A Theory of Justice*.

41. Cf. Fred D'Agostino, *Incommensurability and Commensuration. The Common Denominator* (Burlington: Ashgate, 2003), 100–104.

42. Amartya Sen, 'What Do We Want from a Theory of Justice', *The Journal of Philosophy* 103 (2006): 224.

43. Broome argues that lexical priority of the just to the good is, like all other lexical theories, implausible: 'It is implausible that any benefit to the worst-off person, however small it may be, is always more valuable than a great benefit to someone better-off.' More generally, it is implausible that any value, however small in amount, has lexical priority to any other value, however large in amount. See John Broome, *Weighing Lives* (Oxford: Oxford University Press, 2004), 28–29.

44. Norman Daniels and James Sabin, 'Limits to Health Care: Fair Procedures, Democratic Deliberation, and the Legitimacy Problem for Insurers', *Philosophy & Public Affairs* 26 (1997): 303–350.

45. Cf. Norman Daniels, *Just Health: Meeting Health Needs Fairly* (Cambridge: Cambridge University Press, 2008), 113–117.

46. Amartya Sen, *Inequality Re-examined* (Cambridge, Mass.: Harvard University Press, 1992), 46–49, especially figure 3.1; and Sen, 'What Do We Want from a Theory of Justice', 225. Cf. Sunstein's 'incompletely theorized agreements' and Rawls's 'overlapping consensus'. See Cass R. Sunstein, *Legal Reasoning and Political Conflict* (Oxford: Oxford University Press, 1996); and Rawls, *A Theory of Justice*.

47. Amartya Sen, *The Idea of Justice* (London: Penguin Books, 2009), 95, 109.

48. Sen, *Inequality Re-examined*, 134, fn. 12; Amartya Sen, 'Incompleteness and Reasoned Choice', *Synthese* 140 (2004): 43–59.

49. Cf. Parfit, 'Equality and Priority', 205; and Ruth Chang, *Making Comparisons Count* (New York: Routledge, 2002).

50. Cf. Derrida's *aporia*; and Lyotard's *differend*. See Jacques Derrida, 'Force of Law: The Mystical Foundation of Authority', in *Deconstruction and the Possibility of Justice*, eds. Drucilla Cornell, Michel Rosenfeld, David Gray Carlson (New York/London: Routledge, 1992), 22–26; and Jean-François Lyotard, *The Differend: Phrases in Dispute* (Minneapolis: University of Minnesota Press, 1988).

Chapter 6

Rival Theories of Justice

SUMMARY

Conflicting principles of justice are mirrored in rival theories of justice that select one of them as the ultimate principle. One theory of justice may be better with respect to one principle, while another is better with respect to another principle. The theories may be ranked – some theories are overall better than some others – but this ranking is incomplete and there seems to be no single theory in which all values relevant for justice can be integrated in a way that is complete and optimal. This claim will be further substantiated in chapter 7.

****

Different and conflicting aspects of a fair and efficient distribution of resources and welfare – for example, equality, liberty, utility and need – are mirrored in rival theories of distributive justice that select one of these values as the ultimate or primary principle of justice:

- *Equality*: egalitarian justice (R. Arneson, G.A. Cohen, A. Sen)
- *Liberty*: libertarian justice (R. Nozick), political liberalism (J. Rawls)
- *Utility*: utilitarian justice (J. Bentham, J. S. Mill, H. Sidgwick, P. Singer)
- *Need*: Need-based justice (D. Miller)

Which theory is the best one and how to decide that? The difficulty of the choice between these theories of justice reflects and is analogous to the difficulty of the choice between the relevant principles in the distribution of welfare and the allocation of resources (see, e.g., the discussion of Rawls's theory of justice in chapter 7 and the discussion of allocation of scarce health care resources in chapter 9). The problems of incommensurability of the relevant values and the incomplete comparability of the alternatives for choice equally apply to the comparison of theories of justice in which the conflicting principles play a part. Amartya Sen gives an insightful example of conflicting principles:

> Conflicts of distributive principles that are hard to eradicate can be illustrated with an example. . . . The example is concerned with the problem of deciding which of three children should get a flute about which they are quarrelling. Child *A* is the only one of the three who knows how to play the flute . . .; child *B* is the only one without any toys of his own . . .; child *C* has worked hard to make the flute all on his own. Theorists of different persuasions – utilitarian or egalitarian or libertarian – may believe that a just resolution can be readily spotted here, though, alas, they would respectively see totally different resolutions as being exactly right . . . [T]he different resolutions all have serious arguments in support of them, and we may not be able to identify exactly one of the alternative arguments as being the only one.[1]

John Stuart Mill argues in a similar way:

> I am unable to see how any of these [theories] can be refuted. For in truth every one builds upon rules of justice confessedly true. . . . Each is triumphant so long as he is not compelled to take into consideration any other maxims of justice than the one he has selected; but as soon as their several maxims are brought face to face, each disputant seems to have exactly as much to say for himself as the others. . . . Who shall decide between these appeals to conflicting principles of justice. Justice has . . . different sides, which it is impossible to bring into harmony, and the disputants have chosen opposite sides. Any choice between them, on grounds of justice, must be perfectly arbitrary.[2]

Alasdair MacIntyre writes in *After Virtue*:

> [There is] no method of weighing, no rational criterion for deciding between claims based on [for instance] legitimate entitlement against claims based on need. Thus these two types of claim are indeed, as I suggested, incommensurable, and the metaphor of 'weighing' moral claims is not just inappropriate but misleading.[3]

Robert Sugden concludes his chapter on social justice in *The Theory of Choice*:

> Some readers may feel satisfied to endorse one particular theory of justice and to reject all the others. But I suspect that many, like myself, will feel pulled in different directions. Each theory seems to be based on some ideas about justice that are deeply rooted in Western culture. Each tries to formalize and generalize the ideas on which it is based.[4]

Susan Hurley too demonstrates that 'conflicts within persons are in certain respects like conflicts between persons'.[5] Bernard Williams expresses a similar thought:

> [S]ome one-person conflicts of values are expressions of a complex inheritance of values, from different social sources, and what we experience in ourselves as a conflict is something which could have been, and perhaps was, expressed as a conflict between two societies, or between two historical states of one society. The same point comes out the opposite way round, so to speak: a characteristic dispute about values in society, such as some issue of equality against freedom, is not one most typically enacted by a body of single-minded egalitarians confronting a body of equally single-minded libertarians, but is rather a conflict which one person, equipped with a more generous range of human values, could find enacted in himself.[6]

This idea is already described in Plato's *Republic*. Stuart Hampshire discusses Plato's view that

> there is a clear analogy between conflict and justice in the divided minds of individuals and conflict and justice in the class-divided city. In both cases, justice consists in harmony of the parts or elements, a harmony imposed by reason.[7]

Hampshire contrasts this with the philosophy of Heraclitus who believes that

> every soul is always the scene of conflicting tendencies and of divided aims and ambivalences, and correspondingly, our political enmities in the city or state will never come to an end.[8]

While Plato believed that the conflicts in the minds of individuals and the conflicts between individuals could be resolved into harmony by justice based on reason, Heraclitus believed that justice itself is inherently conflicting and not resolvable into harmony.

INCOMMENSURABILITY AS A KEY PROBLEM

The issue under consideration shows the significance of the incommensurability condition of incomplete comparability. If there is no common standard or super-value to which the contributory values or aspects of justice may appropriately be reduced, incomplete comparability and impossibility of 'objective overall measurement' may result. A core problem for the scales of justice is that the 'scale' of one contributory value of justice (e.g., equality) has another dimension than the 'scale' of another contributory value (e.g., need, priority to the worst-off). How to unite various scales of disparate values with unlike dimensions to a single scale? Mill:

> There must be some standard, by which to determine the goodness or badness, absolute and comparative, [of competing claims or principles]. And whatever that standard is, there can be but one for if there were several ultimate principles, the same decision might be approved by one of these principles and condemned by another; and there would be needed some more general principle as umpire between them.[9]

This shows the strength of utilitarianism, which, according to Mill, is able to supply the required common standard of justice.[10] Henry Sidgwick draws the same conclusion:

> Utilitarianism furnishes us with a common standard to which the different elements included in the notion of Justice may be reduced. Such a standard is imperatively required: as these different elements are continually liable to conflict with each other.[11]

The emphasis Mill and Sidgwick put on the requirement of a single decisive criterion originates from their awareness that incommensurability of the relevant values easily leads to indeterminateness between the competing claims, principles and theories. Plato too was aware of the problem of incommensurability and the need of a single criterion to maintain objective measurability and decidability:

> [I]f we disagree about the larger and smaller, wouldn't we turn to *measurement* and quickly stop our disagreement? . . . But when we differ about the just and unjust . . . and prove unable to turn to any *sufficiently decisive criterion*, aren't these the things that lead to our becoming enemies to one another?[12]

Martha Nussbaum points out that Plato

> shows 'our deep and pressing need for an ethical science of measurement' and believes that 'we will be saved only by something that will assimilate deliberation to weighing and measuring; this in turn requires a unit of measure, some external end about which we can all agree, and which can render all alternatives commensurable.'[13]

However, if utility is not an appropriate measure of justice as, among others, Rawls has demonstrated in his *A Theory of Justice*, it is not plausible that we can make the disparate elements of justice commensurable.

THOMAS KUHN'S PHILOSOPHY OF SCIENCE

The problem of choosing the most adequate theory of justice as described earlier has an interesting analogy in Thomas Kuhn's philosophy of science:

> Scientists who share values for theory-choice may nevertheless make different choices in the same concrete situation. Different values dictate different conclusions, different choices. In such cases of value-conflict (e.g. one theory is simpler but the other is more accurate) the relative weight placed on different values by different individuals can play a decisive role in individual choice.[14]

So one scientific theory may be better with respect to one relevant standard (e.g., simplicity), while another scientific theory may be better with respect to another standard (e.g., accuracy). Compare this with our discussion about theories of justice: one theory of justice may be better with respect to one principle (e.g., need), while another theory of justice is better with respect to another principle (e.g., equality). Kuhn speaks about incommensurable scientific theories[15] and incommensurable standpoints,[16] which make an overall comparability of these theories and viewpoints problematic. Kuhn's philosophy about the overall incomparability of scientific theories is controversial, especially because scientific theories can be tested by experiments of which the factual outcomes may show which theory is (not) in agreement with the facts. However, in the field of justice we can avoid the more controversial part of Kuhn's philosophy. Theories of justice can less easily (if at all) be tested by experiments resulting in factual outcomes showing which theory is in agreement with objectively demonstrable facts. The appraisal of theories of justice is dependent on evaluative comparisons. Therefore, we may be confronted with conflicts of values, of which an impartial resolution may be prevented by the problem of incommensurability. If this problem may apply to theories in natural science, it may a fortiori apply to theories outside the field of natural science, where evaluative comparisons are indispensable. Paraphrasing Robert Nozick's discussion of scientific theories, we can say the following about assessment of theories of justice:

> There are no rules or algorithms to determine the acceptance of a theory of justice. There are different desirable features of a theory that may conflict (such as concern for the worst-off, equality, liberty). There also are different conceptions of each of these desirable features; moreover, different weightings can be given to these features. Theories of justice are under-determined by reason.
> There may be two kinds of reactions to this problem: a radical and a defensive reaction. The radical reaction holds that these features undermine the objectivity of theories of justice. Work within a school of thought makes political theory

'path dependent', in that the past history of political thought and of what theories have been accepted by theorists partly determines our current formulation and acceptance of theories, which therefore is not simply a function of the data available to us. . . . The lack of agreed-upon rules to determine theory acceptance makes such acceptance a matter of subjective judgment, or the product of non-rational social forces, or of other factors such as Gestalt switch and conversion, which are not governed by reason.

The *defensive reaction* follows the following path. Although there are not precisely agreed-upon rules of theory choice, rationality does not require such explicit rule following. Moreover, although there might not be a complete ordering of theory preferability, relative to given data, there might be a partial ordering that is enough to decide the question theorists are facing. One theory might be best according to all the criteria, or it might be that the vague weights that are given to the different criteria are within a range that is constrained enough to determine particular theory choices. Hence, political theory and theories of justice can be rational and objective despite these complicating factors.[17]

An assumption of Nozick's possible 'defensive reaction' is that the relative weights given to the different criteria lie within a limited range – 'a range that is constrained enough to determine particular theory choices'. However, in chapters 1, 4 and 5 we have made plausible that this assumption is unfounded if the relevant criteria and values are incommensurable and the theories are incompletely comparable. Then the range of indeterminateness with respect to the weights of the different criteria and values is very wide.

It is worth emphasizing that the above approach has nothing to do with moral relativism. One theory of justice may be objectively and universally better in one respect, while another is objectively and universally better in another respect. It may also be the case that, with respect to justice, some theories are overall better than some others. The theories may be ranked, but this ranking is incomplete and there seems to be no single theory in which all values relevant for justice can be integrated in a way that is objectively optimal and complete. This claim will be further substantiated in the next chapter, which is devoted to John Rawls's famous theory of justice. As we have discussed in chapter 4, the justification of a choice between incompletely comparable alternatives – in this case, incompletely comparable theories of justice – can only be partial in the double sense of 'incomplete' and 'biased'.

NOTES

1. Amartya Sen, 'What Do We Want from a Theory of Justice?', *Journal of Philosophy* 103 (2006): 224–225.

2. These sentences are to be found in J. S. Mill's *Utilitarianism*, ed. Roger Crisp (Oxford: Oxford University Press, 2002), 100–102. (Adaptations have been made without bending the text.)

3. Alasdair MacIntyre, *After Virtue*, 2nd ed. (Notre Dame, Ind.: University of Notre Dame Press, 1984), 246.

4. Shaun Hargreaves Heap, Martin Hollis, Bruce Lyons, Robert Sugden, Albert Weale, *The Theory of Choice* (Oxford: Blackwell Publishers, 1992), 285.

5. Susan Lynn Hurley, *Natural Reasons, Personality and Polity* (Oxford: Oxford University Press, 1989), 262.

6. Bernard Williams, *Moral Luck* (Cambridge: Cambridge University Press, 1981), 72–73.

7. Stuart Hampshire, *Justice Is Conflict* (Princeton: Princeton University Press, 2000), 3–4.

8. Ibid., 5.

9. John Stuart Mill, *A System of Logic*, 8th ed. (London: Longmans, 1949), 620–621.

10. Mill, *Utilitarianism*, chap. V, 'On the Connection between Justice and Utility'.

11. Henry Sidgwick, *The Methods of Ethics* (Indianapolis/Cambridge: Hackett Publishing Company, 1981), 447.

12. From Plato's *Euthyphro*.

13. Martha C. Nussbaum, *The Fragility of Goodness. Luck and Ethics in Greek Tragedy and Philosophy* (Cambridge: Cambridge University Press, 2001), see chap. 4 (The *Protagoras*: A Science of Practical Reasoning), section IV. In fact, Nussbaum argues, this is also the central motivation of utilitarianism: '[T]he need for commensurability in order to deal with messy deliberative problems.' 'Bentham's arguments that only ... a science of *measure* would eliminate contingency from social life show deep Platonic sympathies,' 112.

14. Thomas Kuhn, 'Reflections on My Critics', in *Criticism and the Growth of Knowledge*, eds. Imre Lakatos and Alan Musgrave (Cambridge: Cambridge University Press, 1999), 262. Compare also what Kuhn says in *The Structure of Scientific Revolutions*, 2nd ed. (Chicago: University of Chicago Press, 1970), 199: 'Two men may disagree, for example, about the relative importance of fruitfulness of their theories, or if they agree that bit disagree about the relative importance of fruitfulness and, say scope in reaching choice.' This is analogous to our problem of *ranking* relevant standards or values. Compare Alexander Bird in his comment on this passage in his book *Thomas Kuhn* (Princeton: Princeton University Press, 2001), 244: 'As a matter of fact Kuhn thinks that certain values are ubiquitous in science – accuracy, simplicity, fruitfulness, consistency and breadth of scope. But even then there is room for difference over what counts as simplicity or fruitfulness and for difference *how these values should be ranked*.'

15. Kuhn, 'Reflections on My Critics', 267–268.

16. Kuhn, *Structure of Scientific Revolutions*, 175, 200.

17. This text is borrowed from Robert Nozick, *Invariances: The Structure of the Objective World* (Cambridge, Mass.: Belknap Press of Harvard University Press, 2001) and adapted to the issue under consideration (e.g., 'scientific theories' are substituted by 'theories of justice').

Chapter 7

Implications of Incommensurability for John Rawls's Theory of Justice

> How is it possible that there can be a stable and just society whose . . . citizens are deeply divided by conflicting and even incommensurable religious, philosophical and moral doctrines?
>
> John Rawls[1]

SUMMARY

John Rawls recognizes the problem of incommensurability for justice. His theory of justice consists of ingenious attempts to resolve this problem. Rawls starts from the given that people in a pluralistic society adhere to conceptions of the good and moral doctrines that are not only conflicting but also incommensurable. These different conceptions of the good and morality are associated with different conceptions of justice, which are conflicting and incommensurable. Rawls thinks he has constructed principles of justice that are neutral with respect to these conceptions and may be affirmed by all reasonable and rational people in an overlapping consensus. In this chapter I show that he has only partly succeeded in achieving this aim, not because of shortcomings of his theory but due to the multidimensional aspects of justice that are not able to be captured in a complete theory of justice.

****

In chapters 5 and 6 we have discussed different criteria – like liberty, equality, need and efficiency/utility – according to which welfare and other advantages can be distributed. We have seen that aggregating these values in order to create a combined measure for a just distribution is problematic due to their incommensurability. Rawls, in whose theory of justice liberty, equality, need and efficiency play a significant role, has tried to overcome the problem of incommensurability by attempting to avoid, rather than resolve, it. He has ingeniously tried to circumvent trade-offs between disparate values in three different ways:[2]

(1) Restriction of distribuenda to a limited number of publicly verifiable and supposedly measurable primary social goods
(2) A scheme of lexical priorities
(3) The difference principle

Here I shall only briefly discuss them. They will be considered more extensively in the subsequent sections.

(1) *Restriction of distribuenda.* Rawls argues that without restriction of distribuenda 'the index problem is known to be insoluble'.[3] He does not concentrate on 'outcomes' like equal welfare, health and capabilities. The thought behind this limitation 'is to find a practicable public basis of interpersonal comparisons based on objective features of citizens' social circumstances'.
(2) *Lexical priorities.* Rawls introduces a scheme of lexical priorities between his three principles of justice:[4] the principle of equal liberty (concerned with basic liberties), the 'principle of fair equality of opportunity' (concerned with equality) and the 'difference principle' (concerned with need [concern for the worst-off] and utility [efficiency]). This scheme of lexical priorities tries to avoid that liberty, equality, need and utility have to be balanced against each other.
(3) The *difference principle.* Rawls argues that 'greater average well-being and a more equal distribution are both desirable ends'. But, he continues, different political views 'balance these ends differently, and we need criteria for determining their relative weights. The fact is that we do not in general agree to very much when we acknowledge ends of this kind.'[5] The difference principle 'is a relatively precise conception' and avoids the problem of different weightings of, on the one side, greater average well-being and, on the other side, a more equal distribution, 'since it ranks all combinations of objectives according to how well they promote the prospects of the least favoured'.[6] According to this principle inequality is allowed only if it is to the advantage of the worst-off. This avoids having to balance efficiency and equality. The difference principle also obviates (or at least restricts) the need of interpersonal cardinal measurements and comparisons. Ordinal comparisons between, on the one side, the worst-off group and, on the other side, better-off persons are

sufficient.⁷ And the problem of the index of primary goods with respect to the worst position seems to be limited, because the basic liberties and fair equality of opportunity need not be balanced against other values and because the remaining primary social goods are strongly correlated in the worst-off position.⁸

So the three 'constructions' (1. restriction of the number of distribuenda; 2. lexical priorities; 3. difference principle) seem to enable integration of liberty, equality, need and utility without having to balance and aggregate them, which would be an insurmountable problem because the relevant values are incommensurable and can, therefore, not be impartially weighed as we discussed in previous chapters.

Although ranking of values avoids the need of aggregation, it does not avoid reasonable disagreement, if values may be ranked in more than one rational way. Because people adhere to different incommensurable conceptions of the good and rank values in line with these conceptions, they will probably arrive at different incompletely comparable rankings. In that case ranking does not solve the problem of incommensurability because the problem of aggregation is replaced by the problem of comparing different possible rankings.

Democratic decision cannot satisfactorily resolve the problem either, because, as Arrow's *theorem* and the *voters' paradox* show, the majority rule easily leads to incoherent results and intransitive rankings. This will be discussed in detail in chapter 8. Again, Rawls tries to overcome this problem by avoiding, rather than resolving, it. Aiming at a solution acceptable to all rational and reasonable people, he tries to avoid the need to compare competing rankings and, instead, to find an agreed-upon ranking. As said already, an important cause of choosing differing rankings of values is adhering to differing conceptions of the good. By means of the device of the *original position*, where the parties are behind a *veil of ignorance* and do not know their conception of the good, Rawls hopes and expects that people will choose the same ranking of values regarding the basic structure of the society. This expectation is based on the so-called Harsanyi doctrine – the claim that people with the same information and experiences will act in the same way – and on the belief that rationality and reasonableness will lead to consensus. The device of the original position avoids Arrow's theorem – the impossibility to satisfy minimal conditions of a rational social choice based on an aggregation of divergent rankings (see chapter 8) – because the different parties are combined to one and the same representative and impartial rational agent, choosing a single superior, complete and transitive ranking of values.

The earlier Rawls of *A Theory of Justice* was optimistic with respect to the capability of reason to achieve consensus on objective principles of justice. He thought that fundamental disagreements between people could be avoided, or at least transcended, by an appeal to reason – an appeal to grounds and political values which are detached from specific personal interests and conceptions of the good. His confidence in the unifying power of reason is based on the Kantian assumption that reason detached from personal interests and aims will lead to 'eternal', universally applicable, single right and complete answers to conflicts of values related to justice. Rawls summarizes his optimistic view on the last page of *A Theory of Justice*:[9]

> Once we grasp this conception [of justice], we can at any time look at the social world from the required point of view. . . . This standpoint is also objective . . . (I)t enables us to be impartial, even between persons who are not contemporaries but who belong to many generations. Thus to see our place in society from the perspective of this position is to see it *sub specie aeternitatis*: it is to regard the human situation not only from all social but also from all temporal points of view. . . . (In this way people) can, whatever their generation, bring together into one scheme all individual perspectives and arrive together at regulative principles that can be affirmed by everyone.

In his *Political Liberalism*, Rawls has moderated this view. Still the later Rawls maintained his belief in an overlapping consensus on his principles of justice among rational and reasonable people who adhere to a liberal democracy.

STRUCTURE

The first part of this chapter investigates the question whether Rawls's principles indeed lead to determinate conclusions. The second part of this chapter investigates the question whether reasonableness and rationality determinately show that his principles are indeed the most reasonable and rational ones and that these principles will be endorsed by all rational and reasonable people in an overlapping consensus. With respect to the first question I shall argue that Rawls's principles lead to insufficiently determinate conclusions. We shall see that, despite Rawls's restriction to a limited number of primary goods and his ingenious system of lexical priorities, he incompletely succeeds in resolving the index problem. The disparity and incommensurability of his distribuenda – basic liberties and other primary social goods – render them incompletely comparable. This prevents the determination of an overall index of liberty or other advantages, and the determination of the overall greatest liberty and the overall least advantaged position. With respect to the second question I shall try to show that reason is less unifying than what Rawls believes, because rationality and reasonableness under-determine the choice between incommensurable alternatives (see chapter 1). My critical comments are not without some diffidence. Rawls has developed an impressive and wonderful theory of justice. Because the theory is complicated, critics run the risk to explain it incorrectly. That is why Rawls may easily become a victim of the 'Straw Man fallacy' – the fallacy of criticizing someone for a position that he does not hold. I am happy that two experts who largely support Rawls's views – Elizabeth Anderson and Adam Swift – undertook the task to defend Rawls's approach against my criticism. This chapter has considerably benefitted from their critique. Still I think that the main points of my critical comments on Rawls may be maintained.

ARE RAWLS'S PRINCIPLES OF JUSTICE INTERNALLY DETERMINATE?

Rawls's principles of justice are concerned with the just distribution of primary social goods. These consist of

- basic liberties
- income and wealth
- equal rights and opportunities to the powers and prerogatives related to positions of responsibility in the political and economic institutions of the basic structure
- social bases of self-respect.

There are several basic liberties like freedom of conscience, freedom of religious or secular belief, freedom of thought and speech, freedom of assembly and association, right to political participation such as the right to vote, right to hold public office and the right to participate in government, and the rights and liberties related to the freedom and integrity of the person (freedom of movement, free occupational choice, right to personal property, freedom from psychological oppression and freedom from physical assault or arbitrary arrest). All rational people have a common interest in these primary social goods because they are required for the advancement of all citizens' rational plans of life, however distinct the content of their conceptions of the good may be.[10] If people have disagreement about justice it is less about Rawls's primary goods as such than about their weights and ranking. The possible problem is formed by the relative weights that have to be assigned to the relevant primary goods in situations in which they lead to conflicting demands. Some of the values related to the primary goods do never clash, and other values only contingently conflict. For instance, the liberty to vote does not conflict with the freedom from arbitrary arrest, and the right to personal property does not conflict with freedom of speech. Increase of one basic liberty or other primary good does not imply here restriction of, or collision with, another basic liberty or primary good. However, as we shall see, some primary goods may lead to conflicting claims.

LEXICAL PRIORITIES

How does Rawls rationally determine the weights and resolve the conflicting claims? He formulates a number of principles of justice, which are lexically ordered according to three *priority rules*. The principles are:

(1) *Principle of equal liberty*

Each person is to have an equal right to the most extensive total system of equal basic liberties compatible with a similar system of liberty for all.

(2) (a) *Principle of fair equality of opportunity*;
    (b) *Difference principle*

Social and economic inequalities are to be arranged so that they are both:

- attached to offices and positions open to all under conditions of fair equality of opportunity (*principle of fair equality of opportunity*)
- to the greatest benefit of the least advantaged (difference principle)

The lexical priority rules are:

1st *priority rule* (*priority of liberty*): principle (1) is lexically prior to principle (2)
2nd *priority rule*: principle (2a) is lexically prior to principle (2b)
3rd *priority rule* (*priority of justice over efficiency and welfare*): principle (2) [(a) and (b)] is lexically prior to efficiency and to maximizing the sum of advantages

Rawls expects that all rational and reasonable people may agree with these principles and their lexical ordering because they are conditions for developing a sense of justice and pursuing a conception of the good – aims that are shared by all rational and reasonable people. Cooperation and reciprocity, necessary to attain these aims, are made possible by the principles and are of interest irrespective of the specific content of a conception of the good. In this context the value that deserves priority is liberty – an as great liberty as possible and compatible with an equal liberty for all. Without this liberty we are not able to optimally pursue or revise our conception of the good and to develop a sense of justice. Basic liberties get lexical priority over other primary goods such as income and wealth (provided that a minimum level of wealth has been achieved). If a basic liberty and another social or economic advantage clash, the former gets lexical priority. Justice requires that liberty may only be limited for the sake of liberty and not for the sake of other social and economic advantages. So liberty gets absolute priority over all other advantages. For instance, improvement of incomes and wealth of all people at the cost of one or more of the basic liberties (however small the decrease of the basic liberty may be) would be unjust. The different distribution rules are supposed not to conflict, because each primary good gets a place in one of the lexically ranked principles of justice. Basic liberties fall within the first principle, equal opportunities within the second principle, the distribution of wealth within the third principle. In this way the primary goods are strictly separated from each other so that there is no need to weigh them because conflicts are supposed to be avoided. The distribution of the primary goods is supposed not to lead to conflicts because the lexical priorities in combination with the difference principle avoid the necessity of an overall judgment of a relative level of well-being. Rawls does not need to make an overall comparison because his aim is not equality between civilians in overall amount of advantage. Inequalities are allowed as long as they maximize the level of well-being of the worst-off and as long as the principles of equal liberty and opportunity are satisfied. Rawls's approach is more practicable than an 'overall advantage' approach in which disparate advantages have to be aggregated to an overall metric of advantage. As Rawls argues:

> as long as we can identify the least advantaged representative man, only ordinal judgments of well being are required from then on. . . . It does not matter how much worse off this representative individual is than the others. The further difficulties of cardinal measurement do not arise since no other interpersonal comparisons are necessary. The Difference Principle, then, asks less of our judgments of welfare. We never have to calculate a sum of advantages involving a cardinal measure.[11]

GREATEST LIBERTY AND WORST-OFF POSITION

As we have seen, Rawls restricts the scope of justice to a limited number of primary goods. In combination with his scheme of lexical priorities he supposes that irresolvable value conflicts are prevented. However, apart from the question whether Rawls's restriction of the scope of justice is warranted and whether resources are an adequate index of well-being and form the right and exhaustive distribuenda, conflicts between the relevant primary goods are not excluded. The scheme of lexical priorities prevents conflicts *between* principles but not clashes of values *within* a principle. For instance, the first principle concerns several basic liberties that are not immune to mutual conflicts. And within the difference principle the overall worst-off position may be impossible to determine in case of bidirectionality of the relevant primary goods present in the states to be compared, because it requires an aggregation of disparate primary goods, like income, wealth, powers and prerogatives of offices and positions of responsibility and the social bases of self-respect.

Let us start with the notion 'greatest liberty'. This is a problematic notion because the exercise of one basic liberty may mean the violation of another. Freedom of speech (in the unrestricted form as adhered to by many liberals) may clash with freedom from psychological oppression, discrimination, race abuse and blasphemy and with freedom from being insulted in one's social standing, reputation, integrity and feeling of self-respect. This tension will be discussed in detail in chapter 11. Freedom of association and conscience (e.g., of confessional school governors) may collide with freedom from discrimination (e.g., of gay teachers in employment). The freedom to set up private schools clashes with equality of opportunity in school education, while prohibition of private schools in order to advance equality of opportunity in education restricts people's liberty.[12] Rawls expected that these conflicts are avoided or resolved by the greatest liberty principle, which states that the decision resulting in the 'most extensive overall liberty' is the just one. The idea is that freedom may be usefully restricted in the sense that restriction of one liberty may increase overall liberty. Let us consider this idea in more detail. Take two different liberties, A (say free speech) and B (say freedom from psychological oppression).[13] Suppose that restriction of liberty A increases liberty B. Does this mean that overall liberty increases, decreases or remains the same? Unlike Rawls's principles, his basic liberties are not lexically ordered. This means that the question cannot be answered if the relevant liberties are incommensurable and have no determinate relative weights. Reduction to an overarching value, expressible in a single metric, will be difficult, due to the disparity of the liberties. Assigning relative weights is an intuitive procedure, which Rawls rejects as unworkable because it may lead to very divergent and even opposite outcomes. Different people assign differing relative and absolute weights to the same values. For instance, for many liberals the value of free speech may be as 'sacred' and non-negotiable as the integrity of religious matters for many Christians, Muslims and other religious believers. Free speech restriction, which may protect against discrimination, blasphemy and harm to self-respect, may lead to more overall liberty for religious believers, but to less overall liberty for non-religious liberals. So increase or restriction of a particular liberty may mean an overall increase of liberty for the one, but an overall decrease of liberty for the other. This illustrates that the greatest liberty principle and the axiom that 'liberty is only allowed to be restricted for the sake of a greater liberty' do not always work. Reference to the common good does not work either because of the different interests of different people. Different individuals may reasonably make divergent choices not only in the light of their different beliefs or conceptions of the good but also in the light of their different temperaments and characters. Some persons might reasonably prefer the exercise of a particular basic liberty, say freedom of speech, in unrestricted form, given their specific temperament and their immunity against the risk of being exposed to the exercise of the same unrestricted liberty on the part of others. Other persons would not pay this price of unrestricted freedom of speech, since, given their temperament, they would value the protections afforded by the restrictions higher than the unrestricted liberty.[14] By the way, this shows that Rawls's idea of a 'representative equal citizen' is hardly helpful because such a citizen, representative for persons with different temperaments and 'background beliefs', does not exist.

Rawls's axiom that 'a liberty may only be restricted for the sake of a greater liberty' is faced with the same problems, again because it is not univocal what the greatest liberty is. Besides, somebody's exercise of a basic liberty may cause harm to others without restricting liberty. If liberty may only be restricted for the sake of liberty, this seems to mean that liberty need not be restricted whatever large the possible harm to others, if this harm forms no restriction of liberty. Many liberals regard free speech as an unrestricted basic liberty including the right to offend. Salman Rushdie says:

> What is freedom of expression? Without the freedom to offend, it ceases to exist. Without the freedom to challenge, even to satarise all orthodoxies, it ceases to exist. Language and the imagination cannot be imprisoned, or art dies, a little of what makes us human.[15]

Unrestricted and openly expressed negative and abusive criticisms – for instance on race, cultural customs, sexual nature or religious belief – may violate the relevant persons' social standing, reputation and feeling of self-respect (what Rawls himself calls 'perhaps the most important primary good')[16] without necessarily restricting their liberty. Parekh says:

> Free speech is not the only great value, and needs to be balanced against such avoidance of needless hurt, social harmony, protection of the weak, truthfulness in the public realm, and self-respect and dignity of individuals and groups. There is no 'true' way of reconciling them; it all depends on the history, traditions, political circumstances, and so on of a society.... No single value trumps

all others, and their relative importance can only be decided in the light of the social and cultural context and the likely consequences.[17]

This issue of free speech is discussed in detail in chapter 11.

IS A GREATER LIBERTY FOR ALL BETTER FOR ALL?

Rawls argues that

> it is rational for men to want as large a share as possible of liberty, since they are not compelled to accept more if they do not wish to, nor does a person suffer from a greater liberty.[18]

But, as Herbert Hart shows, this overlooks the fact that an as great liberty as possible for all is not always an overall and unambiguous advantage for all. The possible advantages of a particular (extension of) liberty for oneself have to be balanced against the possible disadvantages for oneself due to the practice of the same (extension of) liberty by others:

> Distribution of liberty of action necessarily does two things: first, it confers on individuals the advantage of that liberty, but secondly, it exposes them to whatever disadvantages the practice of that liberty by others may entail for them.[19]

After Hart's criticism Rawls has given up the idea of 'most extensive liberty' and has made some adaptations in his argument of the 'basic liberties'. He assumes that there is a coherent scheme of basic liberties which will keep each other in equilibrium because they 'not only limit one another, but they are also self-limiting'. It concerns regulation rather than restriction, Rawls argues. But we have seen that this need not be the case. A coherent scheme and equilibrium may be achieved intrapersonally, but it is implausible that this scheme is the same for all rational people because the point of equilibrium of competing basic liberties depends on the specific weights that are applied to the different basic liberties.[20]

DOES THE DIFFERENCE PRINCIPLE AVOID THE INDEX PROBLEM?

Rawls thinks this question can largely be answered in the affirmative:

> The Difference Principle tries to establish objective grounds for interpersonal comparisons in two ways. First of all, as long as we can identify the least advan-

taged representative man, only ordinal judgments of wellbeing are required from then on. We know from what position the social system is to be judged. It does not matter how much worse off this representative individual is than the others. The further difficulties of cardinal measurement do not arise since no other interpersonal comparisons are necessary. The Difference Principle, then, asks less of our judgments of welfare. We never have to calculate a sum of advantages involving a cardinal measure. While qualitative interpersonal comparisons are made in finding the bottom position, for the rest the ordinal judgments of one representative man suffice.[21]

According to Rawls the problem of the index of primary goods with respect to the worst position is limited:

> Assuming that the two principles of justice are serially ordered, this [index] problem is greatly simplified. The basic liberties are always equal, and there is fair equality of opportunity; one does not need to balance these liberties and rights against other values. The primary social goods that vary in their distribution are the rights and prerogatives of authority, and income and health. But the difficulties are not so great as they might seem at first because of the nature of the Difference Principle. The only index problem that concerns us is that of the least advantaged group. The primary goods enjoyed by other representative individuals are adjusted to raise this index, subject of course to the usual constraints. It is unnecessary to define weights for the more favored positions in any detail, as long as we are sure that they are more favored. But often this is easy since they frequently have more of each primary good that is distributed unequally. If we know how the distribution of goods to the more favored affects the expectations of the most disfavoured, this is sufficient. The index problem largely reduces, then, to that of weighting primary goods for the least advantaged. We try to do this by taking up the standpoint of the representative individual from this group and asking which combination of primary social goods it would be rational for him to prefer. In doing this we admittedly rely upon intuitive estimates. But this cannot be avoided entirely.[22]

So Rawls hopes to resolve the index problem for the difference principle in a similar way as he does for the greatest liberty principle, to wit, by means of a 'representative rational individual'. But if there is no objectively best worst-off position preferred by every rational person, such a representative individual does not exist. Besides, Rawls trivializes here the problem of 'intuitive estimates', which he elsewhere rejects as unworkable because it may easily lead to conflicting judgments.

The applicability of the difference principle depends on the possibility to determine the overall worst-off position from heterogeneous social and economic advantages like income, wealth, powers and prerogatives of offices and positions of responsibility, and the social bases of self-respect. First, for the maximin criterion (= maximizing the minimum/worst-off position) to be applicable, each of these items must be roughly measurable. Income is objectively measurable. But it is less clear how wealth, powers, prerogatives and bases of self-respect are to be measured.[23] Second, and more important, how are we to construct an overall index to be capable of aggregating these multidimensional values? Rawls argues that levels of income and wealth on the one side and levels of other primary social goods on the other side are strongly correlated.[24] But this does not mean that the former are always good proxies for the latter.[25] Suppose labourer *A* earns a low wage but works under circumstances that promote participation and self-respect. Labourer *B* has a higher wage but no say and he works under circumstances that prevent personal involvement and diminish self-respect.[26] Who is overall worse-off? In a similar vein Martha Nussbaum argues that income and wealth are not good proxies for important social goods such as mobility and social inclusion.[27] Philippe van Parijs raises a similar objection:

> [The strong correlation between the levels of various social goods in the worst-off position] is not enough to permit comparison across relevant social states, as some schemes may be designed, for example, so as to give a lower income but greater powers to the worst-off category. A market economy with worker-owned firms may conceivably outperform conventional capitalism in terms of the powers and prerogatives associated with the worst position while doing worse income-wise for everyone.[28]

He continues:

> However, appeal to rational prudence from the standpoint of the least advantaged should enable us, Rawls believes, to appropriately weight the various goods to the extent necessary for the sake of applying maximin to the aggregate index. Contrary to what Rawls suggests, more is required than intrapersonal comparison, since the worst off need not be the same people in all relevant social states.

Still van Parijs thinks that there is no real problem:

> But the interpersonal comparison involved is arguably unproblematic enough for us to be able to determine in which relevant social state the worst off enjoy the best combination of income and wealth, powers and prerogatives, and the social bases of self-respect.

As far as I can see, van Parijs does not give arguments why he believes that the relevant interpersonal comparison is 'arguably unproblematic enough' to be able to determine the best combination of the relevant social goods. Taking his own example, how to determine which combination is the best one, (*A*) a lower income in combination with greater powers and a social basis of self-respect, or (*B*) *vice versa*? Suppose that the welfare level of better-off people further increases while the position of worst-off people changes from *A* to *B* (increase in income but decrease of powers and self-respect) or from *B* to *A*: is the difference principle satisfied in the former, the latter or neither case? Martha Nussbaum summarizes the problem:

> I believe that Rawls already runs into considerably difficulty when he opts for a single linear measure for relative social positions. For he insists that self-respect (or rather its social basis) is 'the most important' of the primary goods. And yet, when it comes to measuring who is least well-off in a society, Rawls ignores self-respect, measuring social positions in terms of income and wealth alone.[29]

ARE RAWLS'S PRINCIPLES EXTERNALLY DETERMINATE?

We have discussed the question whether Rawls's principles are *internally* determinate, that is, whether they lead to determinate conclusions. Now we shall discuss the question whether Rawls's principles of justice are *externally* determinate, that is, whether reasonableness and rationality determinately show that these principles are the most reasonable and rational ones in comparison to others and that these principles will be endorsed by all rational and reasonable people in an overlapping consensus.

REASONABLE DISAGREEMENT

How is it possible, Rawls wonders, that adherents to conflicting beliefs may all be reasonable? Why does reason, at least in the long run or in principle, not lead to one non-conflicting truth? This is caused by the so-called *burdens of judgment* or *sources of reasonable disagreement* of which Rawls formulates six main types, which I will summarize here in a condensed form:[30]

1. Conflicting scientific and empirical evidence make unambiguous evaluations hard.
2. Disagreement about the weights of relevant considerations result in different judgments.
3. Vague political and moral concepts lead to different interpretations.

4. Weighing moral and political values depends on interpersonally differing total experience.
5. Different kinds of normative considerations make an overall assessment difficult.
6. A system of social institutions can only contain a limited number of moral and political values.

The burdens of judgment make it improbable that different people, however reasonable, will come to agreement on conceptions of the good and comprehensive beliefs: many rival conceptions of the good are reasonable and no particular comprehensive belief will be accepted by all reasonable people. The burdens of judgment may cause considerable and irreconcilable disagreements even among the most rational, intelligent and optimally informed people. Therefore, Rawls argues, 'it is not to be expected that conscientious persons with full powers of reason will arrive at the same conclusion.'[31] Burdens of judgment and reasonable disagreement will also prevent consensus on principles of justice as long as they are based on personal comprehensive beliefs and conceptions of the good, as is illustrated in the following summary of the rival conceptions of justice.

Conflicting conceptions of justice

- Justice based on
  - *equality* (Richard Arneson, G. A. Cohen, Ronald Dworkin, Martha Nussbaum, John Rawls, Amartya Sen)
  - *liberty* and *legitimate entitlement* (Robert Nozick)
  - *need* (David Miller)
  - *utility* (John Stuart Mill, Henry Sidgwick, Peter Singer)
- Justice based on
  - *equality* of
    - *basic liberties and other primary goods* (John Rawls)
    - *resources* (Ronald Dworkin)
    - *opportunities* (Richard Arneson)
    - *capabilities* (Martha Nussbaum, Amartya Sen)
    - *resources and welfare* (G. A. Cohen)
- Justice based on
  - *rational consensus* (Jürgen Habermas)
  - *overlapping consensus* (John Rawls)

- *dissensus* (Clifford Geertz, Stuart Hampshire, Chantal Mouffe, Jacques Derrida, Iris Young)
- *modus vivendi* (John Gray)
- Justice as *impartiality* (Brian Barry, John Rawls) versus 'the fiction of impartiality' (Iris Young)
- *The right is prior to the good* (John Rawls) versus *The good is prior to the right* (John Gray, Michael Sandel, Michael Walzer)
- *Perfectionism* (Joseph Raz) versus *anti-perfectionism* (Isaiah Berlin, J Gray, Chantal Mouffe, John Rawls)
- Anti-perfectionism based on *neutrality* (John Rawls) versus anti-perfectionism based on *agonistic pluralism* (Isaiah Berlin, John Gray, Chantal Mouffe)
- *Cosmopolitanism* (Immanuel Kant, John Rawls [of *A Theory of Justice*]) versus *communitarianism* (Michael Walzer, Michael Sandel, Alasdair MacIntyre)

Some thinkers believe that the ultimate criterion of justice is equality, others freedom or legitimate entitlement, still others need-satisfaction, merit or utility. Theorists who agree on a basic principle (say equality) disagree on its content (e.g., equal liberty, equal resources, equal welfare, equal capability or a combination of all these equalities). Some thinkers believe that 'the right is prior to the good', others that 'the good is prior to the right'. Another controversy concerns the feasibility of consensus about justice. Some theorists believe that rational consensus is feasible, while others think that reasonable disagreement cannot be overcome and that only an *'overlapping* consensus' can be achieved. Still others believe that in a pluriform society we can only hope for a modus vivendi or that justice can only be adequately understood as encompassing continuing conflict and *dissensus*. Taking stock of all these, often fundamentally different, conceptions of justice (of thinkers all adhering to a liberal democratic framework), it seems an impossible task to achieve agreement on principles of justice. Still Rawls thinks that an appeal to 'public reason' – an appeal to grounds and political values which are detached from specific and personal interests, moral doctrines and conceptions of the good – will lead to an overlapping consensus on a political, rational and reasonable conception of justice. As said earlier, Rawls's optimism is based on the idea that reason detached from (personal) interests will lead to single right, universally applicable and complete answers to value conflicts. However, in the preceding chapters we have seen that 'reason' often gives ambiguous answers and under-determines decisions between rival rational and reasonable alternatives. I shall argue that this will especially happen if reason is detached from guiding principles originating from conceptions of the good, interests and background beliefs. That is why public reason in Rawls's sense will appear to be more vulnerable to incomplete comparability and indeterminateness than non-public reason. By bracketing conceptions of the good and some basic interests and aims, not only sources of reasonable disagreement but also sources of adequate and complete assignment of weights are cut off.

Interestingly, Rawls uses the burdens of judgment and the absence of consensus on *right* principles of justice as foundations for his overlapping consensus on *fair* principles of justice. According to Rawls, if rational and reasonable people differ in their conceptions of the good and comprehensive beliefs, justice cannot be based on a specific conception of the good or comprehensive belief if it is the aim of justice to be acceptable for all rational and reasonable people. Coercive principles of justice cannot be legitimate if they may reasonably be rejected ('the liberal principle of legitimacy').[32] Because no specific comprehensive belief or conception of the good, however reasonable, will be accepted by all reasonable people, principles must be neutral between comprehensive beliefs and conceptions of the good. The rationale of Rawls's *veil of ignorance* is to ensure that the choice of principles will be independent of, and neutral between, comprehensive beliefs and conceptions of the good. In combination with a detachment from other possible sources of disagreement and biased views based on personal preferences, capacities, predilections, social status and self-interested considerations, about which the parties behind the veil are ignorant as well, Rawls thinks that consensus may be attained about person-independent and therefore neutral basic principles of justice. Although people have different conceptions of justice, influenced by differences in backgrounds, beliefs and interests, an overlapping consensus on basic rules of justice can be reached if these personal backgrounds, beliefs and interests are bracketed. By means of the veil of ignorance basic principles of justice may be constructed which are consensus-based, legitimate and neutral. At least, this is what Rawls expects. However, it is implausible that behind the veil of ignorance reasonable disagreement will disappear. This becomes clear if we again consider the burdens of judgment mentioned previously, now behind the veil of ignorance.

Behind the veil of ignorance

1) 'scientific and empirical evidence' are not less conflicting;
2) it is implausible that people, ignorant of their conception of the good, will assign similar 'weights to relevant considerations' and will arrive at similar judgments;
3) 'political and moral concepts' are not less vague;
4) people have no personal experience, background and history; it has not been demonstrated that this means that they will weigh moral and political values in the same way; by contrast, it is questionable whether any adequate weighing procedure is possible at all, if an adequate frame of reference is lacking;

5) it is not to be expected that people find it less 'difficult to make an overall assessment' about an 'issue containing more than one relevant side';
6) it is not to be expected that all reasonable and rational people select the same values 'from the full range of moral and political values that might be realized'.

Because behind the veil of ignorance virtually all sources of reasonable disagreement remain present, it is implausible that reasonable disagreement change into consensus, even on a political conception of justice. By contrast, it is plausible that the reasonable disagreement, recognized by Rawls with respect to conceptions of the good, will return with respect to conceptions of justice, whether political or comprehensive.[33] Amartya Sen expresses a similar objection:

> Even after vested interests and personal priorities have been somehow 'taken out' of consideration through such devices as the 'veil of ignorance', there may remain possibly conflicting views on social priorities.[34]

In his later work Rawls recognizes that different political conceptions of justice are possible and reasonable.[35] This is an implicit recognition of reasonable disagreement on (even political) conceptions of justice. This recognition is difficult to reconcile with the expectation of an overlapping consensus on a political conception of justice and a single ranking of basic principles affirmed by all reasonable people.

NON-NEUTRALITY

Apart from the fact that the veil of ignorance and the recourse to public reason will not avoid reasonable disagreement, it does not lead to neutrality between comprehensive beliefs either. Rawls's veil of ignorance and his interpretation of public reason are biased in favour of some comprehensive views and to the prejudice of others. Behind Rawls's veil people are ignorant about their conception of the good. Similarly Rawls's public reason prescribes the bracketing of these conceptions. Therefore both Rawls's veil and his conception of public reason form a bias against comprehensive beliefs in which the good is believed to be prior to, or at least inextricably bound up with, the right. Alasdair MacIntyre expresses a similar objection:

> the question has to be asked whether, by adopting this procedure [of detaching oneself from particularities and specific interests], key questions have not been begged . . . [I]ts requirement of disinterestedness in fact covertly presupposes one particular partisan type of account of justice, that of liberal individualism,

which it is later to be used to justify, so that its apparent neutrality is no more than an appearance.[36]

A thick veil of ignorance parallels a relatively narrow public reason. Rawls's public reason largely removes controversial moral, philosophical and religious issues from the agenda of political life. Sandel argues:

> Although political liberalism upholds the right to freedom of speech, it severely limits the kinds of arguments that are legitimate contributions to political debate, especially debate about constitutional essentials and basic justice.... Not only may government not endorse one or another conception of the good, but citizens may not even introduce into political discourse their comprehensive moral or religious convictions, at least when debating matters of justice and rights.

According to, among others, John Finnis, Robert George, Patrick Neal and Christopher Wolfe public reason in the relatively narrow Rawlsian sense 'attempts to put the grounds, and often the substance, of people's deepest moral convictions off-limits in the most important public discourse'. This may lead to a 'truncated doctrine of public reason' which 'excludes what may be of much relevance to basic questions of justice'.[37] In a personal communication Elizabeth Anderson has given the following comment on an earlier draft of this chapter:

> The perspective of public reason (which is the perspective of reasonable citizens in a democracy) and the perspective of the parties in the original position are two distinct perspectives. The doctrine of public reason is prior to any argument to be made in the original position. The original position is not a bias in any sense of unfairness since it is entailed by the joint fundamental commitments to 1) reciprocity; 2) inclusion of all citizens; 3) the fact of reasonable pluralism.... It is no just complaint against public reason that it excludes doctrines inconsistent with reciprocity and inclusion.... One does not need a comprehensive theory of the good to choose among principles. Public reasons are enough, although one must specify a set of such reasons and weights to get determinacy.

These are fundamental points. I do not think they refute the claims of non-neutrality and indeterminateness, but they may be helpful to clarify the issue. I agree with Anderson that the perspectives of public reason and those of the original position are different. Still, as Rawls notices, the guidelines of public reason have 'essentially the same grounds' as the substantive principles of justice adopted in the original position. 'They are companion parts of one agreement.'[38] This is not surprising because Rawls's veil of ignorance is, among others, meant to detach principles of justice from specific comprehensive conceptions of the good not shared by all reasonable people.

Similarly, Rawls's public reason is detached from reasons related to specific conceptions of the good not shared by all reasonable people. So both Rawls's original position and his public reason are significantly related to the detachment of the good from the right.

Most people will agree that a veil of ignorance is a useful device for preventing contingent and morally irrelevant factors like race, gender and social status from playing a role in distributive justice. However, there is much disagreement about the proper thickness of the veil. Rawls's thick veil makes us ignorant not only about morally irrelevant factors but also about the good. There is much controversy about the question whether justice must and can be detached from (conceptions of) the good. A thick veil is unacceptable for, and biased against, adherers to comprehensive beliefs in which justice is regarded as inextricably bound up with the good. As we shall see, they are sometimes to some extent unable, rather than unwilling, to enter the original position.

The disadvantaged persons I have in mind do not deny the requirement of a standard of public reason and reciprocity, but they disagree with the content Rawls gives to these notions. I believe that Rawls's usage of the term 'public reason' is ambiguous and that the content he gives to it, is, although well reasoned, 'partial' in two senses: 'incompletely justified' and 'biased', because there are other possible well-reasoned contents of public reason which can similarly be (partially) justified, but which Rawls calls unreasonable. I shall try to substantiate this view next. It is understandable that Rawls tries to prevent a wider public reason that permits deliberations and decisions based on conceptions of the good, because this would cause continual disagreement. In that case he would have to give up not only the possibility to achieve a rational consensus on specific and single principles of justice (a possibility Rawls has given up in his *Political Liberalism*) but also the possibility to achieve a more general rational consensus on 'reasonable' and 'justifiable' principles of justice. However, the desire to achieve consensus is obviously no legitimate reason to ignore things that matter to people but may prevent consensus. It is true that Rawls has added what he calls a 'proviso', which permits religious and other idealistic discourse and views a place in public discussion as long as these can be 'translated' to *public* reasons, relevant and understandable for people who do not adhere to the relevant beliefs. But this does not really resolve the problem because Rawls ultimately holds on to publicly accessible reasons that are neutral between specific conceptions of the good and comprehensive beliefs. Jürgen Habermas's view on Rawls's political conception of justice, summarized by James Finlayson, is as follows: 'Rawls's political conception of justice sacrifices its cognitive status (its rational acceptability) to its functional or instrumental aim of ensuring [consensus and] social stability. . . . Principles of justice are justified as reasonable simply because they happen to be accepted by all, regardless of whether they deserve to be.'[39]

As mentioned previously, Anderson argues that the original position is not a bias in any sense of unfairness 'since it is entailed by the joint fundamental commitments to 1) reciprocity; 2) inclusion of all citizens; 3) the fact of reasonable pluralism'. And: 'It is no just complaint against public reason that it excludes doctrines inconsistent with reciprocity and inclusion.' However, I think that the relevant doctrines are inconsistent neither with reciprocity nor with inclusion of all citizens and recognition of the fact of reasonable pluralism. They acknowledge the importance and indispensability of these notions for a decent and democratic society, in which fellow citizens are treated as equals. However, they give these notions a content that differs from Rawls's interpretation, in line with the different content they give to the notion of public reason. I shall first discuss reciprocity and inclusion and next the recognition of the fact of reasonable pluralism.

RECIPROCITY AND INCLUSION

Rawls argues that his idea of reciprocity lies between the idea of impartiality and the idea of mutual advantage[40] and that it has the following three aspects:[41]

a) All citizens are regarded as free and equal.
b) They are prepared to offer one another fair terms of social cooperation.
c) In order to be fair the relevant terms of social cooperation must be 'reasonably acceptable' to all citizens.

These aspects of reciprocity are compatible with more than one content. The content of mutual advantage may differ. Some citizens may have mutual advantage of (and may therefore rationally opt for) a reciprocity that excludes comprehensive beliefs and conceptions of the good in constructing rules of justice. I shall call this (*R*awlsian and *r*estrictive) reciprocity 'reciprocity *R*'. Other citizens may have mutual advantage of (and may therefore rationally opt for) a reciprocity permitting them to let their comprehensive beliefs and conceptions of the good play a part, provided that the relevant beliefs belong to reasonable comprehensive beliefs and that basic rights and principles of a liberal democracy are endorsed. I shall call this (*w*ider) reciprocity 'reciprocity *W*'. Rawls writes, 'The criterion of reciprocity is normally violated whenever basic liberties are denied.'[42] Note that not only 'reciprocity *R*' but also 'reciprocity *W*' endorses basic liberties and entails equal inclusion of all citizens. So people who would opt for reciprocity *W* instead of *R* (e.g., most secular or religious idealistic comprehensive believers and most people who believe that the right cannot be detached from the good) endorse inclusion and reciprocity, at least its first two aspects and with a different content. But how should we consider the third aspect of reciprocity, the reasonable acceptability of the terms of social cooperation to all citizens? While 'reciprocity W' may be reasonably acceptable for people with an idealistic comprehensive belief and for people who believe that a conception of justice cannot be detached from a conception of the good, this reciprocity may not be reasonably acceptable for people who don't have an idealistic comprehensive belief (or an idealistic comprehensive belief without idealistic political implications) and for people who believe that a (political) conception of justice can and must be detached from the good. The reverse applies to 'reciprocity R', which may be reasonably acceptable for the latter people but often not for the former. So the third aspect of reciprocity, its reasonable acceptability for the different parties, seems to be determined by its specific content. Some contents of reciprocity are reasonably acceptable to all reasonable people (e.g., the reciprocities related to democratic principles and basic human rights). Other contents of reciprocity are reasonably acceptable to some citizens but not to others and are then, by definition of the criterion of reciprocity (its third aspect), not fair to the latter citizens.

Returning to the question of the neutrality of the original position, in the light of what has been said previously, the Rawlsian original position seems to be a device in favour of people who have an overall mutual advantage of 'reciprocity R' and an overall disadvantage of 'reciprocity W', while the device seems to be unfavourable for people who have an overall mutual advantage of 'reciprocity W' and an overall disadvantage of 'reciprocity R'. In other words, the device of Rawls's original position seems to be predisposed against people who cannot (or find it wrong to) detach justice from the good and of people who run the risk to be harmed in their integrity as a person because they cannot bracket what they regard as the truth.

THE FACT OF REASONABLE PLURALISM

The relevant idealistic, moral, philosophical or religious doctrines belong to Rawls's reasonable comprehensive beliefs, endorse his basic liberties, hold on to the premises of a liberal democracy, entail reciprocity (reciprocity W) and inclusion, and recognize the fact of reasonable pluralism. But they draw other inferences from the fact of reasonable pluralism than Rawls's. The controversy about the content and scope of public reason is extensively discussed in *Natural Law and Public Reason*[43] which reveals the strong disagreement between renowned, honest and respected political theorists about the content and justifiable limits of public reason. In the light of the burdens of judgment with respect to the complicated question of the political consequences to be drawn from the fact of reasonable pluralism, it is plausible that the controversy about this question is an instance of reasonable instead of unreasonable disagreement. Rawls argues that, due to the burdens of judgment, 'it is (with respect to many complicated issues) not to be expected that conscientious persons with full powers of reason will arrive at the same conclusion'. He emphasizes that a 'basic aspect of the reasonable [is] . . . the willingness to recognize the burdens of judgment'.[44] If Rawls states that only one reasonable conclusion can be drawn from the fact of reasonable pluralism, he does not recognize the burdens of judgment. This implies that he is unreasonable according to his own definition. Although attaching much importance to inclusion of all reasonable citizens, Rawls's approach leads to exclusion from deliberation on justice of all people who think that justice is inextricably bound up with the good and who are incapable of bracketing what they regard as the good or the truth. By calling them 'unreasonable' Rawls can maintain that his justice as fairness includes all reasonable people. Apart from the circularity of this reasoning, it means that renowned, honest and respectful theorists and many people with an idealistic comprehensive belief are stigmatized as unreasonable, because they regard justice as related to the good or the truth. These persons recognize the significance of accepting standards of public reason, reciprocity, inclusion, mutual respect and reasonable acceptability but only if these terms receive a different content and are understood in a wider (and more inclusive) sense, leaving room for reasonable comprehensive beliefs to play a part in public deliberations on justice instead of, as George and Wolfe argue, 'largely removing moral, philosophical and religious issues from the most important public discourse.'[45] In a similar way Seyla Benhabib argues that Rawls's public reason is conceived 'not as a process of reasoning among citizens but as a regulative principle *imposing* limits upon how individuals, institutions, and agencies *ought to* reason about public matters'.[46] Michael Sandel too disagrees with Rawls's restrictive version of public reason:

> according to the ideal of public reason advanced by political liberalism, citizens may not legitimately discuss fundamental political and constitutional questions with reference to their moral and religious ideals. But this is an unduly severe restriction that would impoverish political discourse and rule out important dimensions of public deliberation.[47]

And:

> political liberalism . . . leaves little room for the kind of public deliberation necessary to test the plausibility of contending comprehensive moralities – to persuade others of the merits of our moral ideals, to be persuaded by others of the merits theirs.[48]

Implications of Incommensurability for John Rawls's Theory of Justice 119

Concluding his 'Response to Rawls' Political Liberalism' Sandel argues:

> If liberal public reason is too restrictive, it remains to ask whether a more spacious public reason would sacrifice the ideals that political liberalism seeks to promote, notably mutual respect among citizens who hold conflicting moral and religious views. Here it is necessary to distinguish two conceptions of mutual respect. On the liberal conception, we respect our fellow citizen's moral and religious convictions by ignoring them (for political-purposes), by leaving them undisturbed, by carrying on political debate without reference to them. To admit moral and religious ideals into political debate about justice would undermine mutual respect in this sense. But this is not the only, or perhaps even the most plausible, way of understanding the mutual respect on which democratic citizenship depends. On a different conception of respect – call it the deliberative conception – we respect our fellow citizen's moral and religious convictions by engaging, or attending to, them – sometimes by challenging and contesting them, sometimes by listening and learning from them – especially when those convictions bear on important political questions. There is no guarantee that a deliberative mode of respect will lead in any given case to agreement with, or even appreciation of, the moral and religious convictions of others. It is always possible that learning more about a moral or religious doctrine will lead us to like it less. But the respect of deliberation and engagement affords a more spacious public reason than liberalism allows. It is also a more suitable ideal for a pluralist society. To the extent that our moral and religious disagreements reflect the ultimate plurality of human goods, a deliberative mode of respect will better enable us to appreciate the distinctive goods our different lives express.[49]

In sum, in the light of Rawls's idea of reasonable disagreement it is not easy to understand why people who draw other political inferences from the fact of reasonable pluralism and give a different content to public reason are called 'unreasonable', while reasonable disagreement on the inferences to be drawn is not surprising given the burdens of judgment with respect to these complicated issues.

VEIL OF IGNORANCE, PUBLIC REASON AND INCOMPLETENESS

The veil of ignorance is a device to secure that in the choice of principles of justice no one is advantaged or disadvantaged by morally irrelevant matters. Examples of morally irrelevant matters, which must be prevented from playing a part in principles of justice, are social class, race, gender, income and property group, personal characteristics like character and intelligence and so on. They concern contingencies causing undeserved and therefore unjust inequalities if they significantly influence the outcome of the distribution of advantages. However, behind the veil we are ignorant not only of these morally irrelevant matters but also of our comprehensive beliefs, including our conceptions of the good. Although Rawls mentions them simultaneously with morally irrelevant factors like fortuitous advantages or disadvantages, not relevant for the choice of principles, they concern fundamentally different issues. Comprehensive beliefs and conceptions of the good may be relevant for matters of basic justice to the extent that they constitute basic interests.

A veil of ignorance behind which conceptions of the good are unknown may be too thick to be able to see which principles and which rankings of these principles protect all one's fundamental interests most appropriately. Without knowing all these fundamental interests, reason may be indeterminate due to a lack of sufficient data relevant for an adequate and complete assignment of weights. If we do not know our conception of the good or comprehensive belief, how can we judge which conception of justice is the best one, assuming that justice has to do not only with fair cooperation, reciprocity and mutual advantage but also with protection of other basic interests? Basic interests and harm to these interests are difficult to detach from (what is regarded as) the basic good. Different conceptions of the good are not only sources of reasonable disagreement on conceptions of justice (being one of Rawls's reasons to keep conceptions of the good out of deliberations on basic principles of justice) but also sources of the weights to be assigned to the relevant values and principles of justice. A conception of the good is a 'compass', without which we cannot find our way. People with different 'compasses' (conceptions of the good) follow different routes. Depriving them of their 'compasses' does not have the consequence that they follow the same route but that they lose their way. If we remove conceptions of the good from deliberation on rules of justice, we remove not only sources of disagreement but also sources of weight assignment. Reasons have usually no determinate weight from their own but receive their weight in a belief or conception of the good. That is why public reason, which supposes the 'bracketing' of one's comprehensive belief and conceptions of the good, will easily remain indeterminate in selecting and ranking principles. Behind the veil of ignorance and adhering to a narrow version of public reason, the relevant primary goods and values of justice must receive their weight from another source than conceptions of the good or comprehensive beliefs. This source is supposed to be a political aim shared by all rational and reasonable people. This aim is fair cooperation, reciprocity and mutual advantage. There are two problems here. First, even within this common political interest, there may be reasonable disagreement about the way it is optimally promoted. Some rankings of political values may be better than others, but it is not to be expected that there is a single right one. Rawls admits this and argues that there are several reasonable political conceptions of justice.[50] This will result in reasonable disagreement about the right arrangements and about the ranking of political values. But this is difficult to reconcile with Rawls's hope and expectation that reasonable people behind the veil of ignorance will achieve an overlapping consensus. As we have mentioned previously, Rawls states in one of his 'burdens of judgment',

> [t]o some extent . . . the way we . . . weigh moral and political values is shaped by our total experience, our whole course of life up to now; and our total experiences must always differ.

Second, people have not only common but also different vital interests. Cooperation and reciprocity are important political values supporting common basic interests but there is no reason to think that they will always trump other values related to basic interests originating from peoples' conception of the good. As Michael Sandel argues,

> Even granting the importance of securing social cooperation on the basis of mutual respect, what is to ensure that this interest is always so important as to outweigh any competing interest that could arise from within a comprehensive moral or religious view?[51]

And:

> to assess restrictive rules of public reason, we need to weigh their moral and political cost against the political values they are said to make possible; we must also ask whether these political values – of toleration, civility, and mutual respect – could be achieved under less restrictive rules of public reason. Although political liberalism refuses to weigh the political values it affirms against competing values that may arise from within comprehensive moralities, the case for restrictive rules of public reason must presuppose some such comparison.[52]

The tension between the relevant values becomes particularly visible in some fundamental moral questions such as abortion, euthanasia, human cloning, same-sex marriage, environmental questions and capital punishment which cannot be disregarded in issues of basic justice. Let us take as an example the controversy on abortion. It may be described in terms of two conflicting values, namely, the woman's autonomous choice and the worth of protection of, and respect for, unborn human life. According to Rawls we have to consider the question in terms of political values such as the due respect for (unborn) human life and the equality of women as equal citizens. We have to balance these values according to the rules of public reason, without falling back on comprehensive beliefs. But is that possible? Taking for granted that we agree on relevant considerations and values, the weights we assign to them depend on our aims and beliefs, because values and reasons have often, and certainly in the issue under consideration, no determinate relative weight from their own. How do we determine what has to have more weight: the autonomy of the woman or worth of protection of unborn human life if we have no background knowledge from which we can interpret and rank these values? Suppose I believe on philosophical, moral and religious grounds that an embryo is a human being and must be respected as human being from the conception onwards, how could I make a balance of the political values autonomy and inviolability detached from this belief? With respect to this issue Rawls's view seems to lack subtlety with respect to people who deny a right to abortion, where he calls them 'unreasonable', 'cruel' and 'oppressive':

> Any comprehensive doctrine that leads to a balance of political values excluding that duly qualified right [to abortion] in the first trimester is to that extent unreasonable; and depending on details of its formulation, it may also be cruel and oppressive; for example, if it denied the right altogether except in the case of rape and incest. Thus assuming that this question is either a constitutional essential or a matter of basic justice, we would go against the ideal of public reason if we voted from a comprehensive doctrine that denied this right.[53]

Without a comprehensive background belief the options may easily become indeterminate in the strong sense: we lack a frame of reference and a standard of comparison originating from this belief. Both Rawls's original position and his public reason seem inappropriate in the double sense that we are incapable of detaching ourselves from our beliefs and that, *if* we would be able to do so, we would often be unable to come to any determinate judgment. There are more than enough reasons, but they lack the required determinate weights so that these reasons under-determine the choice. The same reasons may result in opposite conclusions dependent on the specific weights assigned to them.

PUBLICLY ACCESSIBLE REASONS

The meaning of 'publicly accessible reasons' is ambiguous. We have, I think, to make a distinction between, on the one side, publicly accessible *values,* and, on the other side, *reasons* attaching specific weights to these values. While many values as such are publicly accessible, the weights assigned to these values are usually comprehensive-belief-based. If a religious believer assigns absolute weight to 'worth of protection' of nascent human life and thinks that abortion has to be prohibited, is his judgment and choice based on a 'publicly accessible reason'? I think that the answer is 'yes' and 'no'.

'Yes', because the reason for the choice is based on a publicly accessible value – 'worth of protection of' unborn human life'. 'No', because the reason for the specific weight (in this case 'absolute weight') of this value is comprehensive-belief-based. The same applies to a liberal believer who assigns absolute weight to the autonomy of the woman, believes that a foetus has little intrinsic value and thinks that abortion has to be legalized. His reason for the choice is based on a publicly accessible value – 'autonomy of the woman'. But the reason for the specific weights (much weight to autonomy and little weight to worth of protection) is comprehensive-belief-based. The reason for choosing one alternative instead of the other seems therefore largely dependent on one's comprehensive belief or conception of the good. Although the relevant reason is based on a publicly accessible value, it is not accompanied by a parallel public reason supporting the same conclusion. Indeed, public reason remains silent about the particular choice. So public reason as such (detached from a conception of the good that supplies the weights) does not guide the choice and 'offers no direction'. The rationally acceptable weights of the relevant conflicting values may range from very small to very large. For instance, the relative weight of 'worth of protection of nascent human life' versus 'autonomy and equality of the woman' may range from very small to very large. Elizabeth Anderson's judgment that 'a ban on abortion would relegate women to an inferior caste status, incompatible with the equality necessary for a democracy',[54] resulting in assigning an overriding weight to the value of autonomy, reveals that her 'moral background belief' is different from, for instance, John Finnis's, who thinks that abortion is murder and assigns an overriding weight to the value of 'worth of protection' of unborn human life.[55] So while the relevant values are publicly accessible, the weights assigned to them and the reasons to legalize or prohibit abortion seem inextricably bound up with comprehensive beliefs, philosophical and moral doctrines and conscious or unconscious conceptions of the good. Rawls and Anderson may maintain that from the perspective of public reason only one side in the abortion controversy is reasonable. In the light of the previous arguments it is questionable whether this is justified. Even Stephen Macedo, a proponent of the Rawlsian public reason, argues for 'a recognition of the reasonableness of both sides of the abortion issue' and to regard it as an instance of reasonable instead of unreasonable disagreement.[56]

Summarizing, we cannot decide between publicly accessible values if they have no determinate weight. Values have usually no determinate weight from their own, detached from a frame of reference or conception of the good. Because a sufficiently common frame of reference is often lacking, we must often rely on personal perspectives in assigning weights. If, except for the 'proviso', we are not allowed to use reasons for weight assignment that originate from our comprehensive beliefs and conceptions of the good, it is not clear where we must find sufficiently determinate reasons.

THE LIBERAL PRINCIPLE OF LEGITIMACY

We ended the previous section with the conclusion that it is difficult or impossible to assign determinate weights to relevant values without falling back on an adequate frame of reference, often being a comprehensive belief. This is one side of the picture. The other side concerns legitimacy and public justification. An important principle, which John Rawls calls the liberal principle of legitimacy,[57] and which is adhered to by many other liberal theorists (among others, Brian Barry,[58] Thomas Nagel[59] and T. M. Scanlon[60]), is that public justification of coercive rules of justice cannot be based on claims that cannot be endorsed by all reasonable people. Scanlon says:

> thinking about right and wrong is, at the most basic level, thinking about what could be justified to others on grounds that they, if appropriately motivated, could not reasonably reject.[61]

Something similar is defended by Jürgen Habermas with his 'Principle (U)' or 'moral principle':[62]

> A norm is valid *if and only if* the foreseeable consequences and side effects of its general observance for the interests and value-orientation of *each individual* could be freely and *jointly* accepted by *all* affected.

So, on the one side, falling back on private reasons is often unavoidable to arrive at determinate choices of principles of justice and their ranking. On the other side, premising that the liberal principle of legitimacy is valid, falling back on private reasons not shared by others cannot lead to publicly justifiable coercive principles of justice. This tension is further enforced because of its association with two important but often conflicting liberties:

(1) The liberty from interference by coercive rules that cannot reasonably be endorsed because they are based on reasons related to some comprehensive beliefs and not to others. Call this liberty N. This liberty is protected and promoted by the liberal principle of legitimacy.
(2) The liberty to live a life in which private and public are interwoven, in which integrated comprehensive and political ends are pursued and in which the weights assigned to relevant values are determined by one's comprehensive belief. Call this liberty P.

While liberty N entails a wider private domain, liberty P entails a wider public domain. Liberty N and liberty P have similarities with Isaiah Berlin's negative and positive liberty described in his famous inaugural lecture 'Two

Concepts of Liberty'[63] and with Benjamin Constant's 'liberties of the moderns' and 'liberties of the ancients'.[64] Constant's distinction is related to two different democratic traditions: (1) the liberal tradition associated with Locke, in which negative liberty and private autonomy, protected by constitutional liberties and rights, play a central part; and (2) the republican tradition associated with Rousseau, which has its roots in the democracy of the old Athens and in which the public autonomy, the sovereignty of the people, is regarded as the highest form of liberty, allowing citizens to participate in the collective self-government of the nation and to pursue the common good of the society.

The following sections are devoted to the question whether liberty N and liberty P are compatible, that is, whether they are simultaneously and optimally realizable in one and the same society. This question will be answered in the negative. As Rawls argues, justice as fairness tries to adjudicate between the contending traditions to which these liberties are related.[65] I shall argue that an impartial adjudication based on a rational comparison is problematic due to incommensurability of liberty N and liberty P and of the two traditions to which these liberties are related, making them incompletely rationally comparable.

THE PUBLIC/PRIVATE SPLIT

As a consequence of the burdens of judgment different rational and reasonable people adhere to different conflicting comprehensive beliefs and disagree about which belief is right or superior. Because of the burdens of judgment 'it is not to be expected that conscientious persons with full powers of reason will arrive at the same conclusion'.[66] Therefore it is not to be expected that, within the foreseeable future (if ever), reasonable disagreement on matters of truth in justice, morality and 'conceptions of the good' will disappear. Disagreement does obviously not entail that a single right judgment does not exist or that one comprehensive belief may be right and another may be wrong or that one may be better or truer than another. But there is no agreed-upon or unambiguously and irrefutably demonstrable criterion to decide *which* comprehensive belief is the right or superior one. Therefore, Rawls argues, it is unreasonable to insist, in the public domain, on one's own belief and to impose this belief on other people who have other reasonable beliefs. In Rawls's own words:

> Since many doctrines are seen to be reasonable, those who insist, when fundamental political questions are at stake, on what they take as true but others do not, seem to others simply to insist on their own beliefs when they have the political power to do so. Of course, those who do insist on their beliefs also

insist that their beliefs alone are true: they impose their beliefs because, they say, their beliefs are true and not because they are their beliefs. But this is a claim that all equally could make; it is also a claim that cannot be made good by anyone to citizens generally. So when we make such claims others, who are themselves reasonable, must count us unreasonable. And indeed we are, as we want to use state power, the collective power of equal citizens, to prevent the rest from affirming their not unreasonable views. To conclude: reasonable people see that the burdens of judgment set limits on what can be reasonably justified to others.[67]

So, when making moral demands on others, personal justification is not sufficient; such demands require public justification. It is clear that *our* beliefs or (rankings of) values do not give reasons to others who do not accept those beliefs or (rankings of) values. Therefore a reasonable citizen refrains from appealing to his private convictions in public justifications if these do not provide other liberal citizens with reasons to accede to his demands. That is why personal justification has to be separated from public justification and why public coercive rules cannot be made dependent on private reasons, however personally justified. It is crucial to make a distinction between what can (personally) reasonably and justifiably be believed and what can reasonably be advanced as the justification of a society's basic institutions. So public justification of basic principles of justice cannot legitimately be based on private claims that are controversial between competing reasonable comprehensive beliefs (the liberal principle of legitimacy). It would be unreasonable, Rawls concludes, if this separation of public and private justification would be ignored.

The public/private split both supports an important liberty and restricts an important liberty. It protects the liberty from interference by coercive rules of the government that cannot publicly be justified (liberty *N*). By contrast, it restricts the liberty to live a life in which private and public are interwoven and in which integrated comprehensive and political ends are pursued (liberty *P*). The important question is whether it is better to accept or to reject this public/private split. To prevent misunderstandings I want to emphasize that the 'public/private split' in the sense in which it is used here is clearly distinct from the separation between religious and political authority ('separation of Church and State'). I premise that all parties – also the parties who do not accept the public/private split – accept the separation between religious and political authority which implies freedom of religion and conscience and excludes the possibility to impose one's religion, theology or secular comprehensive belief on others. The question whether it is better to accept or to reject the public/private split would be answerable in terms of the early Rawls of *A Theory of Justice* if we could decide whether it increases or decreases the (equal) overall freedom of people and the total system of basic liberties. Let us investigate whether this question is indeed answerable in these terms.

'IDEALISTIC' AND 'NON-IDEALISTIC' COMPREHENSIVE BELIEFS

Before we answer this question let us consider the following example. Suppose Larry and Christopher adhere to rival comprehensive beliefs. As an atheist Larry does not regard human life as sacred or absolutely inviolable, and as a convicted believer in the importance of personal autonomy, he is also an active proponent of legalization of abortion and euthanasia. Further he is an advocate of capital punishment and has no objections to genetic engineering for purposes of human enhancement. Christopher is a Christian. On religious and philosophical grounds he believes in the integrity and inviolability of human life starting from the conception. He believes that abortion entails killing an unborn person and that euthanasia, capital punishment and genetic manipulation for human enhancement (and not exclusively for preventing or treating diseases) are morally wrong. He experiences a moral duty to devote himself to trying to prevent these wrongs by legislation.

Neither Larry nor Christopher is a fanatic or fundamentalist. Both endorse liberal democratic principles. Although Christopher is a religious believer, he rejects a confessional state, endorses the separation between Church and State and fully recognizes freedom of thought, conscience and religion. Contrary to Larry and Christopher, Bertrand has no comprehensive belief with religious or secular idealistic social aims and he has no political aspirations. The only thing he wants is to be left alone and not to be hindered by other people's beliefs. Let us call Larry's and Christopher's non-religious respectively religious beliefs 'idealistic' comprehensive beliefs because these beliefs imply an orientation on a supposedly ideal society. Bertrand's belief will be called a non-idealistic comprehensive belief.

Returning to our question whether the public/private split increases or decreases the equal overall freedom of people, this depends not only on the extent to which the respective liberties decrease or increase but also on the weights assigned to them and on the extent to which both liberties influence a person's total freedom. These weights cannot be detached from beliefs, aims, interests, insights and predilections. Bertrand, who has no political aspirations or idealistic social aims, and who only wants to be left alone, will assign less weight to liberty P and more weight to liberty L. For him restriction of liberty P increases his overall freedom. But for Larry who has a non-religious idealistic belief and Christopher who has a religious idealistic belief with implications for the way they think the society has to be organized, the restriction of liberty P in favour of liberty L means a significant decrease of liberty P, possibly resulting in an overall decrease of their freedom. Besides, the public/private split may violate their integrity as a person and may decrease their freedom to live according to their conceptions of the good, strong commitments and what they regard as the truth. So the public/private split (implying the restriction of liberty *P* in favour of liberty *N*) means an increase in overall freedom for people like Bertrand, but may mean a decrease in overall freedom for people like Larry and Christopher.

REASONABLENESS

Rawls would say that 'idealistic comprehensive believers' are personally justified to hold on to their belief. For instance, Christopher is allowed to hold on to his Christian belief, including his belief that abortion and euthanasia are morally wrong. But, Rawls argues, these beliefs are not allowed to play a role in justifying basic public coercive rules like prohibition of abortion because these rules are not reasonably acceptable for and may therefore reasonably be rejected by people who hold on to rival reasonable beliefs. Rawls's support for the public/private split is based on what he understands by 'reasonableness'. The issue is complicated because the notion of 'reasonableness' is complex and ambiguous. Discussions on the correct interpretation of reasonableness easily lead to circular reasoning. Besides, Rawls applies the notion in more than one way, which makes the question still more complicated:

SENSES IN WHICH RAWLS USES THE NOTION 'REASONABLENESS'

(a) Reasonableness in general[68]

- Having the willingness to try to govern one's conduct by a principle from which one and others can reason in common
- Taking into account the consequences of one's actions on other's well-being
- Having the disposition to act morally and not merely egoistically
- Not repressing comprehensive views that are not unreasonable though different from one's own
- Endorsing liberty of conscience and freedom of thought
- Not rejecting the essentials of a democratic regime
- Recognizing the importance of social unity and cooperation and having interest in taking part in fair terms of cooperation
- Having a capacity of a sense for justice and for a conception of the good
- Recognizing equal basic rights and liberties, fair equality of opportunity as social bases for self-respect

(b) Reasonable comprehensive beliefs[69]

Beliefs with the following three features:

- They are exercises in *theoretical* reason covering the major religious, philosophical and moral aspects of human life in a coherent and consistent way, in which a particular primacy and weight are assigned to certain values.
- They are exercises in *practical* reason singling out which values to count as especially significant and how to balance them when they conflict.
- They normally belong to, or draw upon, a tradition of thought and doctrine.

(c) Reasonable disagreement[70]

Disagreement between people about the right comprehensive belief or conception of the good due to the *burdens of judgment* (see above).

(d) Reasonable persons[71]

Persons who

(1) recognize the 'fact of reasonable pluralism' and *burdens of judgment* and 'see that these set limits on what can be reasonably justified to others' and
(2) 'think it unreasonable to use political power, should they possess it, to repress comprehensive views that are not unreasonable, though different from their own';
(3) 'are ready to propose, or to acknowledge when proposed by others, the principles needed to specify what can be seen by all as fair terms of cooperation. Reasonable persons ... understand that they are to honor these principles, even at the expense of their own interests as circumstance may require, provided others likewise may be expected to honor them'.[72]

Let us consider whether Larry and Christopher are reasonable in Rawls's senses. First, they endorse the general characteristics of reasonableness mentioned under (*a*):

- They do not repress comprehensive views that are not unreasonable, though different from their own.
- They endorse liberty of conscience and freedom of thought.
- They do not reject the essentials of a democratic regime.
- They recognize equal basic rights and liberties, fair equality of opportunity as social bases for self-respect.

Second, their belief answers to the three features of reasonable comprehensive beliefs mentioned under (*b*). Rawls says, 'Political liberalism counts many familiar and traditional doctrines – religious, philosophical, and moral – as reasonable even though we could not seriously entertain them for ourselves.' Larry's and Christopher's belief belong to these 'familiar and traditional doctrines counted as reasonable'. They also recognize 'reasonable disagreement' about the right comprehensive belief or conception of the good (*c*). That is why they also recognize the fact of reasonable pluralism and burdens of judgment (*d1*) and do not want to repress comprehensive views that are not unreasonable, though different from their own (*d2*). From the burdens of judgment and the fact of reasonable pluralism Larry and Christopher do not, however, draw the same conclusion as Rawls. Rawls's specific conception of a reasonable person is based on the argument that, on pain of unreasonableness, one ought to draw the same conclusion (namely, that the doctrine of constraint should be accepted). However, the relation between a factual 'is' (the fact of reasonable pluralism) and a moral 'ought' (the doctrine of constraint), between description and prescription, is notoriously dubious. The possible inferences to be drawn from the fact of reasonable pluralism and the burdens of judgment in terms of public demands are far from univocal. This is reflected by the strong disagreements between intelligent and conscientious people about this issue.

Because Larry and Christopher do not draw the same conclusion as Rawls, Rawls regards them as 'unreasonable' in the specific sense mentioned in (*d*). But, as we discussed already in a previous section, the burdens of judgment themselves with respect to the consequences to be drawn from the burdens of judgment and from the fact of reasonable pluralism render it plausible that the disagreement about this question is an instance of reasonable instead of unreasonable disagreement (*c*). As Rawls argues, because of the burdens of judgment, 'it is not to be expected that conscientious persons with full powers of reason will arrive at the same conclusion.' It is implausible that there are no burdens of judgment with respect to such a complicated question as which conclusion must be drawn from the fact of reasonable pluralism. As Rawls himself emphasizes, a 'basic aspect of the reasonable' is 'the willingness to recognize burdens of judgment'.[73] If Rawls states that only one reasonable conclusion can be drawn from the fact of reasonable pluralism, he does not recognize these burdens of judgment and is unreasonable according to his own definition. This incoherence is strengthened by the fact that Rawls regards Larry's and Christopher's comprehensive belief as reasonable while he regards Larry and Christopher themselves, trying to live according to the implications of this reasonable belief, as unreasonable. Christopher is reasonable in his believing that abortion, euthanasia and capital punishment are morally wrong, but unreasonable in his trying to prevent these wrongs (by trying to influence constitutional matters and matters of basic justice through democratic deliberations and procedures). Rawls could reply as follows:

> Christopher has no good reasons for objections because he is free to believe that abortion is killing unborn human beings and that euthanasia and capital punishment are morally wrong. Besides he is free to live according to his belief: because he himself need not exercise the right of euthanasia, abortion, et cetera, in his own case.

But this reply would not do justice to the whole problem. Christopher is only partly free to live according to his belief. He is free to refrain from what he considers as morally wrong but he is not allowed to act upon his commitment and obligation to devote himself to pursuing a society in which the relevant 'wrongs' are prevented. He must set aside some of his deepest convictions that do not belong to an unreasonable belief. To avoid the stigma of being unreasonable he must, when entering the political arena, ignore the truth in which he believes, his conception of the good and his conscience. It is indeed questionable whether this stigma would be justified. Steven Mulhall and Adam Swift give the following comment: 'It is hard not to suspect that, for many, living in accordance with [Rawls's] conception of politics will involve a greater or lesser degree of what might be called schizophrenia, a bracketing off or suspension of their vision of the good.'[74] Indeed, can it reasonably be expected that anyone who takes his convictions and commitments seriously to acquiesce in its being treated as a private matter? The convinced believer does not usually deny the desirability of cooperation and reciprocity and avoidance of conflict, but may be unable to agree to political principles that oblige him to ignore his deepest convictions. Bhikhu Parekh says:

> Secular citizens are able to lead whole and integrated lives whereas religious citizens, who are required to bracket out their deepest beliefs, are subjected to moral incoherence and self-alienation. . . . Allowing them to be guided by their religious beliefs but banning them from using these to defend their views in public does not improve the situation. It introduces self-alienation at a different level by requiring them to speak in a language different to the one in which they think. . . . Religious people generally seek wholeness in their lives and do not think it possible or desirable to separate their private and political concerns.[75]

Christopher Eberle says:

> To stigmatize the theist for refusing to violate his deepest convictions is an instance of unreasonableness. If it is unreasonable and unjustified to impose rules on others, then imposing the doctrine of restraint on religious citizens – requiring of them an extremely burdensome willingness to violate their most fundamental

commitments – is itself unreasonable and unjustified and a violation of the norm of respect and might very well constitute the kind of browbeating associated in some of the literature with those who refuse to exercise restraint.[76]

The stigma of 'unreasonableness', mistakenly suggesting that it is unwillingness instead of inability to give priority to the doctrine of restraint over moral and other strong commitments originating from what Rawls regards as a reasonable comprehensive belief, is difficult to reconcile, not only with freedom of conscience (which Rawls regards as a basic liberty) but also with what he regards as the most important primary good: (the social bases of) self-respect.[77] While Rawls argues that 'it seems evident that parties must choose principles that secure the integrity of their religious and moral freedom',[78] he characterizes the rejection of the doctrine of restraint as unreasonable even where this doctrine violates the integrity of one's religious and moral freedom. If freedom of conscience (and to live according to one's conscience) is a basic liberty, and if a coercive rule forces the religious believer to give absolute priority to something else, this violates a basic liberty. If so, then, the religious believer may reasonably reject the doctrine of restraint – at least *from this perspective* (I emphasize this because, as we shall see next, from a different perspective it is unreasonable to reject the doctrine of constraint). The following 'dialogue', borrowed from Patrick Neal, illustrates the issue better than whatever theoretical analysis does.

Dialogue on the 'Original Position'[79]

Consider specifically the case of the citizen of faith (A) who, we imagine, participates in the following dialogue with the keeper of the keys (B) to the Original Position.

> *A:* So this is the place where we reason together and determine how to live by principles of justice? I'm all for that, and happy to be here.
>
> *B:* Good. You know you'll have to leave your knowledge of matters irrelevant from the point of view of justice behind before you enter in here.
>
> *A:* By all means, by all means! You know, we have a story that this place reminds me of a little bit. It's about the last being made first, and the lion lying down with the lamb. . . .
>
> *B:* Yeah, yeah, well, there are no stories in here. Stories are particular. That's your story, not everybody's. You'll have to leave it behind to come in.
>
> *A:* Well, I suppose, if you say so. Though my particular story is about universal things, you know.
>
> *B:* It's a rule. But hey, it applies to everyone equally, so don't feel put out.
>
> *A:* I see your point. Fair enough. So what shall I leave behind here?

B: Here, put it in this sack and you can pick it up on your way out. Race, gender, occupation, wealth. . . .

A: Yes, yes, if you could just help me a bit with this, it's a bit difficult to remove. But really, this is splendid. It must be like one big family in there.

B: Family? What family do you mean? There's lots of different kinds of families.

A: Yes, I'm sure there are. Well, never mind. Is that everything? I'm feeling rather thin, you know.

B: Almost everything. Put your conception of the good on top of the pile there.

A: I don't believe I have one, though I'm not sure. I never heard of a 'conception of the good' before.

B: Look, don't hold out on me, friend; everybody's got one. We get a lot of folks trying to sneak through with their conception of the good. It says here on my register you're a Christian. Is that right?

A: I try to be.

B: Well, whatever. Look, you have to leave your Christianity here, too. That's your conception of the good.

A: But then how will I be able to talk about justice when I get in there?

B: Don't worry about it. You'll do fine. There are plenty of Christians walking around who talk about justice all the time without bringing religion into it.

A: Well, perhaps, but I'm afraid I'm not one of them. But isn't this the place where we're going to determine the most fundamental rules of political order?

B: Right. You go in and make up the rules. Then you come out and we give you your personal stuff back, at least all that's admissible within the rules.

A: You mean I don't necessarily get it all back?

B: Hey, look, what do you want, special treatment? You believe in justice, don't you?

A: Absolutely.

B: Well, do you think people ought to be allowed to do things that violate justice?

A: No, not at all.

B: Well there you go. Take your conception of the good, for example. If it's within the rules of justice, then they stamp it with a big machine that says 'REASONABLE,' and you get it back. If not, it gets stamped

'UNREASONABLE,' and you have to talk with some counselors about some of the problems you might face when you leave.

A: Let me make sure I have this right. You want me to take off my Christianity, and then make up some rules, and then see whether my Christianity fits the rules or not before I put it back on? And if it doesn't fit the rules, I'm not supposed to put it back on?

B: Yeah, that's about it. Hey, look, what do you want? Everybody does the same. The boss says when we get Christians who don't like the idea, we should give them this book to read, to help them see things more clearly. Here, take a copy. [Hands him Kant's *Religion within the Limits of Reason Alone*]

A: [Taking the book] Oh, I'm afraid I prefer Kierkegaard. I just can't do it. I don't even know if I could get this Christianity off of me even if I wanted to.

B: Sure you could. Jeez, you sound like some of those feminists over there, who say they can't remove their gender.

A: Well, it doesn't matter. There's no way I'm taking it off.

B: Yeah? Well, I guess I had you figured wrong. I didn't take you for a guy who won't play by the rules unless he's sure he's going to win. You can line up over there, beside the rich folks hanging on to their money. You know what? They all have big, fine conceptions of the good, too, which they claim shows how they deserve what they have. Anyway, just go on over there. If you can't live on the basis of equality and respect for people different from you, you can't come in here.

A: I think there must be some misunderstanding. I believe in the equality of all people, and I certainly think we ought to try to respect people who are different from us.

B: Well, apparently you don't believe in it as much as you claim. If you did, you'd take off your religion. After all, what are you so worried about? If your religion is all you take it to be, you won't have any problems. Seems to me the fact you're afraid to take it off shows that you know it might not pass muster. Otherwise, you wouldn't be afraid.

A: I don't think you understand. I'm not afraid of anything, and I don't want anything for myself. But Christianity is *why* I believe in these things, and it is *how* I know about justice. When I saw your flyer about 'people who want to live together in freedom and equality,' I thought, boy, this is the place for a guy like me. Now I'm not so sure.

And one more thing. It's not 'my' conception of the good, or 'my' religion. It's not a personal possession of mine. I wish you'd quit referring to it like that.

B: [Sighing] Just a minute. [Shouting off to the side]: Hey, boss, we got another one of them fanatics here.

REASONABLE BELIEF AND UNREASONABLE BELIEVER

Rawls tries to avoid the discrepancy between the reasonableness of belief and the reasonableness of the believer by making the reasonableness of the former dependent on the reasonableness of the latter in the sense described under (*d*) in the previous list of senses of reasonableness.[80] But this means that the same objections raised against Rawls's exclusive definition of a reasonable person may be raised against his narrowed explanation of reasonable comprehensive beliefs. Rawls has two ways to escape incoherence. The first is denying the reasonableness of being convinced of the truth of one's belief. But his 'epistemic abstinence' prevents this escape. Rawls emphatically states:

> Political liberalism does not question that many political and moral judgments of certain specified kinds are correct and it views many of them as reasonable. Nor does it question the possible truth of affirmations of faith. Above all, it does not argue that we should be hesitant and uncertain, much less sceptical, about our own beliefs.[81]

The second possible way out is denying the reasonableness of comprehensive beliefs that involve public commitments naturally stemming from these beliefs. But this would mean that Rawls has to deny the reasonableness of many religious and non-religious comprehensive beliefs from which these public commitments naturally result. By contrast, he says (as we have just quoted):

> Political liberalism counts many familiar and traditional doctrines – religious, philosophical, and moral – as reasonable even though we could not seriously entertain them for ourselves.[82]

The reader may get the impression that I take sides with religious and secular idealistic believers who will reject the public/private split, against liberals who will endorse it. But this is not true. There are good reasons for the public/private split. But, as shown previously, there are also good reasons to reject it. I only want to emphasize the difficulty that Rawls himself describes as follows:

> How can it be either reasonable or rational, when basic matters are at stake, for citizens to appeal only to a public conception of justice and not to the whole truth as they see it? Surely the most fundamental questions should be settled by appealing to the most important truths, yet these may far transcend public reason.[83]

Rawls tries to resolve this 'paradox' by invoking his liberal principle of legitimacy.[84] In the next chapter I will try to show in more detail that this is doomed to fail. To avoid misunderstandings, I want to emphasize again that the public/private split under consideration concerns separation of public rules of basic justice from ideas about justice that are based on private comprehensive beliefs or conceptions of the good. This public/private split should be distinguished from the separation between religious and political authority – the separation of 'Church and State'. The recognition of the separation of 'Church and State' need not entail the recognition of the public/private split. The possible objections of the relevant religious believers to the public/private split do not concern this separation of 'Church and State': these believers do recognize and want to maintain this separation, which is an important characteristic of a liberal democratic society.

POSITIVE AND NEGATIVE LIBERTY

Liberty N and liberty P show similarities with Isaiah Berlin's negative and positive liberty. By positive liberty – sometimes called 'freedom *to*' – Berlin understands the freedom of self-mastery, of rational control of one's life, the freedom to participate in political activities and collective self-government and to be involved in making the laws under which one lives. By negative liberty – sometimes called 'freedom *from*' – he understands the freedom *from* interference by others. Berlin argues that people who attach more importance to negative liberty 'want to curb authority as such', while people who attach more importance to positive liberty want authority 'placed in their own hands'. According to Berlin negative and positive liberties are not only incompatible and conflicting but also incommensurable.[85] What does this mean?

INCOMMENSURABILITY AND INCOMPATIBILITY

Incommensurability and incompatibility are unrelated. Incompatible things may be commensurable, while incommensurable things may be compatible. For instance, the liberty to unrestrictedly interrupt each other in a debate is incompatible with the liberty from being hindered by interruptions, but both liberties may be commensurable with respect to efficiency of the debate. Conversely, liberty of conscience and liberty of movement are incommensurable but obviously not incompatible. Incommensurable values are no problem if they are compatible. Conversely, incompatible values are no problem if they are commensurable. A possible problem arises only if the relevant values are both incompatible (or incompletely compatible) and incommensurable. Indeed, if the values are not incompatible although they are incommensurable, there is no conflict. And if the values are not incommensurable although they are incompatible, their conflict is rationally resolvable: a rational comparison can be made and the better option can be chosen.

The possibility of incompatible or conflicting values is not self-evident. Originally Isaiah Berlin adhered to the 'Platonic ideal' that all questions about human values and about central problems of life have one true answer. According to Condorcet, quoted by Isaiah Berlin, all values must, in the end, be compatible, and perhaps even entail one another: 'Nature binds truth, happiness, and virtue together as by an indissoluble chain.' Condorcet spoke in similar terms of liberty, equality and justice. He thought that the task of social science is to show that ideals that are truly good are inseparable instead of incompatible. As in the sciences there could be no conflict between right answers. These answers must necessarily be compatible and form a single whole. Indeed, how could one truth be incompatible with another? In *The Pursuit of the Ideal* Isaiah Berlin tells about his conversion from his belief in the harmony of values to the belief in their possible incompatibility.[86] Reading Machiavelli Berlin's original faith was shaken. Machiavelli described two societies, the cultures of which were shaped by values which differed in 'some profound, irreconcilable ways': a society shaped by 'Christian virtues' of humility, self-denial and submission to the will of God and a society shaped by 'pagan virtues' of courage, excellence, self-assertion and power. The outlooks and ends of these societies differ profoundly and, Berlin says, their values – being not means to ends but ends in themselves – cannot be combined in any final synthesis. Berlin summarizes his view as follows: 'Not all good things are compatible, still less the ideals of mankind.'[87] John Rawls, referring to Berlin, expresses a similar view:

> The full range of values is too extensive to fit in any one social world and there is no social world without loss. It is a basic error to believe that values, if they are true, must be compatible. In the realm of values, as opposed to the world of fact, not all truths can fit into one social world.[88]

According to Berlin negative and positive liberty form an important instance of these incompatible values and ideals:

> [Negative and positive liberty] are not two different interpretations of a single concept, but two profoundly divergent and irreconcilable attitudes to the ends of life. . . . it is often necessary to strike a compromise between them. [E]ach of them makes absolute claims. These claims cannot both be fully satisfied. But it is a profound lack of social and moral understanding not to recognize that the satisfaction that each of them seeks is an ultimate value which, both historically and morally, has an equal right to be classed among the deepest interests of mankind.

INCOMPATIBLE AND INCOMMENSURABLE LIBERTIES

Isaiah Berlin's positive and negative liberty have the following four characteristics:

1) They are two different concepts or kinds of liberty instead of two interpretations of the same liberty.
2) Both belong to the 'deepest interests of mankind'.
3) They are incompatible: they cannot both be optimally realized or fully secured and protected in one and the same society, regime or system of justice. 'They cannot be combined in any final synthesis' and 'it is often necessary to strike a compromise between them'.
4) They are incommensurable: they 'cannot be drawn up on a single scale of magnitude'[89] so that it is not possible to determine which balance or combination of these liberties constitutes the largest overall liberty.

Liberty N – freedom from interference by coercive rules that cannot reasonably be endorsed – has affinity with Berlin's negative liberty. Liberty P – freedom to live a life in which private and public are interwoven and in which integrated comprehensive and political ends and self-government are pursued – shows similarities with positive liberty. It has a strong affinity with one of Rawls's basic liberties: the freedom of political participation, including the right to participate in government and 'to take part in, and to determine the outcome of, the constitutional process that establishes the laws with which they are to comply'. Rawls explains this basic liberty in terms of positive liberty.[90]

The four characteristics claimed by Berlin with respect to negative and positive liberty seem equally to apply to liberty N and liberty P: they are two different, important, incompatible and incommensurable kinds of liberty. They 'cannot both be optimally realized or fully secured and protected in one and the same regime or system of justice' so that 'it is necessary to strike a compromise between them'. Because they are incommensurable it cannot rationally and determinately be decided which 'balanced combination' is the best one. To put it differently, if we want to compare two different systems of justice of which one has more liberty N and another more liberty P, it cannot determinately be concluded which system is the better one because they are incompletely comparable, given the fact that all conditions of incomplete comparability – incommensurability, significant bidirectionality and significant symmetry – are satisfied. This explains the impossibility of a determinate, impartial or objective judgment in terms of the relative worth of different systems in the sense of the greatest overall liberty or most extensive combination of liberties represented by the relevant systems. One system is better in one respect, while another is better in another respect, but there seems to be no objectively determinable system in which the relevant liberties are integrated in a way that is optimal for all rational and reasonable people. This is summarized by John Gray in his *Two Faces of Liberalism*:[91]

> Only if basic . . . liberties cannot make incompatible demands can justice be insulated from conflicts of value. If basic liberties clash, there is no way of avoiding judgments of importance among the human interests they protect. Manifestly, such judgments will vary with different conceptions of the good. The argument of which among a set of rival liberties is to be protected, and in what degree, is then inescapably an argument about the good. At that point, conflicts of value re-emerge at the core of political philosophy, and the Rawlsian enterprise faces ruin. Once it is allowed that important liberties may be rivals, we are not far from accepting that their conflicts have no solutions which are acceptable to all reasonable persons. In that case, different mixes of liberties may be right in different societies. Even in a single society, people may reasonably differ as to how the claims of rival freedoms, or rival components of the same freedom, are best reconciled. . . . As a result, liberal regimes can no longer be marked off from all others by protecting any particular combination of liberties. All regimes embody particular settlements among rival liberties. That is a result which illustrates the accuracy of Isaiah Berlin's observation, when he wrote: 'If the claims of two (or more than two) types of liberty prove incompatible and if this is an instance of the clash of values at once absolute and incommensurable, it is better to face this intellectually uncomfortable fact than to ignore it, or automatically attribute it to some deficiency on our part which could be eliminated by an increase in skill or knowledge; or, what is worse still, suppress one of the competing values altogether by pretending it is identical with its rival – and so end by distorting both.'

THEORY OF JUSTICE VERSUS POLITICAL LIBERALISM

In the first part of this chapter we have seen that Rawls's theory is *internally* indeterminate: taking for granted that Rawls's principles are right, these do not lead to complete rankings and determinate conclusions. In the present part we have seen that Rawls's theory is *externally* indeterminate as well: reason does not show that Rawls's principles are determinately superior. There are good reasons to accept, in the original position, Rawls's thick veil of ignorance and in line with this, to accept, in the public domain, the narrow scope Rawls gives to public reason. However, there are also good reasons to choose another approach of an original position in which the veil of ignorance is less thick, that is, in which the agent is ignorant of morally irrelevant matters but not ignorant of her conception of the good and comprehensive belief.

The earlier Rawls of *A Theory of Justice* is different from the later Rawls of *Political Liberalism*. Given the adaptations in *Political Liberalism* one may wonder whether the core of his original theory has not considerably been changed. Rawls's original aim was to achieve consensus on complete principles of justice. Remember the quotations referred to earlier, in which the earlier Rawls articulates conditions for rational, stable and viable principles of justice and for developing a 'complete' conception and theory of justice:

> a conception of right must impose an ordering on conflicting claims. This requirement springs directly from the role of its principles in adjusting competing demands. . . . It is clearly desirable that a conception of justice be complete, that is, able to order all the claims that can arise (or that are likely to in practice). And the ordering should in general be transitive: if, say, a first arrangement of the basic structure is ranked more just than a second, and the second more just than a third, then the first should be more just than the third.[92]

And:

> Institutions are just when . . . the rules determine a proper balance between competing claims . . . [I]f men balance final principles differently, as presumably they often do, then their conceptions of justice are different. The assignment of weights is an essential part of a conception of justice. If we cannot explain how these weights are to be determined by reasonable ethical criteria, the means of rational discussion have come to an end.[93]

And:

> The principles must be specified so that they yield a determinate conclusion.[94]

The later Rawls seems to have given up these aims and to have replaced them by the aim to achieve consensus on the content of public reason and on a *set* of *reasonable* principles rather than on one concrete system of determinate principles. This seems to mean that the later Rawls admits the external indeterminacy of his principles and the reasonable disagreement not only on comprehensive-belief-based principles of justice but also on political ones. While the earlier Rawls emphasized the importance of an overlapping consensus on complete, determinate and stable principles of justice, the later Rawls contents himself with a consensus on the content of public reason and a set of different possible reasonable principles.

This change in approach leads to two problems. First, we have seen that there *is* no consensus but, instead, reasonable disagreement, not only on specific principles of justice but also on the content of public reason. Second, how do we choose concrete principles given the fact of reasonable disagreement? Rawls's 'solution' is a final democratic decision if reasonable reasons continue to collide.[95] This leads to a choice of principles not endorsed by all reasonable people for the very reason that there is often severe (although reasonable) disagreement about the right principles of justice. In other words, the recognition that there is a set of reasonable principles does not lead to agreement on and endorsement of principles chosen from this set. Although the relevant principles belong to the set of reasonable principles, they may be regarded as being wrong, similarly to the fact that reasonable conceptions of the good may simultaneously be regarded as being mistaken.

A rule of justice being 'one reasonable candidate among others' has little authority because it can just as well, and legitimately, be replaced by other, even opposite, not less justifiable rules. The resulting instability and contingency of principles of justice further increase if the latter are based on democratic decisions: what is just today is unjust tomorrow due to the variability of majorities. Another objection against the dependence of rules of justice on democratic decisions is the susceptibility to incoherent and intransitive rankings as described in Arrow's theorem.[96] This problem is discussed in detail in chapter 8.

CONSENSUS?

In his *Political Liberalism* Rawls has given up his belief in the possibility to achieve consensus on specific principles of justice and admits that several principles are 'reasonable'. Reasonableness and rationality do not offer an agreed-upon solution precisely because there are many reasonable and rational solutions even within Rawls's 'public reason'. This will *a fortiori* apply to a wider public reason like the one discussed previously. As Anderson notes, '*Political Liberalism* extends the idea of "the fact of reasonable pluralism" entailing a kind of "fragmentation of reason" or existence of rival but reasonable views beyond the sphere of the good to the sphere of the right itself.'[97] This 'fragmentation of reason' within the sphere of the right is precisely the problem. The relevant reasonable principles of justice may have divergent and conflicting contents and may therefore cause reasonable disagreement instead of consensus. In that case the same reasonable disagreement preventing consensus on a conception of the good prevents consensus on principles of justice. The fact that the disagreement on reasonable conceptions of justice is reasonable does not alter the fact that there is (often fierce) conflict about the question which reasonable but conflicting principles of justice are to be chosen.

Summarizing, Rawls's recourse to 'consensus on the content of public reason' in combination with democratic decisions seems to fail in different respects: First, there is simply no consensus on the content of public reason. Second, even if consensus on the content of public reason could be achieved, this would not lead to consensus on principles of justice because public reason as such (both in Rawls's relatively narrow sense and *a fortiori* in a wider sense) is indeterminate. Third, democratic decisions cannot take away this predicament because they do not lead to stable and consistent principles of justice and do not turn reasonable disagreement into consensus.

CONCLUSIONS

The conditions of complete and stable principles of justice as formulated by the earlier Rawls in his *A Theory of Justice* are not satisfied in the later Rawls's *Political Liberalism*. We have seen that reasonableness and rationality do not offer the required single agreed-upon solution because there are many reasonable and rational but conflicting solutions. Reasonable and rational people assign different weights to competing claims, and they balance final principles differently. Reason under-determines the choice between rival claims because these claims and the values on which they are based are incompletely comparable. As we have discussed, the assignment of weights in case of incommensurability is an intuitive procedure, strongly influenced by one's conception of the good and easily resulting in conflicting conclusions. The rival weightings do not entail that one ranking must be right or the best and the others must be wrong or less good.

Terms like 'equal advantage', 'least advantage', 'equal liberty' and 'greatest liberty' play a central role in egalitarian and Rawlsian theories of justice. They can be usefully applied only if the relevant amounts of advantage and liberty can, at least roughly, be measured and compared. The problem is that multidimensional aspects, instead of a one-dimensional standard, play a role in determining 'overall equality', 'greatest liberty' and 'worst-off position'. We have seen that this easily leads to ambiguous and conflicting conclusions if, apart from the first condition for incomplete comparability (the 'diversity' condition: a plurality of relevant multidimensional values), the other three conditions for incomplete comparability ('bidirectionality', 'incommensurability' and 'significance') are satisfied as well. The presence of two or more significant, incommensurable and bidirectionally divided values confronts us with the problem of incomplete comparability and a possibly wide range of indeterminateness implying indeterminate equivalence relations and the absence of even rough comparability. Incommensurability is not merely one of the conditions of incomplete comparability but the central one because it means that there is no *overall measurable* and therefore no determinate and objective equivalence relation between the relevant conflicting values. In this light we may explain Socrates's question referred to in the beginning of this chapter:

if we disagree about the larger and smaller, wouldn't we turn to *measurement* and quickly stop our disagreement? . . . But when we differ about the just and unjust, the good and the bad . . . and prove unable to turn to any *sufficiently decisive criterion*, aren't these the things that lead to our becoming enemies to one another?[98]

As Martha Nussbaum formulates it,

[Socrates] claims to have enabled us to see our deep and pressing need for an ethical science of measurement'. He believes that 'we will be saved only by something that will assimilate deliberation to *weighing* and *measuring*; this in turn requires a *unit of measure*, some external end about which we can all agree, and which can render all alternatives *commensurable*.[99]

The same problem of incommensurability – the lack of a 'unit of measure' and a single scale – is emphasized by H. L. A. Hart, who writes:

When a choice has been made between . . . competing alternatives it may be defended as proper on the ground that it was for the public good or the common good. It is not clear what these phrases mean, since there seems to be no *scale* by which contributions of the various alternatives to the common good can be *measured* and the greater identified.[100]

Incommensurability appears to be the core problem for the 'scales of justice'. The 'scales' of the disparate aspects of justice have different incommensurable dimensions. Absence of an equivalence relation and 'unitary scale resistance'[101] interfere with a determinate assessment of the weights of conflicting claims by Justitia's scales. This leads to, what Amartya Sen calls, 'incomplete rankings of justice'.[102] Sen distinguishes 'tentative incompleteness' – which is based on *inconclusiveness* and awaits resolution – from 'assertive incompleteness' – which is based on *indeterminateness* and is impossible to resolve even in principle. The results of the investigation described in this book suggest that the relevant 'incomplete rankings of justice' are not based on inconclusiveness but on indeterminateness, which means that they are irresolvable in principle.

IS COMPLETE JUSTICE UNACHIEVABLE?

This chapter and the two previous ones focus on shortcomings, rather than virtues and achievements, of theories of justice. Still several theories represent important insights and ingenious constructions. A marvellous exemplar is Rawls's *A Theory of Justice* as we have seen in this chapter. The shortcomings and incompleteness of theories revealed in the light of incommensurability are not attributable to (the authors of) the theories but to their subject matter. As I have tried to show, multifaceted values and multidimensional aspects of justice constitute an incomplete coherence, not able to be captured in an objective and impartial harmonious synthesis and a complete theory of distributive justice. We have seen that one distribution or theory is better in one respect, while another is better in another respect, and some may be overall worse or better than some others. The systems and theories may be ranked, but this ranking is incomplete and there seems to be no single superior and objectively determinable perfect system and theory in which all aspects and values relevant for justice are integrated in an objectively optimal way. In this context it is revealing that Rawls calls his masterwork '*A*' *Theory of Justice*. It is indeed 'a' theory among many possible others. It belongs to a set of theories that can only be partially ordered. The justification of a choice between incompletely comparable theories or rules of justice is partial in the double sense of 'incomplete' and 'biased'. This does obviously not mean that we can never make unanimous and determinate comparative judgments of justice and assess whether some distributions of advantages are just, unjust, more or less just. Amartya Sen points out, for instance, that persistence of endemic hunger or exclusion from medical access are clearly unjustifiable and, although there exist indeterminate conflicts of liberties, some limitations of liberty are univocally unjust.[103] Assessments of unambiguous injustices and of minimal requirements of justice do not require complete rankings and complete theories of justice. Besides, incomplete rankings do not mean that local and temporary agreement cannot be achieved even on more than minimal requirements of justice. However, they do mean that principled and theoretical solutions to conflicts between incommensurable demands of justice are unattainable.

NOTES

1. John Rawls, *Political Liberalism* (New York: Columbia University Press, 1996), 133.
2. As Russell Hardin argues, 'Making his own theory overcome indeterminacy is a central, driving concern that has largely been neglected in the voluminous literature responding to Rawls's theory.' See Russell Hardin, *Indeterminacy and Society* (Princeton/Oxford: Princeton University Press, 2003), 105.
3. Rawls, *Political Liberalism*, fn. 8, 180, 181.
4. John Rawls, *A Theory of Justice*, revised edition (Cambridge, Mass.: Belknap Press of Harvard University Press, 1999), 266.
5. Ibid., 279.
6. Ibid., 280.

7. Ibid., 79.
8. Ibid., 80.
9. Ibid., 514.
10. Rawls, *Political Liberalism*, 180.
11. Rawls, *A Theory of Justice*, 79.
12. See for further examples John Gray, 'Rival Liberties' in his *Two Faces of Liberalism* (Cambridge/Oxford: Polity Press, 2000), 69–104; and Herbert Hart, 'Rawls on Liberty and its Priority', *University of Chicago Law Review* 40 (1973).
13. Rawls, *A Theory of Justice*, 53.
14. I owe this point to Herbert Hart, 'Rawls on Liberty and its Priority'.
15. Quoted by Bhikhu Parekh, *Rethinking Multiculturalism. Cultural Diversity and Political Theory* (New York: Palgrave, 2000), 317.
16. Rawls, *Theory of Justice*, 386.
17. Parekh, *Rethinking Multiculturalism*, 320.
18. Rawls, *A Theory of Justice* (Cambridge, Mass.: Belknap Press of Harvard University Press, 1971), 143.
19. Hart, 'Rawls on Liberty and its Priority'.
20. I agree with John Gray that Rawls's revision obscures rather than avoids the necessity of making controversial judgments about the greatest liberty. See Gray, *Two Faces of Liberalism*, 81.
21. Rawls, *A Theory of Justice*, 79.
22. Ibid., 80.
23. Philippe van Parijs, 'Difference Principles', in *The Cambridge Companion to Rawls*, ed. Samuel Freeman (Cambridge: Cambridge University Press, 2003), 212.
24. Rawls, *A Theory of Justice*, 83.
25. Compare Norman Daniels, 'Democratic Equality: Rawls's Complex Egalitarianism', *The Cambridge Companion to Rawls*, 261; Philippe van Parijs, 'Difference Principles', *The Cambridge Companion to Rawls*, 212; Martha C. Nussbaum, *Frontiers of Justice: Disability, Nationality, Species Membership* (Cambridge, Mass.: Belknap Press of Harvard University Press, 2006), 431, fn. 5.
26. I owe this (somewhat revised) example to Daniels, 'Democratic Equality'.
27. Nussbaum, *Frontiers of Justice*, 116.
28. van Parijs, 'Difference Principles', 212.
29. Nussbaum, *Frontiers of Justice*, 114–115.
30. Rawls, *Political Liberalism*, 56–57.
31. Ibid., 58.
32. Ibid., 137.
33. Compare Richard J. Arneson, 'Rawls versus Utilitarianism in the Light of Political Liberalism', in *The Idea of a Political Liberalism: Essays on Rawls*, eds. Victoria Davion and Clark Wolf (Lanham, M.D.: Rowman & Littlefield, 2000). And Michael J. Sandel, *Liberalism and the Limits of Justice*, 2nd ed. (Cambridge: Cambridge University Press, 1998), 202–210.
34. Amartya Sen, 'What Do We Want from a Theory of Justice', *Journal of Philosophy* 103 (2006), 224.

35. Rawls, *Political Liberalism*, 240, 241.

36. Alasdair MacIntyre, *Whose Justice? Which Rationality?* (Notre Dame: University of Notre Dame Press, 1988), 3, 4.

37. Robert P. George and Christopher Wolfe, 'Introduction', in *Natural Law and Public Reason*, eds. Robert P. George and Christopher Wolfe (Washington, D.C.: Georgetown University Press, 2000), 1, 2, 4.

38. Rawls, *Political Liberalism,* 225, 226.

39. James Gordon Finlayson, *Habermas: A Very Short Introduction* (Oxford: Oxford University Press, 2005), 102.

40. Rawls, *Political Liberalism*, 16.

41. Ibid., xliv.

42. Ibid., li.

43. George and Wolfe, *Natural Law and Public Reason*.

44. Rawls, *Political Liberalism*, 54.

45. George and Wolfe, 'Introduction', 1.

46. Seyla Benhabib, 'Deliberative Rationality and Models of Democratic Legitimacy', *Constellations: An International Journal of Critical and Democratic Theory* 1 (1994), 36.

47. Sandel, *Liberalism and the Limits of Justice*, 196.

48. Ibid., 211.

49. Ibid., 217, 218.

50. Rawls, *Political Liberalism*, 240, 241.

51. Sandel, *Liberalism and the Limits of Justice*, 196.

52. Ibid., 215.

53. Rawls, *Political Liberalism*, 243, fn. 32.

54. Elizabeth Anderson, personal communication.

55. John Finnis, 'Abortion, Natural Law, and Public Reason', eds. George and Wolfe, 75–105.

56. Stephen Macedo, 'In Defense of Liberal Public Reason: Are Slavery and Abortion Hard Cases?' eds. George and Wolfe, 33.

57. John Rawls, *Political Liberalism*, 23, 61, 124, 137.

58. Brian Barry, *Justice as Impartiality* (Oxford: Clarendon Press, 1999), chap. 3.

59. Thomas Nagel, 'Moral Conflict and Political Legitimacy', *Philosophy and Public Affairs* 16 (1987), 221.

60. Thomas Scanlon, *What We Owe to Each Other* (Cambridge, Mass.: Belknap Press of Harvard University Press, 1998), 5; and Scanlon, 'Contractualism and Utilitarianism', in *Utilitarianism and Beyond*, eds. Amartya Sen and Bernard Williams (Cambridge: Cambridge University Press, 1982), 110.

61. Ibid., 5.

62. James Gordon Finlayson, *Habermas: A Very Short Introduction*, 81.

63. Isaiah Berlin, 'Two Concepts of Liberty', in his *Four Essays on Liberty* (Oxford: Oxford University Press, 1969).

64. See Benjamin Constant, 'Liberty of the Ancients Compared with that of the Moderns', in *Political Writings*, ed. Benjamin Constant (Cambridge: Cambridge University Press, 1988).

65. Rawls, *Political Liberalism*, 5.
66. Ibid., 58.
67. Ibid., 61.
68. Rawls, *Political Liberalism*, 48–9, fn. 1; 50–54.
69. Ibid., 58–60.
70. Ibid., 55, 56.
71. Ibid., 60, 61.
72. John Rawls, *Justice as Fairness: A Restatement* (Cambridge, Mass.: The Belknap Press of Harvard University Press, 2001), 6–7.
73. Rawls, *Political Liberalism*, 54.
74. Stephen Mulhall and Adam Swift, *Liberals and Communitarians*, 2nd ed. (Oxford: Blackwell, 1997), 197.
75. Parekh, *Rethinking Multiculturalism*, 323, 324.
76. Christopher J. Eberle, *Religious Conviction in Liberal Politics* (Cambridge: Cambridge University Press, 2002), 150, 151.
77. Rawls, *Theory of Justice*, 386.
78. Ibid., 181.
79. From Patrick Neal, 'Political Liberalism, Public Reason, and the Citizen of Faith', eds. George and Wolfe, 185–188.
80. Rawls, *Political Liberalism*, 60, 61.
81. Ibid., 63.
82. Ibid., 59, 60.
83. Ibid., 216.
84. Ibid., 216–220.
85. Berlin, 'Two Concepts of Liberty', in *Four Essays on Liberty*, 166, 130, fn. 1.
86. Isaiah Berlin, 'The Pursuit of the Ideal', in *The Proper Study of Mankind*, eds. Henry Hardy and Roger Hausheer (London: Pimlico, 1998), 8.
87. Berlin, 'Two Concepts of Liberty', 167.
88. Rawls, *Political Liberalism*, 197, n. 32.
89. Berlin, 'Two Concepts of Liberty', 130, fn. 1.
90. Rawls, *A Theory of Justice*, 194.
91. Gray, *Two Faces of Liberalism*, 81, 82.
92. Rawls, *A Theory of Justice*, 115–116.
93. Ibid., 37.
94. Rawls, *A Theory of Justice*, 56, 65.
95. Rawls, *Political Liberalism*, 216ff.
96. Kenneth J. Arrow, *Social Choice and Individual Values* (New Haven, Conn.; and London: Yale University Press, 1963).
97. Elizabeth Anderson, personal communication.
98. From Plato's *Euthyphro*.
99. Martha C. Nussbaum, *The Fragility of Goodness: Luck and Ethics in Greek Tragedy and Philosophy* (Cambridge: Cambridge University Press, 2001), see chap. 4, section IV.
100. Herbert Hart, *The Concept of Law* (Oxford: Oxford University Press, 1997), 167, my emphasis.

101. I owe this phrase to Cass Sunstein, 'Incommensurability and Kinds of Valuation: Some Applications in Law', in *Incommensurability, Incomparability, and Practical Reason*, ed. Ruth Chang (Cambridge, Mass.: Harvard University Press, 1997).

102. Amartya Sen, 'Incompleteness and Reasoned Choice', *Synthese* 140 (2004), 55, 56 and fn. 28 and 29, 59.

103. Amartya Sen, 'What Do We Want from a Theory of Justice', *Journal of Philosophy* 103 (2006), 224.

Chapter 8

Do We Need a Theory of Justice?
A Reply to Amartya Sen

Note: The text of this chapter is nearly completely copied from 'The Aim of a Theory of Justice', *Ethical Theory and Moral Practice* 15 (2012): 7–21.

SUMMARY

Amartya Sen argues that for the advancement of justice identification of perfect justice is neither necessary nor sufficient. He replaces perfect justice with comparative justice. Comparative justice limits itself to comparing social states with respect to degrees of justice. Sen's central thesis is that identifying perfect justice and comparing imperfect social states are 'analytically disjoined'. This chapter challenges Sen's thesis by demonstrating that to be able to make adequate comparisons we need to identify and integrate criteria of comparison. This is precisely the aim of a theory of justice (e.g., John Rawls's theory): identifying, integrating and ordering relevant principles of justice. The same integrated criteria that determine perfect justice enable us to compare imperfect social states. Sen's alternative approach, which is based on social choice theory, is incapable of avoiding contrary, indeterminate or incoherent directives where principles of justice conflict.

*****

Suppose we are confronted with the question which of two social states is more just. Amartya Sen argues that, to be able to answer this question, identification of perfect justice is neither necessary nor sufficient.[1] What moves us in pursuing justice is not 'that the world fails short of being completely just . . . but that there are clearly remediable injustices around us which we want to eliminate'. Gandhi, Martin Luther King and all other persons who have dedicated themselves to pursuing a more just society, 'were not trying to achieve a perfectly just world . . . but they did want to remove clear injustices to the extent they could'.[2] Sen does not deny the need of any theory, but the need of a theory that identifies a perfectly just society. The latter is a society that is completely just – a society in which all possible injustices have been removed. The aim of a theory of perfect justice, Sen says, is 'to offer resolutions of questions about the nature of perfect justice'.[3] Compliance with the principles formulated by such a theory is supposed to render a society or its basic structure completely just. Sen presents as an alternative 'a theory of justice in a very broad sense. Its aim is to clarify how we can proceed to address questions of enhancing justice and removing injustice'. According to Sen, identifying perfectly just arrangements and determining whether a particular social change would enhance justice 'do have motivational links but they are nevertheless analytically disjoined'. Determining whether a particular social change would enhance justice, is a 'comparative exercise': different social states are compared in order to see whether one is more just than the other. Sen believes that it is 'entirely incorrect' to assume that 'this comparative exercise cannot be undertaken without identifying, first, the demands of perfect justice'.[4] Sen argues that theories of perfect justice are not only redundant but also insufficient for realizing justice. Several other theorists have written about the putative shortcomings of ideal theories.[5] One of the differences is that Sen explicitly denies the need of an ideal theory at all, while the other critics argue that such a theory has to be supplemented by 'non-ideal theory', which takes into account non-ideal circumstances.

Sen's argument demonstrates that many injustices can be combated without taking a theory of perfect justice as our guideline. Therefore, the (possible) lack of an agreed upon theory of perfect justice cannot be an alibi for not trying to enhance justice in many distressing and unambiguous cases of injustice. This is obviously true and worth emphasizing. However, Sen's view seems to overshoot the mark where he generalizes from particulars. If Sen is right, it implies that theories of justice such as those developed by John Rawls – which Sen calls 'transcendental' theories of perfect justice – are largely superfluous. The aim of this paper is to investigate whether this is true. I will argue that the pertinent question is not whether, to be able to advance justice, we need the identification of perfect justice. The question is rather whether, to be capable of adequately comparing different social states with respect to degrees of justice, we need to identify and order criteria of justice that can serve as standards of comparison. I will answer this question affirmatively. Determining or constructing ordered and integrated principles of justice is precisely the aim of a theory of perfect justice. The same integrated principles that identify perfect justice enable adequate comparisons of imperfect social states. If so, this refutes Sen's central thesis that identifying perfect justice and comparing imperfect social states are 'analytically disjoined'. Also some other thinkers have questioned Sen's view that an ideal theory of justice is not needed to advance justice.[6] Unlike their criticisms, my approach is to a large extent a conceptual analysis, which mainly concentrates on Sen's central thesis of the analytical disjunction between perfect and comparative justice. The analysis demonstrates that the thesis is fallacious. In addition, I comment on Sen's alternative approach, which is based on social choice theory. I will try to show that, unlike Rawls's theory of justice, a social-choice-based approach is incapable of avoiding contrary, incoherent and unstable directives where principles of justice conflict.

STANDARDS OF COMPARISON

Although there is large agreement on the importance of justice, there is much disagreement on its requirements. It is not always self-evident which principles are relevant to justice and how they have to be ordered. For instance, some theorists claim that merit and desert are aspects of distributive justice, while others deny this. Further, most theorists think that some kind of 'equality' is a central criterion of justice. But, as Sen rightly asks: 'Equality of what?'[7] Without an answer to this question, we do not know with respect to which kind of equality we have to compare social states in order to determine their comparative degrees of justice. Some theorists believe that justice requires equal distribution of welfare, others find equal distribution of resources more appropriate. Besides, more than one kind of equality, and principles other than equality, may be relevant to justice. In other words, we have to determine which criteria have to be taken into account. If more than one criterion or principle is relevant, we have to find out how they cohere and how they must be ordered. Without answers to these questions we cannot know which social state is more just, A or B, if A is more just with respect to one principle and B is more just with respect to another. As David Miller argues, '[W]e need to develop a theory, because there are going to be cases in which our intuitions conflict, or perhaps run out altogether.'[8]

A theory of justice such as John Rawls's is meant to answer precisely the previous questions. Rawls's theory orders and integrates competing criteria or principles of justice. It assigns lexical priority to equal basic liberties over equal opportunities and it ranks the latter over the difference principle. The difference principle, in turn, integrates efficiency of welfare distribution with concern for the worst-off. According to Rawls, a theory of justice should provide the standards and their ordering for a proper assessment of the distributive aspects of the basic structure of society. The social ideal is a complete conception defining principles for all the virtues of the basic structure, together with their respective weights when they conflict. A complete or ideal theory of justice is necessary for resolving the problems resulting from, what Rawls calls, 'intuitionism'. Rawls understands by intuitionism

> the doctrine that there is an irreducible family of first principles which have to be weighed against one another by asking ourselves which balance, in our considered judgment, is the most just. While the complexity of the moral facts requires a number of distinct principles, there is no single standard that accounts for them or assigns them their weights. Intuitionist theories have two features: first, they consist of a plurality of first principles which may conflict to give contrary directives in particular types of cases; and second, they include no explicit method, no priority rules, for weighing these principles against one another: we are simply to strike a balance by intuition.[9]

Intuitions about the right balance of principles differ between persons, however rational and reasonable they are. This creates a problem. Rawls:

> If men's intuitive priority judgments are similar, it does not matter, practically speaking, that they cannot formulate the principles, which account for these convictions, or even whether such principles, exist. Contrary judgments, however, raise a difficulty, since the basis for adjudicating claims is to that extent obscure.[10]

According to Rawls, decisiveness, consistency, transitivity, stability and non-arbitrariness are important requirements of justice. One of the tasks of a theory of justice is to satisfy these conditions and avoid contrary directives by offering an explicit method to formulate principles and priority rules.

NECESSITY

To support his view that a theory of perfect justice is neither necessary nor sufficient for comparing two less perfect social states, Sen gives examples of comparative judgments outside the domain of justice. Assume that the *Mona Lisa* is the most ideal painting in the world. Knowing this perfect painting does not give us *sufficient* information about how we should compare and rank less perfect paintings. In addition it is not *necessary* to know the most perfect painting to be able to compare and rank less perfect paintings. Similarly, it is not necessary to know the height of the tallest mountain in the world to compare the height of two smaller mountains.

For the moment leaving aside Sen's claim that a theory of perfect justice is not sufficient, let us concentrate on his claim that such a theory is not necessary. Sen notices that '[t]here would be something odd in a general belief that a comparison of any two alternatives cannot sensibly made without a prior identification of a supreme alternative'.[11] '[I]n general the identification of a transcendental alternative does not offer a solution to the problem of comparison between any two non-transcendental alternatives.'[12] Sen suggests that the aim of a 'transcendental' theory of justice is to identify a perfectly just society. This suggestion is not wrong but incomplete and does not reveal how this identification takes place. As said, the aim of a theory of justice such as Rawls's is to specify the criteria of justice, their mutual relationship and their scope. These connected criteria determine which kind of society would be perfectly just. In addition – and this shows the incompleteness of Sen's suggestion – these are the same criteria with respect to which the degrees of justice of different imperfect social states can be compared. So, if Sen argues that we need no theory of perfect justice to compare social states that are not perfectly just, he suggests that we do not need to know the specific relevant criteria of justice and their interconnectedness to know which social state is less or more just than another. It is true that we often do not need a specific theory of justice, namely, in those cases of flagrant injustice in which all reasonable theories would give the same answer. But, as we will discuss later, in many other cases we cannot get an unambiguous answer to this question without knowing the relevant criteria of comparison and their mutual relation.

The results of comparing the relevant social states will differ to the extent to which conceptions or theories of ideal justice differ – that is, to the extent to which the conceived relevant criteria of justice and their orderings differ. For instance, if advantages are distributed according to equality and concern for the worst-off, or according to liberty and legitimate entitlement, or according to efficiency and utility, the answer to the question which distribution is (more) just, depends on the relevance of these criteria for justice and on their relative weights specified by a conception or theory of justice. It is clear that egalitarian, libertarian and utilitarian conceptions or theories of justice will easily arrive at quite different and often opposing judgments. Similarly, if person P has less resources and person Q less welfare, the answer to the question who is worse-off depends on the specific criteria of distributive justice defined by the theory. If the criterion is 'equal resources', P is worse-off; if the criterion is 'equal welfare', Q is worse-off. And if both criteria are relevant, the answer depends on their relative weights. So, the task of a theory of justice is to specify the criteria of justice, their mutual connectedness and their comparative importance. Consequently, in more complex cases of multidimensional justice, such a theory is necessary to know which persons are worse-off and which social states are less just. In addition the theory has to identify the *scope* of justice. For instance, there is much controversy about the question whether the same principles apply to domestic and global justice. The answer to this important question requires a theoretical underpinning.

JUSTICE AS A COMPLEX CONCEPT

As argued in the previous section an adequate theory of justice gives us information on (1) the relevant criteria of justice, (2) their ranking and integration, (3) their scope. What we ought to do in the name of justice crucially depends on these three factors. A comparison of alternatives cannot be made without criteria of comparison and the result of the comparison depends on the nature of, and mutual relation between, the criteria. Ruth Chang calls the value or criterion with respect to which we want to compare alternatives the 'covering value'.[13] Most covering values are multifaceted in the sense that they contain several contributory values – values that integrally contribute to the covering value. Without an implicit or explicit covering value it remains unclear with respect to *what* we want to compare the alternatives. For instance, if we compare two paintings, say, a Picasso and a Van Gogh, we need a covering value. The specific covering value needed for comparing these paintings is the same as the one with respect to which we can determine whether a particular painting (say, the *Mona Lisa*) is the most perfect one in the world. Similarly, if we want to compare two mountains, we need to know the criterion with respect to which we want to compare them. In Sen's example this criterion is 'height'. It determines not only which mountain is the supreme one in the world (Mount Everest) but also which of two smaller mountains is superior; for instance, with respect to 'height' Mont Blanc is superior to Matterhorn. If we take a different criterion of comparison – say, the difficulty to climb the mountains – the results may significantly differ: it may turn out that not Mount Everest but K2 is the 'supreme' one in the world and that Matterhorn scores higher than Mont Blanc. Most comparative evaluative judgments are made with respect to covering values that comprise more than one aspect or, in Chang's terminology, more than one 'contributory value'. If justice is a multifaceted concept (i.e., if justice is not one principle or rule but several, which is recognized by most theorists, including Sen), the same applies to comparative judgments of justice. Therefore, comparing two social states with respect to their degree of justice is more similar to comparing two paintings with respect to their artistic quality (which is a covering value that comprises more than one contributory value) than to comparing two mountains with respect to 'height' (which is a single and one-dimensional value). Comparing two alternatives with respect to a multifaceted concept like justice means comparing them with respect to a covering value in which the contributory values are integrated according to their relative importance. This is precisely what we want from a theory of justice: that it identifies both the criteria of justice and their ranking, relative weight and mutual connection, so that we can compare different social states with respect to the integral conception of justice explicated by the theory. Rawls:

The assignment of weights is an essential part of a conception of justice. If we cannot explain how these weights are to be determined by reasonable ethical criteria, the means of rational discussion have come to an end.[14]

[A] conception of right must impose an ordering on conflicting claims. This requirement springs directly from the role of its principles in adjusting competing demands.... It is clearly desirable that a conception of justice be complete, that is, able to order all the claims that can arise.[15]

If justice is a multifaceted concept, and if it concerns an integrated goal, '[T]here is no reason to suppose that justice in one dimension or domain is independent of justice in other dimensions or domains.'[16] In that case we need a theory that specifies and integrates the relevant aspects. Without this specification and integration, we cannot determine whether an increase in the realization of one aspect of justice means a small or large increase, or even decrease, of overall justice. That is why the pursuit of justice cannot be done in a piecemeal fashion.

Of course, different conceptions or theories of justice may share basic requirements, and divergent arguments may lead to the same conclusion of injustice, so that we do not need a specific theory to determine whether one social state is better than another with respect to these minimal and basic requirements.[17] As said already, some flagrant injustices are injustices according to all possible theories and all possible reasonable criteria of justice. This does not mean that we do not need a theory of justice, but only that, in this case, all reasonable theories arrive at the same conclusion with respect to some basic requirements. The fact that in those cases a specific theory is not necessary (because of the overlap between widely different conceptions or theories of justice) does obviously not mean that a specific theory is not necessary in the many equivocal cases in which it is not evident what justice requires and in which individual and intuitive conceptions of the relevant covering value do not overlap.

INTERRELATION BETWEEN PERFECT AND COMPARATIVE JUSTICE

As indicated in figure 8.1, a theory of justice (A), which identifies the relevant criteria of comparison, their ordering and scope, determines not only perfect justice (B) but also 'comparative' justice (C).

The criteria of comparison originating from the theory determine both perfect justice ('the supreme alternative') and comparative justice of imperfect social states. Sen thinks that if B does not determine C, A does not determine C either. This does not follow. Sen overlooks the fact that, although C may not be determined by B, both are determined by A. Comparative justice (C)

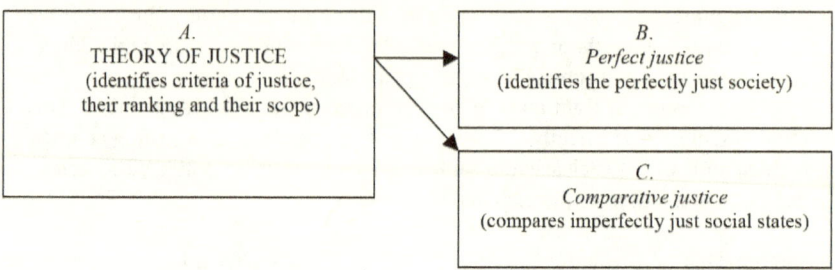

Figure 8.1. Relation between a theory of justice on the one side and perfect justice and comparative justice on the other

is not deduced from, or determined by, but strongly associated with, perfect justice (*B*), because the same criteria of comparison that are generated by the theory (*A*), determine both perfect justice (*B*) and the degrees of justice of less perfect social states (*C*). Remember that Sen's central thesis is that perfect justice and comparative justice are 'analytically disjoined'. The earlier analysis demonstrates that the thesis is mistaken.

SUFFICIENCY

According to Sen a theory of perfect justice is not only not necessary but also not sufficient for comparing two social states with respect to their degree of justice, just as knowing the most perfect picture in the world (say, the *Mona Lisa*) is not sufficient for comparing a Picasso and a Van Gogh. Sen argues that the right, the perfect or the best do 'not tell us much about the comparative merits' of 'non-best societal arrangements'.[18] However, like the question of necessity, the question of sufficiency does not concern knowledge of an ideal or supreme alternative but knowledge of the relevant and integrated criteria of comparison. The latter knowledge may suffice to answer the question of comparative justice. Of course, a theory of perfect justice need not be sufficient with respect to the question what has to be done *all things considered* if justice is not the only value or interest to take into account and has to be weighed against other values or interests. Similarly, a theory need not be sufficient with respect to the question whether perfect justice, defined by the theory, is feasible in non-ideal situations of non-compliance or unfavourable conditions. But these are different questions. What we are considering is Sen's claim that perfect and comparative justice are 'analytically disjoined' and that a theory of perfect justice does not suffice to show which of two imperfect social states contains the largest degree of justice. If we want to compare mountains, it is *sufficient* to know the criterion, say 'height', with respect to which we want to compare them: it suffices to determine both whether the Mont Blanc is superior to the Matterhorn and whether the Mount Everest is the supreme mountain in the world. Similarly, if there would be a single one-dimensional criterion of justice and we would know this criterion (say, 'utility', which according to John Stuart Mill is the right criterion of justice), specified by the theory, this would be sufficient, at least in principle, to determine which of two social states is more just. If justice is a multi- rather than one-dimensional concept, it becomes more complicated. In that case it is not sufficient to know the relevant criteria. We need to know their interrelationship or ranking as well. Returning to Sen's example, the quality of a painting is multifaceted concept as well, which implies that multiple criteria play a role in determining this quality. If we know the relevant criteria and we can integrate them, we have the tools to evaluate the quality of paintings, irrespective of whether they are perfect or not. The integrated criteria that enable a person to identify the *Mona Lisa* as the best picture in the world are the same that enable her to rank imperfect paintings. In other words, and in contrast to what Sen claims, there is an analytical connection between the identification of 'the best' on the one side and the identification of 'the better' of two non-best alternatives on the other. Sen puts the following question:[19]

> [I]s the specification of an entirely just society sufficient to give us rankings of departures from justness in terms of comparative distances from perfection, so that a transcendental identification might *inter alia* entail comparative gradings as well?

Sen agrees that 'the distance-comparison approach' 'has some apparent plausibility', but 'does not actually work':

> The difficulty lies in the fact that there are different features involved in identifying distance related . . . to different fields of departure, varying dimensionalities of transgression, and diverse ways of weighing separate infractions.

Sen concludes that a 'transcendental' theory of perfect justice 'does not yield any means of addressing these problems'. 'The characterization of spotless justice . . . would not entail any delineation whatever of how diverse departures from spotlessness would be compared and ranked.'[20] But this conclusion is not correct. As we already emphasized, a 'transcendental' theory not only formulates but also integrates principles of justice and tries 'to order all the claims that can arise (or that are likely to in practice)'.[21] To the extent that the attempt is successful, the theory suffices to determinately compare two imperfect social states. For instance, if one social state conforms more to one principle, while the other social state conforms more to another, an adequate theory gives a determinate answer to the question which of the two imperfect social states is superior with respect to these integrated principles. For instance, if freedom of speech is an important principle of a transcendental theory of justice (as in Rawls's theory) and if there is less freedom of speech in imperfect social state A than in imperfect social state B, then, other things being equal, the transcendental theory is able to determine that imperfect social state B is more just than imperfect social state A. Suppose further that another principle of a transcendental theory of justice is 'concern for the worst-off' in the sense that interpersonal inequality of welfare is only allowed if it is to the benefit of the worst-off (the 'difference principle' in Rawls's theory). In that case the transcendental theory is again able to determine that imperfect social state C is more just than imperfect social state D, if, other things being equal, C has more concern for the worst-off in line with the difference principle while D has more total welfare at the cost of concern for the worst-off. To further illustrate this, let us scrutinize one of Sen's examples of the putative impotence of a transcendental theory:

> We have to consider . . . departures in procedural equality (such as infringements of fair equality of public opportunities or facilities) which figure within the domain of Rawlsian demands of justice. . . . To weigh these procedural departures against infelicities of emergent patterns of interpersonal distribution (for example, distribution of primary goods), which also figure in the Rawlsian system, would require distinct specification . . . of relative importance. . . . But these valuations . . . lie beyond the specific exercise of the identification of transcendence and are indeed the basic ingredients of a 'comparative' rather than a 'transcendental' approach to justice.[22]

However, Rawls's theory is largely devoted to weighing and ranking competing demands of justice. In Sen's example Rawls's theory gives an answer to the question of relative importance. If imperfect social state A is better with respect to fair equality of opportunity (e.g., fair educational opportunities) while imperfect social state B is better with respect to equal distribution of goods, Rawls's theory makes it possible to determine which social state is 'all things considered' more just. The answer depends on the kind of the relevant goods to which the 'infelicities of emergent patterns of interpersonal distribution' applies. If it concerns the distribution of basic liberties, then social state B is more just than social state A because, in Rawls's theory, the distribution of equal basic liberties is the first principle of justice, which has lexical priority to fair equality of opportunity. If, by contrast, it concerns primary goods other than basic liberties, such as income or wealth, then social state A is more just than social state B because A is in line with the fair equality of opportunity principle, and 'fair opportunity is prior to the difference principle'.[23] In other words, the better of two imperfect social states is the one that is more in line with the integrated principles of justice of the relevant theory (in this case, in line with the lexical ordering of Rawls's principles of justice). The previous illustration shows the importance of justice as an integrated goal and the danger of trying to improve one aspect of justice in isolation, that is, detached from justice as an integrated goal.

Of course one may disagree with the specific principles formulated in a particular theory or with the specific ordering or relative importance attached to these principles. But this is a different question. The question under consideration is whether a 'transcendental' theory is incapable of comparing imperfect social states, rather than whether we agree with the theory. Also a different question is whether a theory always *succeeds* in completely ordering all relevant principles. I think Sen is right that there is a plurality of impartial reasons and competing principles of justice and that some competing demands cannot be unambiguously ranked or integrated because neither seems definitely stronger than the other.[24] However, the question whether a 'transcendental' theory is a panacea for the resolution of all conflicts between competing demands of justice is again not the question under consideration. The claim that a 'transcendental' theory of justice is not sufficient for comparing two imperfectly just social states differs from the claim that a theory may not always, or not entirely, succeed in arriving at an ordering or integration of all possible conflicting claims. The truth of the latter does not automatically imply the truth of the former: to the extent that a theory of justice succeeds in ordering conflicting claims or principles the theory suffices to determinately compare imperfect social states with respect to these claims or principles. And where a theory fails to completely order the relevant claims, this need not be related to the 'transcendental' nature of the theory but, rather, to the very impossibility of a complete integration or ordering of all relevant demands of justice due to their equal strength. In that case, not only 'transcendental' justice but also comparative justice fails to give a determinate and agreed upon answer. Besides, if a transcendental theory does not always succeed in constructing an ordering of demands, this does not mean that it seldom does. Below we will further elaborate on the difference between necessity and sufficiency of a theory on the one hand and its success or failure on the other.

SOCIAL CHOICE

Sen grounds comparative justice on social choice theory:[25] '[S]ocial choice theory as discipline is concerned with arriving at overall judgments for social choice based on a diversity of perspectives and priorities.' And 'The outcomes of the social choice procedure take the form of ranking different states of affair from a "social point of view", in the light of the assessments of the people involved'. Sen writes that 'this is very different' from a search for a 'perfectly' just society. 'Transcendental' theories cannot, on their own, address questions about advancing justice and compare alternative proposals for having a more just society, at least not in a way that differs from the utopian proposal of taking an imagined jump to a perfectly just world. The answers that those theories give 'are quite distinct from the type of concerns that engage people in discussions on justice and injustice in the world', Sen concludes. Sen recognizes that there is an 'inescapable plurality' of reasons and competing principles of justice, 'each of which survives critical scrutiny, but yields divergent conclusions'. Individuals may find it difficult or impossible to completely rank and integrate the principles (= 'personal incompleteness'). In addition, *if* they are able to make a complete ordering for themselves, the orderings may easily differ interindividually. Individually differing rankings of reasons and principles are often difficult or impossible to combine in a single, coherent and complete ordering (= 'collective incompleteness'). Sen argues that even collective incompleteness would not prevent making comparative judgments about a great many cases. Indeed, collective incompleteness does not exclude, what Sen calls, dominance-partial and intersection-partial orderings. 'Dominance' means that one option is better or worse with respect to all relevant criteria. If all criteria lead to 'the same diagnosis of a huge mistake or injustice, then that specific conclusion need not await the determination of the relative priorities to be attached to these criteria.'[26] 'Intersection' means that, although neither of two options or states is better or worse than the other with respect to all relevant criteria, and although different parties attach different weights to these criteria, one and the same option or state may be better or worse than the other according to all parties. Thus, with respect to the question of justice, 'dominance' entails that the relevant social state is more just with respect to all aspects of justice, and 'intersection' implies that there is an overlap between interpersonally different orderings of principles of justice, leading to an overlapping consensus with respect to the particular point under consideration.[27] Of course, in those cases we do not need a theory that determines the relative priorities to be attached to the relevant criteria. Then we do not need rational deliberation and social choice either, because there is no disagreement to be resolved. However, these unproblematic cases do, of course, not make the frequent cases to which dominance- and intersection-partial ordering do not apply less problematic. In a pluralistic society dominance and intersection are often lacking, due to the plurality of competing moral outlooks and conceptions of the good, resulting in a collectively incompletely ordered plurality of divergent principles. In those cases we have to determine the priorities to be attached to relevant principles before we can make adequate comparative judgments. Here social choice is impotent because it reflects rather than resolves collectively incomplete rankings of principles, as will be shown in the next section.

ARROW'S THEOREM

Condorcet's voters' paradox and, more generally, Arrow's theorem demonstrate the fundamental impossibility of combining the minimal requirements of a rational social choice.[28] The theorem states that there is no satisfactory rational way of *collectively* choosing between rival rankings of values or preferences.[29] Below we will discuss a concrete example to show the problem. Sen has devoted seminal articles to collective choice and is, of course, fully aware of this problem. Still, it is useful to discuss the example in more detail for the following reasons. The example reveals that social choice reflects rather than resolves the problem of collective incompleteness. Besides, it demonstrates the relevance of Rawls's emphasis on the importance of a theory of a complete and transitive conception of justice. Further, the example illustrates how Rawls's theory completely and determinately orders relevant principles of justice, where Sen's social-choice-based approach remains incomplete and indeterminate. A final reason to discuss social choice in more detail is that Sen thinks that the impasses 'can be, in most cases, largely resolved by making the social decision procedures more informationally sensitive' and by interpersonal rational deliberation, instead of merely aggregating isolated individual choices.[30]

To start with the latter, although adequate exchange of information and collective rational deliberation are obviously important requirements for rational social choice, it is not to be expected that they, in most cases, lead to a determinate ordering of conflicting principles of justice. Incomplete rankings of justice are usually not the result of insufficient information and insufficient deliberation, but instead, as Sen recognizes, the result of the plurality of reasoned principles and multiple reasoned rankings of these principles. Equally rational people rank principles in different ways, especially if they have different backgrounds and rival moral and political outlooks. As Rawls emphasizes, the differences in intuitive weight assignment to the relevant principles 'are not by any means trivial variations but often correspond to profoundly opposed political convictions'. According to Rawls, the task of an ideal theory of justice is precisely to 'set forth ethical criteria that account for the weights which, in our considered judgments, we think appropriate to give to the plurality of principles'.[31] Sen's social choice approach fails because it is incapable of giving a determinate and unambiguous answer to the question how to avoid, resolve or transcend the different intuitive rankings people make. The impotence of the social choice approach can be shown by the following concrete example of collective choice with respect to the ranking of principles of justice.

Suppose three parties A, B and C take part in a deliberation about how to organize the basic structure of society in a just and collectively acceptable way. Let us assume that collective deliberation results in agreement between the parties that the following aspects should be taken into account with respect to the distribution of welfare: need (priority to the worst-off), utility and liberty. Suppose the parties have to assess three different imperfect social states P, Q and R with respect to their overall degree of justice. In social state P more attention is paid to need, in Q to utility and in R to liberty. How to rank these social states with respect to their overall degree of justice by social-choice-based 'comparative justice'? The ranking depends on the weights assigned to the values need, utility and liberty. As said, the problem is that assignment of weights is an intuitive procedure, largely determined by one's conception of the good and comprehensive moral or philosophical belief. Obviously, in a pluralistic society the considerably different backgrounds, beliefs and moral outlooks easily lead to interpersonally conflicting conclusions. Suppose that the parties differ in assigning weights to the values or principles as follows. Party A ranks need over utility and utility over liberty. B makes the following ranking: first liberty, second need and third utility. C chooses the remaining alternative ranking (table 8.1).

The outcomes show that a unanimous result is not possible. Does social choice or the majority rule resolve this problem? Assuming that a combination of two parties represents a majority, a majority (A and B) ranks need over utility *and* a majority (A and C) ranks utility over liberty *and* a majority (B and C) ranks liberty over need. This creates two problems: (1) the social choice fails to produce consistent and transitive results; (2) it fails to produce any result at all. To start with the second problem, the majority rule does not produce an answer to the question which criterion or value must be ranked first: a majority ranks need over utility so that we cannot give priority to utility; a majority ranks utility over liberty so that we cannot give priority to liberty; and a majority ranks liberty over need so that we cannot give priority

Table 8.1. Rival rankings of principles

Principles	Parties		
	A	B	C
Need	First	Second	Third
Utility	Second	Third	First
Liberty	Third	First	Second

to need. This voters' paradox means that we cannot give priority to any of these values. In other words, social choice is susceptible to yielding vacuous results.[32] With respect to the first problem, it is clear that if need is ranked higher than utility and utility higher than liberty, then liberty cannot consistently be ranked over need. Still this is what happens. This creates problems for a consistent and complete conception of justice, the importance of which Rawls stresses in his *A Theory of Justice*. The requirements of rationally determined weights and transitive orderings of values and principles, as pointed out by Rawls, are not satisfied in the previous example. Social choice reflects rather than resolves the problem of collective incompleteness.[33] This shows one of the reasons why we need a theory of justice. In Rawls's words, we need a complete ordering of conflicting claims, such as those based on need, liberty, equality and utility as indicated in table 8.1. Rawls applies the devices of the original position and the 'veil of ignorance', in which the agents are detached from their conceptions of the good and comprehensive beliefs, expecting that it promotes an overlapping consensus on the ranking of principles. The various individual and partial perspectives are replaced by the perspective of an 'impartial spectator' (see chapter 7). In this way Rawls's theory tries to construct an unambiguous, impartial and stable ordering of principles agreed upon by all reasonable and rational people. It tries to integrate the plurality of principles in a coherent system, making use of a scheme of lexical priorities and the difference principle. For instance, equal basic liberties receive lexical priority to need and utility, and the tension between need and utility is resolved by the difference principle. In this way the predicament resulting from social choice as illustrated in table 8.1 is avoided or resolved. This shows that Rawls's theory offers solutions where Sen's approach remains indeterminate. For instance, when need clashes with utility or efficiency, Rawls's theory shows that a social state in which the neediest citizens get priority is more just than a social state with a more utilitarian or efficient distribution of welfare at the cost of concern for the worst-off. To give another example, above a minimum level of welfare a society with more extensive basic liberties at the cost of economic growth, is shown to be more just than a society with more economic growth at the cost of one or more basic liberties.

Sen denies that Rawls's theory has succeeded in yielding complete rankings of principles. I think Sen is right (see chapter 7). However, the question whether a theory is (entirely) successful differs from the question whether we need a theory. The latter question is the issue under consideration. Besides, even if a complete ordering of all possible claims is unattainable, a partial success or partial ordering may give directives where social choice gives ambiguous, indeterminate and inconsistent results. A final fundamental point is that Sen's approach does not answer the question Rawls asks: How can we resolve disagreement, intellectually rather than socially? Indeed, even if social choice can generate a social ordering of our conflicting individual rankings, we still haven't answered the question Rawls was asking, namely, why the particular ranking is right and how we can justify this ranking. To answer this question is precisely what a theory of justice is for. Sen's recourse to aggregation methods and social choice theory doesn't answer this question.[34]

CONCLUSIONS

We can draw three main conclusions:

1. The aim of a theory of justice is to determine principles of justice, their ordering and scope. Integration is necessary to avoid or resolve conflicts between rival principles. Therefore, priority rules are an essential part of a theory of justice as developed by Rawls.
2. Sen's central thesis that perfect justice and comparable justice are 'analytically disjoined' is mistaken. The integrated principles of an adequate 'transcendental' theory of justice enable not only identification of perfect justice but also comparisons of imperfect social states.
3. Sen's social-choice-based approach fails because the results of collective choices reflect rather than resolve incomplete rankings of principles. That is why his alternative cannot avoid indeterminate, inconsistent and unstable directives where principles of justice conflict.

NOTES

1. Amartya Sen, 'What Do We Want from a Theory of Justice', *Journal of Philosophy* 103 (2006): 216–226; Amartya Sen, *The Idea of Justice* (London: Penguin Books, 2009), 15–18, 98–105.
2. Sen, *The Idea of Justice*, vii.
3. Ibid., ix.
4. Ibid.
5. See, for instance, the contributions to the special issue 'Social Justice: Ideal Theory, Non-Ideal Circumstances', in *Social Theory and Practice* 34 (2008); guest editors Ingrid Robeyns and Adam Swift.
6. Ingrid Robeyns, 'Ideal Theory in Theory and Practice', *Social Theory and Practice* 34 (2008): 341–362; A. John Simmons, 'Ideal and Nonideal Theory', *Philosophy and Public Affairs* 38 (2010): 5–36; Zofia Stemplowska, 'What Is Ideal about Ideal Theory?', *Social Theory and Practice* 34 (2008): 319–340; Adam Swift, 'The Value of Philosophy in Nonideal Circumstances', *Social Theory and Practice* 34 (2008): 363–387.

7. Amartya Sen, *Inequality Re-examined* (Cambridge, Mass.: Harvard University Press, 1992), 12–30.
8. David Miller, *Political Philosophy: A Very Short Introduction* (Oxford: Oxford University Press, 2003), 78.
9. John Rawls, *A Theory of Justice*, revised edition (Cambridge, Mass.: Belknap Press of Harvard University Press, 1999), 30.
10. Ibid., 39.
11. Amartya Sen, *The Idea of Justice* (London: Penguin Books, 2009), 102.
12. Ibid., 17.
13. Ruth Chang, 'Introduction', in *Incommensurability, Incomparability, and Practical Reason*, ed. Ruth Chang (Cambridge, Mass.: Harvard University Press, 1997), 1–34.
14. Rawls, *A Theory of Justice*, 37.
15. Ibid., 115–116.
16. A. John Simmons, 'Ideal and Nonideal Theory', *Philosophy and Public Affairs* 38 (2010): 22.
17. Sen, *The Idea of Justice*, 2–3.
18. Ibid., 98–101.
19. Ibid., 98.
20. Ibid., 99.
21. Rawls, *A Theory of Justice*, 115.
22. Sen, *The Idea of Justice*, 99.
23. Rawls, *A Theory of Justice*, 266.
24. Sen, *The Idea of Justice*, 106, 194–201.
25. Ibid., x, 95–109.
26. Ibid., 3–4.
27. Sen, *Inequality Re-examined*, 46–49, especially figure 3.1. See also Sen, 'What Do We Want from a Theory of Justice', 225; and Sen, *The Idea of Justice*, 2–3: 'A number of distinct and divergent arguments can still lead to the same conclusion.' Cf. Sunstein's 'incompletely theorized agreements', discussed in Cass R. Sunstein, *Legal Reasoning and Political Conflict* (Oxford: Oxford University Press, 1996); and Rawls's 'overlapping consensus' discussed in John Rawls, *Political Liberalism* (New York: Columbia University Press, 1996).
28. Kenneth Joseph Arrow, *Social Choice and Individual Values* (New Haven and London: Yale University Press, 1963).
29. For a proof see Michael Allingham, *Choice Theory: A Very Short Introduction* (Oxford: Oxford University Press, 2002), 99–101. A clear and concise summary and explanation of the problematic issue of rationality and coherence of democratic decisions in general and with respect to distributive justice in particular are given in chapter 6, 'Democracy and dictatorship', 106–110.
30. Sen, *The Idea of Justice*, 93ff.
31. Rawls, *A Theory of Justice*, 35.
32. Allingham, *Choice Theory*, 94. See also the concise and illuminating discussion of this problem by R. P. Wolff, *In Defense of Anarchism* (Berkeley: University of California Press, 1998), 58–67 ('Appendix: The Irrationality of Majority Rule').

33. Allingham, *Choice Theory*, 105–106. See also Shaun Hargreaves Heap et al., *The Theory of Choice* (Oxford: Blackwell Publishers, 1992), 212–214; Susan Hurley, *Natural Reasons, Personality and Polity* (Oxford: Oxford University Press, 1989), 228; Fred D'Agostino, *Incommensurability and Commensuration. The Common Denominator* (Burlington, Verm.: Ashgate, 2003), 6–20, 28; Lewis Kornhauser, 'No Best Answer?', *University of Pennsylvania Law Review* 146 (1998): 1599–1637. Decisions of multi-judge courts are confronted with similar problems. See Lewis Kornhauser and Lawrence Sager, 'The Many as One: Integrity and Group Choice in Paradoxical Cases', *Philosophy and Public Affairs* 249 (2004).

34. I owe this fundamental criticism to an anonymous referee.

Chapter 9

Equity and Efficiency in Health Care

SUMMARY

Because health care resources are not unlimited, it is essential to use them efficiently in order to maximize total health benefit. With the same budget, total health benefit depends on cost-effectiveness of the treatment. However, patient selection purely based on cost-effectiveness and utility of treatment may be at the expense of equity (fair chance of treatment; concern for the worst-off). By contrast, patient selection purely based on equity may be at the cost of total health benefit. The possible conflict between equity and efficiency suggests that a selection procedure that is simultaneously the most just *and* the most useful does not always exist. If we would conclude that neither equity nor efficiency can be ignored, we have to choose a combined approach in which both fairness and outcome are taken into account. In this approach a complete ordering of overall eligibility for treatment is not achievable without assigning relative weights to equity and utility. However, these values are incommensurable so that objective relative weights do not exist, as we have discussed in chapter 1. Because reason under-determines the choice, equally rational and well-informed people may assign considerably different weights to equity and efficiency.

****

An important issue, suitable for illustrating the problem of conflicts of justice (see chapter 5), is the distribution of limited health care resources. Allocation of scarce health care resources may be based on different aspects of equity and efficiency (table 9.1).

Table 9.1. Criteria for allocation of scarce health care resources

Criteria with respect to equity	Criteria with respect to efficiency
• *Need* or priority to the worst-off • *Urgency* • *Equality*: equal chance of treatment • *Liberty*: freedom to independently arrange and pay treatment	• *Utility*: aggregate health benefit in terms of overall gain in • Quantity of life (life expectancy) • Quality of life • QALYs • *Cost-effectiveness* (QALYs per unit of cost)

Patient selection purely based on cost-effectiveness and utility of treatment may be at the expense of equity (fair chance of treatment, concern for the worst-off).[1]

While the tension between total welfare and equal/fair distribution of welfare, described by Rawls, is caused by the fact that equal distribution of welfare decreases the incentive to produce more welfare, the conflict between fair distribution of scarce health care resources and total health benefit, by contrast, is caused by the fact that outcome and cost-effectiveness of medical treatment depend on the characteristics of the disease and the patient. This means that, in case of scarcity of health care resources, total health benefit may be smaller if patients are selected for treatment according to equity criteria instead of on the basis of cost-effectiveness.

NEED VERSUS OUTCOME

The following example shows that utility or cost-effectiveness (QALYs gained per given amount of cost or resources) as selection criterion for treatment may be in tension with selection of patients who are worse-off and in larger need of treatment. Consider patients *A* and *B* who suffer from heart failure, requiring heart transplantation. Patient *A* is younger, has a more serious version of the disease and has a lower life expectancy (and is therefore worse-off and in larger need of treatment) than patient *B*. Treatment of patient *B* is as expensive as that of patient *A* but yields a much larger increase in life expectancy (20 years versus 2 years). Only one heart becomes available for transplantation (suitable for each patient). Which patient has to be selected for transplantation: *A*, who is worse-off, or *B*, who has significantly more benefit from transplantation? Must we choose for equity (concern for the worst-off) or for efficiency (maximizing health benefit)? The possible conflict between equity and efficiency suggests that a selection procedure that is simultaneously the most just *and* the most useful does not always exist.

If we would conclude that neither equity nor efficiency can be ignored, we have to choose a combined approach in which both fairness and outcome are taken into account. This approach seems the most appropriate but is also the most difficult one. Efficiency and equity are disparate values. This makes it difficult to rank patients with respect to overall eligibility for treatment. In the combination approach a complete ordering of overall eligibility for treatment is not achievable without assigning relative weights to equity and utility. Frances Kamm proposes relative weight assignment according to her 'outcome modification procedure for allocation':

> [W]e assign multiplicative factors ... in accordance with the moral importance of ... factors relative to each other and relative to outcome. We multiply the outcome points by these factors. The candidate with a sufficiently high point score gets the resource.[2]

However, as we have discussed in previous chapters and as Rawls has argued in *A Theory of Justice*,[3] dependence on the assignment of weights is problematic because it is based on intuitions, which may widely differ among reasonable and rational people, who may arrive at different and opposite conclusions. In chapter 1 we discussed that there is a large 'range of indeterminateness' with respect to the comparative value of options that bear incommensurable values. In the present case, there is a large range of indeterminateness regarding the trade-off between, and relative weights of, outcome and concern for the worst-off.[4] This is reflected in the fact that different persons assign different relative weights. This is confirmed by Erik Nord's study. The interpersonal differences in weights assigned to need (related to seriousness of the disease/disorder) compared with benefit from treatment may extremely vary, even a factor of 70.[5] This is shown in figure 9.1, which I have deduced from the answers given by different participants in Nord's study.

This implies considerably different sizes of Kamm's multiplicative factor for need versus outcome and considerably different conclusions about the eligibility for the treatment of patients of whom some are needier while others have more health benefit. Nord shows that even one and the same person may significantly vary in his assignment of relative weights. As guiding criterion for treatment selection, Nord applies a combined measure (the so-called SAVE) in which both seriousness of the disease and treatment effect are taken into account by making use of the median weights assigned to these factors by different people. I do not think that this adequately and legitimately resolves the problem under consideration. As Madison Powers and Ruth Faden argue, '[A]ggregate statistics can mask deep moral and political

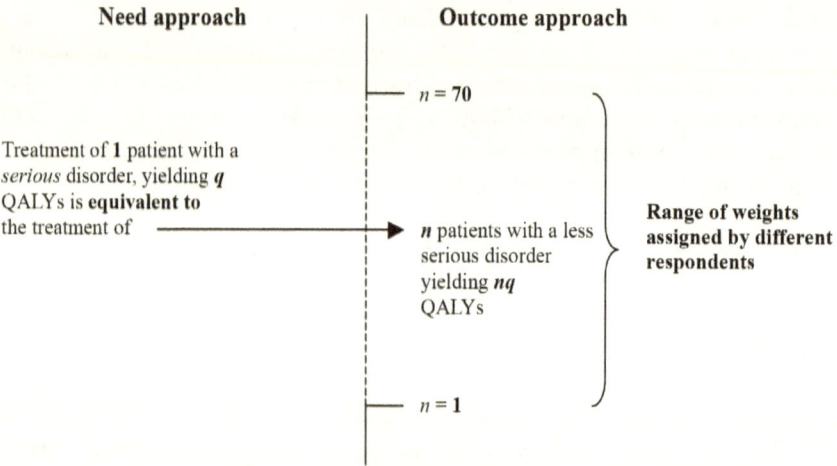

Figure 9.1. Relative weights assigned to need and outcome in Nord's study

divisions.'[6] Daniels and Sabin describe similar observations as those by Nord, among students and medical professionals:

> [P]eople ... vary considerably in how much benefit they are willing to sacrifice in order to give priority to worse-off patients.[7]

Therefore, it seems important to avoid intuitive weight assignment and aggregation of different values if we want to achieve distribution rules acceptable to all rational and reasonable people. Rawls himself has ingeniously tried to escape trade-offs between disparate values by means of his three principles of justice[8] (see chapter 7). A scheme of lexical priorities between these principles enables integration of liberty, equality, need and utility (total welfare) without having to balance and aggregate them. For instance, under the difference principle welfare and equality are combined without needing to balance them. Inequality is allowed if it benefits the least advantaged people. But this solution is not available for the present problem of distribution of scarce health resources: (1) obviously inequality in the distribution of health care resources cannot 'be arranged to the benefit of the least advantaged' as meant by the 'difference principle'. (b) In the context of distribution of health care resources most people reject assignment of lexical priority to one of the relevant values.[9] I had an interesting discussion with Dan Brock and Norman Daniels about this issue. They put the question whether it would perhaps be possible, by deliberation, to narrow down the wide range of weights assigned to need and outcome. Their question suggests that the wide range of differences in weight assignment is, at least partially, due to inconclusiveness rather than to indeterminateness and that increase in knowledge and exchange of insights could, at least in principle, promote convergence to consensus. I answered that, according to me, this is not plausible for two reasons. First, increase in information and knowledge would probably not make much difference because all participants to Nord's study were well informed, intelligent and acquainted with issues of health care distribution and they understood the questions well. Second, even the extremes of the zone of different weight assignments are not manifestly irrational or unreasonable. The wide range is the result of reasonable rather than unreasonable disagreement, and this makes a significant narrowing-down of the range of 'rationally permissible' weights improbable. This is supported by Daniels's own findings:[10]

> There is a considerable disagreement [amongst students and health professionals]: a definite but very small minority is inclined to be maximizers and a definite but very small minority is inclined to be maximiners. Most people fall in between and they vary considerably in how much benefit they are willing to sacrifice in order to give priority to worse-off patients.

Daniels further argues that the large interpersonal differences in weights which people assign to different moral concerns 'probably depend on how these moral concerns fit within wider conceptions of the good. . . . If so, there is good reason to think these disagreements will be a persistent feature of the situation'. In sum, not a lack of rationality, reasonableness or knowledge (inconclusiveness) seems to underlie the width of the range of different weights, but rather the deep moral divisions and the incommensurability of the competing relevant values themselves (indeterminateness). Madison Powers and Ruth Faden conclude: '[T]hese data encounter, in effect, the same philosophical impasse that moral theorists . . . have reached.'[11] If so, then it is not probable that deliberation may significantly narrow down the width of the range of divergent weights.

CONCLUSION

Finite health care resources may be allocated according to competing distribution systems in which the relevant aspects of justice and utility are weighed and ranked differently. Because these aspects are incommensurable, these distribution systems may be incompletely comparable. In that case we cannot say that one of the rival distributions of scarce health care resources is unambiguously and objectively better, worse or equally good as another. This means that reason under-determines the choice: each of the rival distribution systems is rationally permissible while none is rationally required. This is a perplexing conclusion because the distributions may have considerably different consequences for the health and lives of a great many people. Because our choice has such weighty and even tragic consequences, we would want to have the possibility to be guided by reason and to find a principled solution. The under-determination by reason is reflected in the divergent ways in which equally rational and intelligent people make different choices between the possible distributions. Similarly, different *societies* choose different distribution systems as has been shown by Calabresi and Bobbit in their insightful study about the divergent ways in which different countries try to resolve the conflicts with respect to allocation of 'tragically scarce resources'.[12] Steven Lukes has shown that these tragic choices are the result not of trade-offs – which are impossible due to the incommensurability of the relevant values – but of sacrifices.[13]

NOTES

1. Dan Brock, 'Ethical Issues in the Use of Cost Effectiveness Analysis for the Prioritisation of Health Care Resources', in *Public Health, Ethics, and Equity*, eds. Sudhir Anand, Fabienne Peter and Amartya Sen (Oxford: Oxford University Press, 2006); and Helga Kuhse and Peter Singer (eds.), *Bioethics: An Anthology* (Oxford: Blackwell Publishers Ltd, 2006), Part V, 'Resource Allocation', 399–474.

2. Frances Kamm, 'Deciding Whom to Help, Health-Adjusted Life Years and Disabilities', eds. Anand, Peter and Sen, 232.

3. John Rawls, *A Theory of Justice*, revised edition (Cambridge, Mass.: Belknap Press of Harvard University, 1999), especially section 7, 'Intuitionism', 30–36.

4. Compare Dan Brock, 'Ethical Issues in the Use of Cost Effectiveness Analysis for the Prioritisation of Health Care Resources', 213.

5. Erik Nord, 'The Trade-Off between Severity of Illness and Treatment Effect in Cost-Value Analysis of Health Care', *Health Policy* 24 (1993), 227–238. See especially table 1, 231, the first five rows in which treatment effect is assumed to be the same, while the seriousness of the disease (the need of treatment) differs.

6. Madison Powers and Ruth Faden, *Social Justice: The Moral Foundations of Public Health and Health Policy* (Oxford: Oxford University Press, 2006), 186.

7. Norman Daniels and James Sabin, 'Limits to Health Care: Fair Procedures, Democratic Deliberation, and the Legitimacy Problem for Insurers', *Philosophy & Public Affairs* 26 (1997), 320.

8. Rawls, *A Theory of Justice*, 266.

9. This is, among others, shown by Daniels and Sabin, 'Limits to Health Care: Fair Procedures, Democratic Deliberation, and the Legitimacy Problem for Insurers', 303–350: '[A] . . . very small minority is inclined to be maximizers and a . . . very small minority is inclined to be maximiners.'

10. Daniels and Sabin, 'Limits to Health Care', 303–350.
11. Powers and Faden, *Social Justice*, 186–187.
12. Guido Calabresi and Philip Bobbitt, *Tragic Choices: The Conflicts Society Confronts in the Allocation of Tragically Scarce Resources* (New York, London: W.W. Norton & Company, 1978), especially chap. 6 ('The Tragic Dilemma: Mixtures of Approaches').
13. Steven Lukes, 'Comparing the Incomparable: Trade-Offs and Sacrifices', in *Incommensurability, Incomparability, and Practical Reason*, ed. Chang (Cambridge Mass.: Harvard University Press, 1997).

Chapter 10

Legitimacy versus Integrity

SUMMARY

According to the liberal principle of legitimacy, basic principles of justice are legitimate only if all people affected can reasonably endorse them. An implication of this principle is the demand of restraint: basic principles of justice should not be based on reasons that are not justifiable in terms of public reason. The demand of restraint seems justified but may create problems. According to what might be called the principle of integrity, citizens should not be coerced to comply with principles, procedures and rules that violate their moral integrity and freedom of conscience. The aim of this chapter is to show that the liberal principle of legitimacy and demand of restraint may infringe the principle of integrity, *and* vice versa. This creates a moral dilemma or paradox in the sense that, in the relevant cases, the demand of restraint is simultaneously justified and unjustified. The upshot is that, in those cases, neither decision can avoid a moral deficit or element of injustice because either the liberal principle of legitimacy or the principle of integrity will be violated.

****

In his *Political Liberalism* John Rawls defends the so-called liberal principle of legitimacy:

> Our exercise of political power is fully proper only when it is exercised in accordance with a constitution the essentials of which all citizens as free and equal may reasonably be expected to endorse in the light of principles and ideals acceptable to their common human reason. . . . Only a political conception of justice that all citizens might be reasonably expected to endorse can serve as a basis of public reason and justification.[1]

The *liberal principle of legitimacy* may be summarized as follows:

> Constitutional essentials and principles of basic justice are legitimate only if they are capable of being endorsed by all reasonable people.

The principle has important implications. It entails that basic principles of justice cannot be legitimately founded on claims that are controversial between competing reasonable comprehensive beliefs and cannot be publicly justified with political reasons acceptable for all reasonable people. When we make moral demands on others, our personal justification is not sufficient: such demands require public justification. Not only Rawls but many other contemporary political theorists emphasize the moral significance of public justification and endorse the liberal principle of legitimacy in one form or another.[2] An important implication of the principle is that 'we refrain from building our basic political principles around any one of the contested comprehensive doctrines',[3] because such principles lack a public justification. Let us call this requirement of public justification the 'public/private split' or 'demand of restraint':[4]

> Matters of basic justice and constitutional essentials should not be based on reasons that are not justifiable in terms of public reason.

If the liberal principle of legitimacy is correct, the demand of restraint is justified because the latter is a logical corollary of the former. However, the demand of restraint may cause problems, even moral dilemmas and conscientious objections, for some citizens who have commitments and obligations that originate from their specific religious or moral beliefs. They cannot always translate their reasons to political reasons that are acceptable for all reasonable citizens. For instance, many theistic believers think euthanasia, abortion, in vitro fertilisation and genetic engineering are wrong and should be constitutionally prohibited, because they are supposed to be against the will of God. The latter reason originates from their specific contested comprehensive belief and is not justifiable in terms of public reason because it cannot be translated to political reasons that are acceptable for all reasonable citizens. That is why the demand of restraint does not permit it. This reveals that, in particular circumstances and for particular citizens, a conflict may occur between the demand of restraint and what might be called the 'principle of integrity'. This principle runs as follows:

> Citizens should not be coerced to act against their moral integrity, freedom of conscience and fundamental moral commitments naturally originating from a moral belief that is not irrational or unreasonable.

As we will discuss in the next section, many philosophers have shown the importance and reasonableness of (the idea behind) this principle.[5] Also Rawlsians and other adherers to the moral requirement of public justification will not deny the validity of the principle of integrity. In his *A Theory of Justice* Rawls emphasizes the significance of moral integrity and regards freedom of conscience as one of the basic liberties. We will show that denying the moral significance of the principle of integrity is in some respects even against the spirit of the liberal principle of legitimacy itself, and that if the former principle is violated, the latter is in a way violated as well. As we will see, this does not mean that the principle of integrity defeats the liberal principle of legitimacy, *and vice versa*. If so, we are confronted with a possible moral dilemma or paradox because, in the relevant cases, the demand of restraint seems simultaneously both justified and unjustified: it is justified as the natural consequence of the principle of legitimacy; it is unjustified because of the principle of integrity. This is revealed in the following two arguments – the *legitimacy argument* and the *integrity argument*. Both arguments seem sound but they lead to conflicting conclusions:

The legitimacy argument

Premise 1: Coercive principles of basic justice and constitutional essentials imposed on people who cannot reasonably endorse them, are not justified (the liberal principle of legitimacy).

Premise 2: Coercive principles of basic justice and constitutional essentials based on reasons that are not justifiable in terms of public reason cannot reasonably be endorsed by all reasonable people.

Premise 3: The demand of restraint ('public/private split') prevents that coercive principles of basic justice and constitutional essentials are based on reasons that are not justifiable in terms of public reason.

∴ The demand of restraint ('public/private split') is justified (conclusion 1).

The integrity argument

Premise 1: Coercive principles of basic justice and constitutional essentials imposed on people who cannot reasonably endorse them, are not justified (liberal principle of legitimacy).

Premise 2: Coercive principles of basic justice and constitutional essentials that may require the willingness to violate one's moral integrity, freedom of conscience and moral commitments originating from reasonable ethical comprehensive beliefs, cannot reasonably be endorsed.

Premise 3: Coercive principles of basic justice and constitutional essentials that are controlled and partly determined by the demand of restraint ('public/private split') may require the willingness of persons who adhere to reasonable religious or secular idealistic comprehensive beliefs to violate their moral integrity, freedom of conscience and moral commitments that naturally originate from these beliefs.

∴ The demand of restraint ('public/private split') is unjustified (conclusion 2).

If the two arguments are sound, the demand of restraint ('public/private split') is, in the relevant cases (where the demand of restraint clashes with the principle of integrity), both justified (conclusion 1) and unjustified (conclusion 2). In a comment on the previous two rival arguments G. A. Cohen argued that 'the conclusion is too vague' for him 'to be able to assess the contrasting trains of reasoning and to decide whether it is possible to affirm both. More than one thing can be meant by the public/private split'. However, what is meant by the public/private split in both arguments is defined earlier: it concerns the separation between, on the one side, public rules of basic justice and, on the other side, comprehensive-belief- and conception-of-the-good-based reasons for rules of basic justice: in the public private split the latter reasons are not allowed to determine rules of basic justice that cannot be reasonably accepted by people who have other reasonable comprehensive beliefs and do not share the relevant comprehensive-belief-based reasons. This formulation may leave room for ambiguities but the same meaning of the public/private split can be premised in both argumentations, without resolving the conflicting conclusion. Therefore, the ambiguity of the phrase 'public/private split' is an implausible explanation of the tension between both argumentations. Indeed, there is a real tension between, on the one side, the demand not to impose on other people principles of basic justice that they cannot reasonably endorse and, on the other side, the unacceptability of rules that require the violation of a reasonable conception of justice. This will further be discussed later.

The conclusion that the Doctrine of Restraint is both justified and unjustified, seems at odds with the non-contradiction rule of logic that the same proposition or thing (in this case, the demand of restraint) cannot be simultaneously true and not-true – in this case, 'justified' and 'not-justified'. If so, this would mean that at least one of the two conclusions must be false. However, as I will try to show, both arguments are sound and reveal a moral paradox rather than a contradiction. The paradox is caused by the fact that, in the relevant cases, the principle of legitimacy and the principle of integrity are simultaneously both right and wrong. They are right because the arguments supporting them are sound. They are wrong, because, in the relevant cases, the demand of restraint infringes the principle of integrity and, conversely, the principle of integrity infringes the demand of restraint. The upshot is that, in those cases, neither resolution can avoid a moral deficit or element of injustice because it violates either the liberal principle of legitimacy or the principle of integrity.

MORAL INTEGRITY

A citizen's moral or religious commitments may constitute an essential component of his identity. With respect to religious commitments Nicholas Wolterstorff writes:

> It belongs to the religious convictions of a good many religious people in our society that they *ought to base* their decisions concerning fundamental issues of justice on their religious convictions. They do not view it as an option whether or not to do so. It is their conviction that they ought to strive for wholeness, integrity, integration, in their lives. . . . Their religion is not, for them, about *something other* than their social and political existence.[6]

If so, bracketing religious and other moral commitments may mean bracketing essential aspects of one's very self. Rawls argues that 'it seems evident that parties must choose principles that secure the integrity of their religious and moral freedom'.[7] Still he characterizes the rejection of the demand of restraint as unreasonable, even if this happens by conscientious religious believers.[8] However, if freedom of conscience is a basic liberty, and if a coercive rule forces the moral/religious believer to give priority to the demand of restraint, this seems to violate a basic liberty. If so, then it is understandable and not unreasonable – at least according to the principle of integrity, but *not* according to the liberal principle of legitimacy – if believers reject – or cannot even but reject[9] – the demand of restraint where it conflicts with their conscience and moral commitments. Bhikhu Parekh summarizes this as follows:

> [R]eligious citizens, who are required to bracket out their deepest beliefs, are subjected to moral incoherence and self-alienation. . . . Allowing them to be guided by their religious beliefs but banning them from using these to defend their views in public does not improve the situation. It introduces self-alienation at a different level by requiring them to speak in a language different to the one in which they think. . . . Religious people generally seek wholeness in their lives and do not think it possible or desirable to separate their private and political concerns.[10]

Many other political philosophers have emphasized this problem, among others Christopher Eberle, John Finnis, Robert George, Christopher Wolfe, Patrick Neal, Michael Sandel and Nicholas Wolterstorff.[11] Also Rawls himself is aware of this tension, which he describes as follows:

> How can it be either reasonable or rational, when basic matters are at stake, for citizens to appeal only to a public conception of justice and not to the whole truth as they see it? Surely the most fundamental questions should be settled by appealing to the most important truths, yet these may far transcend public reason.[12]

Rawls recognizes 'that the roots of democratic citizens' allegiance to their political conceptions lie in their respective comprehensive doctrines, both religious and nonreligious'. Therefore, he has mitigated the condition of 'publicly acceptable reasons' by formulating his so-called proviso: 'Reasonable comprehensive doctrines, religious or nonreligious, may be introduced in public political discussion at any time, *provided* that in due course proper political reasons are presented.'[13] However, this means that the problem is transferred to the future rather than resolved, because the demand of restraint has to be satisfied 'in due course'.

CONFLICTING LIBERTIES

The conflict between the liberal principle of legitimacy and the principle of integrity concerns two competing fundamental human liberties: (1) the liberty from interference by coercive rules that cannot be reasonably endorsed (call this *negative* liberty 'liberty N'); (2) the liberty to live a life in which private and public are interwoven and in which integrated comprehensive political and moral ends are pursued (call this *positive* liberty 'liberty P'). While liberty N entails a wider private domain at the cost of liberty P, the latter entails a wider public domain at the cost of the liberty N; see also chapter 7. The demand of restraint increases liberty N and decreases liberty P. Doing away with this Demand induces the reverse. How should the dilemma between accepting and rejecting the demand of restraint be resolved? Rawls speaks of a paradox,[14] which he tries to resolve by invoking his principle of liberal legitimacy. But the two previous arguments make it implausible that this principle is capable of resolving the paradox, because both arguments take the principle of liberal legitimacy as starting point (premise 1), but lead to accepting *and* rejecting the public/private split. The approach of the earlier Rawls of finding the best total system of liberty from the perspective of the representative citizen will not offer a way out either. As Herbert Hart argues[15]

> Rawls says that when liberties conflict, the adjustment which is to secure 'the best total system' is to be settled from the standpoint of 'the representative equal citizen', and we are to ask which adjustment 'it would be rational for him to prefer'. This, he says, involves the application of the principle of the common interest or common good.

Hart continues:

> But . . . conflicts between basic liberties will be such that different resolutions of the conflict will correspond to the interests of different people who will diverge over the relative value they set on the conflicting liberties.

In other words, Rawls's 'representative rational agent' does not exist because the interests of rational citizens are divergent, leading to different rational assignments of weights, so that these citizens cannot be represented by one and the same rational agent. Rawls's own remarks about rational choice in the original position are relevant:[16]

> I have . . . assumed that [the persons in the original position] do not know their conception of the good. . . . How, then, can they decide which conceptions of justice are most to their advantage? . . . To meet this difficulty, I postulate that . . . they assume that they normally prefer more primary social goods rather than less. . . . [F]rom the standpoint of the original position, it is rational for the parties to suppose that they do want a larger share, since in any case they are not compelled to accept more if they do not wish to.

As Hart argues, this approach overlooks the fact that the same increase of a particular liberty for all does not always result in the same increase of overall liberty for all. For instance the same increase in positive liberty for all may mean a significant increase in overall liberty for religious and other ethical believers but it may mean a smaller increase, or even a decrease in overall liberty for 'non-idealistic believers'.[17] As Hart argues, the possible advantages of an increase in liberty for the relevant person has to be balanced against the possible disadvantages for this person due to the practice of the same increased liberty by others. Rawls continues that

> even though the parties are deprived of information about their particular ends, they have enough knowledge to rank the alternatives. They know that in general they must try to protect their liberties, widen their opportunities, and enlarge

their means for promoting their aims whatever these are. Guided by the theory of the good and the general facts of moral psychology, their deliberations are no longer guesswork. They can make a rational decision in the ordinary sense.

However, it is not always clear how determinate weights can be assigned to different liberties – in this case to liberty P and liberty N – without knowledge about the basic characteristics of one's plan of life. In some cases public reason needs all relevant sources for weight assignment to become sufficiently determinate (see chapter 7).

Rawls:

> a rational person is thought to have a coherent set of preferences between the options open to him. He ranks these options according to how well they further his purposes; he follows the plan which will satisfy more of his desires rather than less, and which has the greater chance of being successfully executed.

However, the plan 'satisfying more desires rather than less' of a particular rational agent (e.g., a non-idealistic believer) may differ from that of another rational agent (e.g., an idealistic religious believer) and there is no single rational plan representative for all rational plans. Rawls: '[In the original position] The parties must choose principles that secure the integrity of their religious and moral freedom.'[18] But principles that secure the integrity of citizens' freedom are not the same for idealistic and non-idealistic believers. For instance, as we have discussed, the doctrine of restraint (the public/private split) may secure the integrity of the freedom of non-idealistic believers but may violate the integrity of the freedom of idealistic believers.[19] Rawls:

> [T]he parties do not know how their religious or moral view fares in their society, whether, for example, it is in the majority or the minority. The question they are to decide is which principle they should adopt to regulate the liberties of citizens in regard to their fundamental religious, moral, and philosophical interests.[20]

Also religious believers and other 'idealistic believers' do not know how their belief 'fares in their society, whether, for example, it is in the majority or the minority'. Still they may assign much weight to liberty P and reject the public/private split although they know that they may belong to a minority, so that their liberty N may decrease due to possible coercive rules based on the dominant belief and made possible by liberty P exercised by the majority in the absence of the public/private split. Rawls:

> [T]he persons in the original position ... cannot take chances with their liberty by permitting the dominant religious or moral doctrine to persecute or to suppress others if it wishes.[21]

However, by rejecting the public/private split the religious and idealistic believers under consideration do not 'take chances with their liberty' because they do not reject the separation between Church and State (which should be distinguished from the public/private split): they agree with Rawls that all rational and reasonable people in the original position will choose for liberty of thought, religion and conscience and for democratic principles.

John Gray summarizes the problem as follows:[22]

> If basic liberties clash, there is no way of avoiding judgments of importance among the human interests they protect. Manifestly, such judgments will vary with different conceptions of the good. The argument of which among a set of rival liberties is to be protected, and in what degree, is then inescapably an argument about the good. . . . Once it is allowed that important liberties may be rivals, we are not far from accepting that their conflicts have no solutions that are acceptable to all reasonable persons.

This quotation puts into words not only that solutions to the conflict between the relevant liberties will not be similarly acceptable for all reasonable people, but also that solutions depend on judgments about the weights of the human interests these liberties protect. These weights, in turn, depend on the conceptions of the good people adhere to.

Elizabeth Anderson, who commented on an earlier version of the present text, replied as follows:

- Making every conscience a law unto itself, not just for oneself, but for others, entitled to exercise coercive power over others, is anarchy. This is not reasonable. On that view, jihadist terrorist are reasonable in asserting a right to murder random civilians.
- The social basis of self-respect does not require that people bow down to anyone's theological principles as authoritative for them. The only bases of self-respect that count are ones that are consistent with treating fellow citizens, who dissent from one's views, as equals. This is the core lesson of the wars of religion that Europe fought. If you reject that, then you toss out liberalism and democracy altogether.
- It is unreasonable to set up an individual's private conscience as a basis for asserting power over others.

Anderson's objections refer to views that are not the views under consideration in the present discussion, but they are helpful to further clarify the following three points. *First*, the relevant religious persons adhere to moral, philosophical, religious or secular beliefs that all belong to Rawls's reasonable comprehensive beliefs. They respect the principles of a liberal democracy, are not fanatic or fundamentalist, endorse the separation between religious and political authority and fully recognize freedom of thought, conscience and religion. They treat fellow citizens, who dissent from their views, as equals. They have more interest in liberty of religion and conscience than many others. This is not incompatible with having one's comprehensive belief played a significant part in public, politics and matters of basic justice. Compare Bhikhu Parekh's distinction between two 'secularist theses', on the one side the weaker version, which concerns separation between religion and *state* (separation of religious and political *authority*), and on the other side the stronger version, which concerns separation between religion and *politics* (separation of religion and political *decisions*).[23] The former does not automatically entail the latter. As Parekh notices, Montesquieu, Lord Acton and even Tocqueville advocated the separation between state and religion but rejected the separation between politics and religion. The rejection of the latter separation is perfectly compatible with a peaceful society without 'religious wars'. Kent Greenawalt writes:

> in this society [USA] religious divisiveness has occasionally been a serious problem, but one that has overwhelmed the capacity of the society to work. It has never been widely assumed that religious convictions are impermissible grounds for political decisions. The dangers of religious divisiveness that do exist can be largely countered by firm adherence to principles of religious liberty, nonsponsorship, and separation of religious and political authority.[24]

In my native country, the Netherlands, confessional political parties – such as the CDA (Christian Democratic Appeal) and the 'Christian Union'[25] – play (and have always played) a significant role without resulting in religious wars or anarchy. Adherents of these parties treat fellow citizens who dissent from their views as equals. *Second*, my claim is not that no constraints follow from the fact of reasonable pluralism but that, as discussed earlier, differing conclusions may be drawn from this fact, leading to differing constraints. *Third*, I do not 'set up an individual's private conscience as a reasonable basis for asserting power over others'. The legitimacy argument argues that coercive rules of justice based on reasons specifically related to particular comprehensive beliefs cannot reasonably be endorsed by people who adhere to rival reasonable comprehensive beliefs conflicting with these reasons. The integrity argument shows the other side but does not refute the legitimacy argument. I myself do not adhere to a religious or secular idealistic comprehensive belief and I do not take sides in favour of one of the two arguments. By contrast, I argue that both arguments are valid, but result in opposite conclusions. These opposite conclusions of equally valid arguments create the problem under consideration. This chapter tries to show this conflict between two kinds of reasonable (un)acceptability, which seems rationally irresolvable. This is different from regarding an individual's private conscience or commitment as a reasonable basis for asserting power over others, which is obviously not the case and is refuted by the legitimacy argument.

INDETERMINATENESS VERSUS INCONCLUSIVENESS

Let 'A' be a total system of liberties that adopts the public/private split and assigns more weight to liberty N and less to liberty P than system 'B' which rejects the public/private split (on the condition that the parties adhere to liberal democratic principles and support the separation of Church and State). For most non-idealistic comprehensive believers system A is better than system B. For many idealistic comprehensive believers B is better than A. How do we decide which system is, all things considered, the better one? Adam Swift, with whom I discussed this topic, gives the following answer:

> The issue is which of these freedoms is the *more important and more valuable*. Does any liberal theorist think that liberty P is more important than liberty N? By careful argument we can come to see which liberty is more valuable. I wonder whether there is a better solution than the one Rawls offers.

We have seen that Swift's question 'which of the freedoms is the more important and more valuable' cannot be objectively or determinately answered because these freedoms are 'incompletely comparable'. Swift's rhetorical question assumes that the relative weights of the relevant freedoms are objective data, to be found by thorough investigation and 'careful argument', independent of interests, aims, conceptions of the good or comprehensive beliefs. Because the relevant values are incommensurable, they have no objective or determinate relative weight. Therefore, the answer to the question 'Which liberty is more important and more valuable?' depends on the answer to the question 'More important and valuable for whom'? It is not surprising that Swift and many other liberal theorists – given their own 'background belief' – 'wonder whether there is a better solution than the one Rawls offers'. Unlike persons who adhere to religious or non-religious idealistic beliefs, Swift need not 'bracket' some of his convictions or violate some of his commitments. Bhikhu Parekh, Simon Blackburn and Herbert Hart are aware of this. Parekh:

> Secular citizens are able to lead whole and integrated lives whereas religious citizens, who are required to bracket out their deepest beliefs, are subjected to moral incoherence and self-alienation.[26]

Blackburn:

> As a liberal myself, I think that morally and politically Rawls is roughly right . . . But that is because I have no other independent principles that I have been asked to jettison as I think myself into the initial position.[27]

Hart:

> resolutions of the conflict [between different liberties] will correspond to the interests of different people who will diverge over the relative value they set on the conflicting liberties.[28]

Even within the premises of liberal democracy it is difficult to demonstrate that Rawls's principles are rationally superior to all other liberal sets of principles.[29] There are several political theorists who endorse the principles of a liberal democracy and do not regard Rawls's solution as the best one.[30] It is not my aim to take sides, but to investigate whether it is possible at all to speak in terms of overall, impersonal, impartial and rational superiority of a theory or 'solution' if the relevant multidimensional values are incommensurable which entails that they can be ranked in more than one rational and reasonable way.

Let us return to the question which system of liberties is, all things considered, the better one: system 'A' in which more weight is assigned to liberty N or system 'B' in which more weight is assigned to liberty P. According to the legitimacy argument, which concludes that the public/private split is justified, A is better than B. According to the integrity argument, which concludes that the doctrine is unjustified, B is better than A. So it seems to be the case that A is simultaneously better *and* worse than B. But this seems a logical contradiction. Seung and Bonevac defend the possibility of an option A being simultaneously better and worse than another option B:

> The ranking of A and B is indeterminate just in case it is reasonable to conclude that A is better than B, that A is worse than B, and that A and B are of equal value.[31]

Gerald Gaus disagrees:

> The essence of [Seung's and Bonevac's] indeterminate ranking is that there is 'more than one right solution for your choice'. For the moment let us take this as meaning that the following sentences all are justifiably accepted within the same system of belief: (1) A is better than B; (2) B is better than A; (3) A and B are of equal value. If we suppose that A is better than B implies that not (B is better than A), then (1) and (2) are inconsistent and thus believing both violates a

basic rationality condition. In something of an understatement, Seung and Bonevac admit that this 'sounds paradoxical'. This conception of indeterminacy ... commits them to strictly inconsistent beliefs. This seems a consequence worth avoiding.[32]

Gaus adds the following footnote:

Of course this inconsistency can be avoided by analyzing the situation in terms of having a reason to choose A over B, and a reason to choose B over A. As we have seen, reasons can come into conflict.

This footnote articulates the very problem. The legitimacy argument constitutes a reason to choose system A over system B, while the integrity argument constitutes a reason to choose system B over system A. Similarly, if two agents have conflicting aims and interests the comparative value judgments may put both parties in the right without becoming inconsistent. Compare this with what Lyotard calls a *differend*:

A *differend* (in contrast to a litigation) is a case of conflict that cannot be equitably resolved for lack of a rule of judgment applicable to both arguments. One side's legitimacy does not imply the other's lack of legitimacy. A single rule would do wrong one of both.[33]

Take as 'a single rule' the Doctrine of Restraint (public/private split). Starting from the *Liberal Principle of Legitimacy* 'one side's legitimacy does not imply the other's lack of legitimacy'. This seems to mean that the controversy has no objectively right answer. The resistance against this 'indeterminacy' is understandable, because it has serious consequences. In Ronald Dworkin's words:

We claim not just that there is no right answer, 'no decisive reason to take one side or the other, and may never have one, but that, no matter how hard we look and think, we will not find any consideration or argument that would make the case on one side even marginally stronger than the case on the other.[34]

Dworkin rightly argues that even persistent controversy is no reason to suppose that right choices among values are impossible.[35] It may be the case that, if we continue in our research, we may find a (single) right answer. It is true that from persistent disagreement as such – even disagreement between competent, well-informed and rational people – one cannot conclude that the issue is indeterminable in principle, that is, that there is no right answer or that both sides are right. If there is disagreement between two competent weather forecasters about the question whether it will rain tomorrow, this does obviously not show that there is no right answer or that both weather forecasters are right.[36] Here the disagreement does obviously not mean that the issue is indeterminable instead of inconclusive: there is one right answer, which will become clear tomorrow. Gaus:

> It is by complexity that inconclusiveness arises. . . . As the complexity of the issue and the number of variables increase, so does disagreement.[37]

It is questionable, however, whether, in the issues under consideration, an explanation in terms of 'inconclusiveness due to the complexity of the issue of public justification' is adequate and sufficient. The popularity of the inconclusiveness view is not only explainable from the (for many unacceptable) implications of indeterminateness but can also be explained by the pervasive assumption, that there are only three possible value relations between two alternatives A and B: (1) A is better than B, (2) A is worse than B and (3) A and B are equally good. This excludes the possibility that A is neither better nor worse than B while A and B are not equivalent either. The latter possibility means that A and B are 'incompletely comparable' due to their incommensurability. The rival 'liberty systems A and B', mentioned earlier, are incompletely comparable because liberties N and P, which are differently balanced in the two systems, are incommensurable and therefore incapable of being weighed on a single scale. This means that it is objectively indeterminate rather than inconclusive which system of liberties is overall the best, most reasonable or legitimate one. Bhikhu Parekh:

> arguments involve reasons. Since the latter cannot always be disengaged from moral values some of which are incommensurable, arguments are often mutually irreducible and incapable of being weighed on a single scale. To talk of 'weighing-up' arguments and opting for ones that are 'weightier' or 'stronger' is to take a naively homogeneous view of them.[38]

The final choice between the relevant liberty systems A and B can only be partially justified. The argument that a partial justification 'is at least a justification' does not resolve the predicament, because 'partial justification' means that there is no overall justification for the choice of one alternative *rather than* the other and that the alternative decision would not have been less justified than the actual decision. Amartya Sen summarizes the key problem:

> Would a sequence of pairwise comparisons invariably lead us to the very best? That presumption has some appeal, since the superlative might indeed appear to be the natural end point of a robust comparative. But this conclusion would, in general, be a *non sequitur*. In fact, it is only with a 'well-ordered' ranking (for example, a complete and transitive ordering over a finite set) that we can

be sure that the set of pairwise comparisons must also identify a 'best' alternative.... Incompleteness may be of the lasting kind for several different reasons, including ... judgmental unresolvability involving disparate considerations that cannot entirely eliminated, even with full information.[39]

And:

> When there are several objects of value, one alternative course of action may be more valued in one respect but less so in another ... [We may be] faced with an irreducible conflict of compelling principles [and] ... admit both the superiority of one alternative over the other and the converse ... [N]eeds of policy do require that something or other must be ultimately done.... However, it does not follow – and this is the important point to get across – that there must be *adequate reason* for choosing one course rather than another. Incompleteness ... in overall judgements might well be a damned nuisance for decisions, but the need for a decision does not, on its own, *resolve* the conflict. This implies that sometimes even institutional public decisions may have to be taken on the basis of partial justification.[40]

PRIMA FACIE DUTIES

It seems that the legitimacy argument and the integrity argument are based on two valid moral principles: the principle of legitimacy and the principle of integrity. Moral principles – and the duties that originate from them – may conflict. In order to know what's the right thing to do, we may be required to weigh them against each other. If one principle or duty outweighs the other, satisfying the former is the right thing to do. This does not necessarily mean that the outweighed duty did not concern a real obligation. It means, what Ross calls, a *'prima facie* duty', which has to be satisfied only if it does not clash with a weightier duty.[41] We have seen that the liberal principle of legitimacy and the principle of integrity are generally recognized as sound moral principles. It is true that Rawls (like many other political philosophers) emphasizes the importance of the liberal principle of legitimacy. But, as discussed earlier, he simultaneously argues, '[I]t seems evident that parties must choose principles that secure the integrity of their religious and moral freedom.'[42] Similarly, other thinkers who emphasize the importance of the principle of integrity do not generally deny the importance of public justification. However, the fact that the two principles may clash suggests that the moral obligations originating from these principles concern *prima facie* rather than absolute duties. If so, this seems to entail that the conflict between the two principles should be resolved by determining which principle outweighs the other. Many liberals (especially those for whom the demand of restraint does not cause conscientious objections) may assign more weight to the liberal principle of legitimacy than to the principle of integrity. By contrast, many religious believers (especially those for whom the demand of restraint does cause conscientious objections) will do the opposite. However, it does not seem plausible that one of the two principles definitely, unambiguously and impartially outweighs, or deserves lexical priority to, the other. If so, neither principle is definitely defeated by the other and both principles remain valid: it remains wrong to impose rules of basic justice on people who cannot reasonably endorse them *and* it remains wrong to infringe a person's integrity, moral identity and freedom of conscience (provided that they are related to a belief that is not irrational or unreasonable). Interestingly, even the liberal principle of legitimacy itself supports, in some respects, the principle of integrity. Remember that the liberal principle of legitimacy means that constitutional essentials and principles of basic justice are legitimate only if they are capable of being endorsed by all reasonable people. As formulated in premise 2 of the integrity argument, '[C]oercive principles of basic justice and constitutional essentials that may require the willingness to violate one's moral integrity, freedom of conscience and moral commitments cannot reasonably be endorsed.' And as formulated in premise 3 of this argument, '[C]oercive principles of basic justice and constitutional essentials that are controlled and partly determined by the demand of restraint may require the willingness of persons who adhere to reasonable religious or secular idealistic comprehensive beliefs to violate their moral integrity, freedom of conscience and moral commitments that naturally originate from these beliefs.' Citizens cannot reasonably be expected to act against their moral integrity and freedom of conscience. So, even from the spirit of liberal principle of legitimacy itself, we cannot deny the moral significance of the principle of integrity, because violation of the latter principle entails to some extent the violation of the former principle.

MORAL PARADOX

Taking together the liberal principle of legitimacy and the principle of integrity we seem to be confronted with a contradiction, revealed by the two opposing arguments – the legitimacy argument and the integrity argument, mentioned in the introduction: the demand of restraint is both justified (according to the former argument) and unjustified (according to the latter argument). We indicated that this seems at odds with the non-contradiction rule of logic: the same thing cannot be simultaneously p *and* not-p. Also G. A. Cohen, who commented on an earlier version of the text, struggled with the two arguments, because he thinks that they form a contradiction. He argued: 'If one of these arguments is sound, it refutes the other. The only way it can fail to do so is through being unsound.' However, the two arguments reveal a paradox rather than a contradiction. Aristotle's principle of logical non-contradiction runs as follows: The same thing cannot be true and not true at the same time in the same respect. In the present case the conclusion 'justified' and 'not justified' refers to the same thing (demand of restraint) at the same time but not with respect to the same 'value' and not with respect to the same agents. It is with respect to basic liberty N and with respect to non-religious and other 'non-idealistic' believers (who rightly resist coercive rules they cannot reasonably endorse) that the demand of restraint is 'justified'. By contrast, it is with respect to basic liberty P and with respect to religious and other 'idealistic' believers (who cannot reasonably ignore their comprehensive conception of justice, moral commitments and obligations, and their conscientious objections) that the demand of restraint is 'unjustified'. The controversy cannot be reduced to merely conflicting interests of different parties. The conflicting interests are closely related to the conflicts between the relevant principles and values themselves on which these interests are based. That is why this conflict or tension may occur not only between, but also within, individuals. Indeed, few people will deny the importance and at least *pro tanto* validity of each of the two principles.[43] Religious or other 'idealistic' believers may experience a dilemma between the demands of their moral commitments and the demand of public justification.[44] Besides, these believers may acknowledge that their specific moral reasons may not satisfy the liberal principle of legitimacy. Even if, for themselves, their personal moral commitments outweigh the demand of public justification, they need not deny the importance of the latter. Similarly and conversely, 'non-idealistic' believers may acknowledge that the reasons for the demand of restraint may not be sufficient for religious and other 'idealistic' believers to infringe their conscience and refrain from their moral commitments with respect to the basic structure of society (although these commitments cannot be justified by political reasons).

If the previous reasoning is correct, the conclusion that the demand of restraint is *both* justified *and* unjustified concerns a paradox instead of a logical contradiction or incoherence.[45] A paradox is 'an apparently unacceptable conclusion derived by apparently acceptable reasoning from apparently acceptable premises'.[46] As Saul Smilansky shows, '[W]e can have paradox with logical impunity.'[47] There are different kinds of paradox.[48] The legitimacy argument and the integrity argument seem to form two kinds of paradoxes: (1) A paradox that W. V. Quine calls a *paradox of antinomy*, which means that two chains of argument lead to conflicting results, each of which seems to be well supported. We cannot see a way of giving up either, but neither can we hold on to both. (2) A paradox which Smilansky calls an *existential paradox*, which he describes as follows:

> In an existential paradox the conclusion appears absurd even after due reflection, but it needs to be simply accepted as true in spite of its absurdity.... The fault is not in the assumptions or in the argumentation that leads from them to the paradoxical conclusion, . . . but in the 'reality' this conclusion describes. Philosophers who encountered non-moral paradoxes were led, historically, by the emphasis on strict contradiction to focus on exploring what has gone wrong, namely, the premises of the argument or its validity.... But . . . in the 'existential paradox' . . . we do not need to backtrack desperately and examine how we got to the conclusion, in order to dispose of it, but on the contrary – the paradoxical result is a revelation of how things are.[49]

If the liberal principle of legitimacy does not determinately and impartially outweigh the principle of integrity, and vice versa, the paradox constitutes a dilemma, because, in the relevant cases, the demand of restraint is partially justified and partially unjustified. Then we seem incapable of completely justifying the ultimate decision by arguing that it is, all things considered, the right thing to do. In those cases an element of injustice or violation of a moral obligation may not be avoided, whether we take a decision according to the liberal principle of legitimacy or according to the principle of integrity. If so, there is no fault in the reasoning, but a paradoxical conflict in reality. The conclusion from the two argumentations shows similarities with a conflict between two 'oughts' described by Bernard Williams.[50] In our case it concerns an 'ought' (of not imposing rules of justice on people who cannot reasonably endorse them) towards two different kinds of persons mentioned earlier. It is impossible to optimally meet the 'ought' towards one group without interfering with the 'ought' towards the other group. However, as Williams argues, the incompatibility of two oughts does not show (e.g., by an '*ought* implies *can*' reasoning) that one of the 'oughts' is mistaken and should be rejected. Whatever may be the case with respect to the validity of two 'oughts', we have seen that the two arguments (whether they concern 'oughts' or not) do not contain a contradiction or another fault, but reflect a real and rationally irresolvable conflict between two incommensurable and incompletely compatible liberties.

NOTES

1. John Rawls, *Political Liberalism* (New York: Columbia University Press, 1996), 137.
2. For instance, Brian Barry, *Justice as Impartiality* (Oxford: Clarendon Press, 1999), chap. 3; Jürgen Habermas, *The Inclusion of the Other: Studies in Political*

Theory, eds. Ciaran Cronin and Pablo De Greiff (Cambridge, Mass.: MIT Press, 1998), 42; Charles Larmore, *Patterns of Moral Complexity* (Cambridge: Cambridge University Press, 1988); Thomas Nagel, 'Moral Conflict and Political Legitimacy', *Philosophy and Public Affairs* 16 (1987): 221; Martha Nussbaum, 'Political Objectivity', *New Literary History* 32 (2001): 886–887; Thomas Scanlon, 'Contractualism and Utilitarianism', in *Utilitarianism and Beyond*, eds. Amartya Sen and Bernard Williams (Cambridge: Cambridge University Press, 1982), 110; Thomas Scanlon, *What We Owe to Each Other* (Cambridge, Mass.: Belknap Press of Harvard University Press, 2000), 5.

3. Nussbaum, '"Political Objectivity," 886–887.

4. This name is borrowed from Christopher Eberle's 'doctrine of restraint'. See Christopher Eberle, *Religious Conviction in Liberal Politics* (Cambridge: Cambridge University Press, 2002), 68.

5. Cf. Eberle, *Religious Conviction in Liberal Politics*; John Finnis, 'Abortion, Natural Law, and Public Reason', in *Natural Law and Public Reason*, eds. Robert P. George and Christopher Wolfe (Washington, D.C.: Georgetown University Press, 2000); Robert P. George and Christopher Wolfe, 'Introduction', eds. Robert P. George and Christopher Wolfe; Patrick Neal, 'Political Liberalism, Public Reason, and the Citizen of Faith', eds. Robert P. George and Christopher Wolfe; Bhikhu Parekh, *Rethinking Multiculturalism: Cultural Diversity and Political Theory* (New York: Palgrave, 2000); Michael Sandel, *Liberalism and the Limits of Justice* (Cambridge: Cambridge University Press, 1998); Nicholas Wolterstorff, 'The Role of Religion in Decision and Discussion of Political Issues', in *Religion in the Public Square: The Place of Religious Convictions in Political Debate*, eds. Robert Audi and Nicholas Wolterstorff (London: Rowman & Littlefield, 1997).

6. Audi and Wolterstorff, *Religion in the Public Square*, 105.

7. John Rawls, *A Theory of Justice*, revised edition (Cambridge, Mass.: Belknap Press of Harvard University Press, 1999), 181.

8. Rawls, *Political Liberalism*, 240–247.

9. The 'dialogue on the original position' in Neal, 'Political Liberalism, Public Reason, and the Citizen of Faith', 185–188, which I have quoted in chapter 7, gives an insightful illustration of this problem.

10. Parekh, *Rethinking Multiculturalism*, 323–324.

11. Eberle, *Religious Conviction in Liberal Politics*; Finnis, 'Abortion, Natural Law, and Public Reason'; George and Wolfe, 'Introduction'; Neal, 'Political Liberalism, Public Reason, and the Citizen of Faith'; Sandel, *Liberalism and the Limits of Justice*; and Wolterstorff, 'The Role of Religion in Decision and Discussion of Political Issues'.

12. Rawls, *Political Liberalism*, 216.

13. John Rawls, 'The Idea of Public Reason Revisited', *University of Chicago Law Review* 64 (1997); John Rawls, 'The Idea of Public Reason Revisited', in *The Law of Peoples*, ed. John Rawls (Cambridge, Mass.: Harvard University Press, 2000), 152.

14. Rawls, *Political Liberalism*, 216.

15. Herbert Hart, 'Rawls on Liberty and its Priority', *University of Chicago Law Review* 40 (1973): 544.

16. John Rawls, *A Theory of Justice*, 123–124.

17. Non-idealistic believers in the sense that their comprehensive beliefs do not contain strong moral and other idealistic commitments with respect to the society and the public domain.

18. Rawls, *A Theory of Justice*, 181.

19. Cf. Parekh, *Rethinking Multiculturalism*, 323; Simon Blackburn, *Ruling Passions: A Theory of Practical Reasoning* (Oxford: Oxford University Press, 2000), 273–274; and Hart, 'Rawls on Liberty and its Priority', 545. Cf. David Reidy: '[T]here is no obvious way to adopt a view wider than Rawls's without revising or abandoning his understanding of political autonomy and liberal legitimacy.' Reidy notes that this issue may concern 'serious, perhaps the most serious, questions raised by Rawls's ideal of public reason'. See David Reidy, 'Rawls's Wide View of Public Reason: Not Wide Enough', *Res Publica* 6 (2000): 52, 53, 72.

20. Rawls, *A Theory of Justice*, 181.

21. Ibid., 181.

22. John Gray, *Two Faces of Liberalism* (Cambridge/Oxford: Polity Press, 2000), 81–82.

23. Parekh, *Rethinking Multiculturalism*, 322.

24. Kent Greenawalt, *Religious Convictions and Political Choice* (Oxford: Oxford University Press, 1988), 160.

25. The latter party denies that there is a 'right' to abortion.

26. Parekh, *Rethinking Multiculturalism*, 323.

27. Simon Blackburn, *Ruling Passions: A Theory of Practical Reasoning* (Oxford: Oxford University Press, 2000), 273–274.

28. Hart, 'Rawls on Liberty and Its Priority', 545.

29. Compare Kent Greenawalt, *Religious Convictions and Political Choice*, 186.

30. To mention some renowned theorists: John Finnis, John Gray, Michael Sandel, Jerry Cohen, Robert Nozick, Robert George, Christopher Wolfe, Christopher Eberle, Kent Greenawalt, Bhikhu Parekh, Chantal Mouffe and Iris Young.

31. Seung and Bonevac, 'Plural Values and Indeterminate Rankings', *Ethics* 102 (1992): 799–813, 802.

32. Gerald Gaus, *Justificatory Liberalism* (Oxford: Oxford University Press, 1996): 154.

33. Jean-François Lyotard, *The Differend: Phrases in Dispute* (Minneapolis: University of Minnesota Press, 1988), xi.

34. Ronald Dworkin, 'Indeterminacy in Law', in *The Oxford Companion to Philosophy*, ed. Ted Honderich (Oxford: Oxford University Press), 399. Dworkin speaks about indeterminacy in law, but his comment is equally applicable to justice.

35. Ronald Dworkin, *Taking Rights Seriously* (Cambridge, Mass.: Harvard University Press, 1978), 331–338.

36. I owe this example to Gerald Gaus.

37. Gaus, *Justificatory Liberalism*, 156.

38. Parekh, *Rethinking Multiculturalism*, 310.

39. Amartya Sen, 'What Do We Want from a Theory of Justice', *Journal of Philosophy* 103 (2006): 223.

40. Amartya Sen, *On Ethics and Economics* (Oxford: Blackwell Publishers, 2003), 67.

41. William David Ross, *The Right and the Good* (Oxford: Oxford University Press, 1930).

42. Rawls, *A Theory of Justice*, 181.

43. Cf. Amartya Sen, *The Idea of Justice* (London: Penguin Books, 2009), x, who writes with respect to plural principles of justice: 'Pluralities can survive even within a given community, or even for a particular person.' The intrapersonal tension between legitimacy and integrity that may occur within a religious believer is described by Greenawalt, *Religious Convictions and Political Choice*, 5.

44. This tension is described by Kent Greenawalt which he calls his 'personal and professional dilemma'. See Greenawalt, *Religious Convictions and Political Choice*, 5.

45. Interestingly, Rawls himself speaks in this context about a paradox which he tries to resolve by the liberal principle of legitimacy. We have seen that this fails because this principle works in two opposite directions and contributes to, rather than resolves, the paradox.

46. R. M. Sainsbury, *Paradoxes* (Cambridge: Cambridge University Press, 1996), 1. Quoted by Saul Smilansky in *Ten Moral Paradoxes* (Oxford: Blackwell Publishing, 2007).

47. Smilansky in *Ten Moral Paradoxes*, 128.

48. Willard Van Orman Quine, *The Ways of Paradoxes and Other Essays* (Cambridge, Mass.: Harvard University Press, 1976). Quoted by Saul Smilansky, *Ten Moral Paradoxes*.

49. Smilansky in *Ten Moral Paradoxes*, 4–5.

50. Bernard Williams, *Problems of the Self* (Cambridge: Cambridge University Press, 1999), chap. 11, 'Ethical Consistency', 166–186.

Chapter 11

Partial Justice

SUMMARY

Impartiality is a central feature of justice. Therefore, 'partial justice' seems a contradiction in terms. Still it is questionable whether jurisdiction can always avoid partiality. In chapters 5–10 we have seen that there are conflicts of justice that cannot be completely and impartially resolved due to incommensurability of competing principles. In this light it is conceivable that judges cannot always give a complete and impartial justification of a decision between conflicting claims, if these are based on incommensurable principles of justice. The trials against the Dutch Member of Parliament and anti-Islam campaigner Geert Wilders will be taken as an example to investigate this issue. I will argue that it may happen that two rival parties in a judicial dispute may both have a legitimate claim neither of which outweighs the other. In those cases the justification of the final decision cannot always avoid being 'partial' in the double sense of 'incomplete' and 'biased'. A possible way out is a paradigm shift in our thinking about justice.

****

The aim of this chapter is to discuss the question whether justice and jurisdiction are always capable of being impartial, at least in principle. If there are conflicts of justice that cannot be completely and impartially resolved, as we have seen in chapters 5–10, then it is conceivable that judges cannot always give a complete and impartial justification of a decision between conflicting claims based on rival aspects of justice. This would mean that in the relevant cases the realization of justice would be 'partial' in the double sense of 'incomplete' and 'biased'. Impartiality is a central feature of justice, which is symbolized by Justitia's blindfold. Therefore, 'partial justice' and 'partial jurisdiction' seem to be contradictions in terms.

The trials in 2010 and 2016 against the Dutch member of parliament and anti-Islam campaigner Geert Wilders offer an opportunity to investigate this question. Wilders was on trial for the charge of discrimination, group insult and inciting hatred against Muslims and Moroccans. Wilders's trial seems related to a clash between different aspects of justice. As the public prosecutor in the second trial put it, the case is about a conflict between freedom of speech and the freedom from discrimination. Freedom of expression is a basic liberty and a form of autonomy, the protection of which concerns an important aspect of justice. However, freedom from psychological oppression, protection against hate speech and discrimination, protection of human dignity and the social basis for self-respect are important aspects of justice as well. John Rawls calls self-respect one of the most important primary goods (see chapter 7). And mutual respect is a basis of advanced democracies. It is plausible that the kind of speech used by Wilders undermines this fundamental value and forms a threat to social peace. It makes life much more difficult for many of those to whom the speech is directed. It may undermine the assurance that people need to rely on: '[T]he assurance that they can go about their daily life and their ordinary business without fear of being denigrated and excluded as subhuman or second-class citizens.'[1] So Wilders's trial seems to concern a conflict between important aspects of justice, which may be summarized as the right to free speech versus the right not to be discriminated and the 'right to dignity', in the sense of a person's basic entitlement to be regarded as a full member of society.[2] John Rawls was aware that without a determinate ranking of conflicting principles of justice serious decision problems couldn't be avoided. In *A Theory of Justice* he argues that

> a conception of right must impose an ordering on conflicting claims. This requirement springs directly from the role of its principles in adjusting competing demands.[3]

And

> [i]nstitutions are just when . . . the rules determine a proper balance between competing claims. . . . The assignment of weights is an essential part of a conception of justice. If we cannot explain how these weights are to be determined by reasonable ethical criteria, the means of rational discussion have come to an end.[4]

As we have discussed in chapter 7 Rawls recognized the difficulty of impartial weight assignment to competing claims of justice. Therefore, he has tried to avoid the need of weight assignment and to construct a hierarchy or system of *lexical* priorities between rival principles. Because the Dutch constitution does not give a ranking – and does not indicate the relative weights – of the competing rights and aspects of justice, judges themselves will have to balance them in order to determine which one outweighs the other in concrete cases. Some think that it is merely a question of correctly interpreting and applying the rules of the law. But if principles conflict, the law does not always give an unambiguous answer, so that weighing them cannot always be avoided. The question to be answered is whether judges are capable of doing this in an impartial way.

THESIS

I will argue that it may be the case that the justification of the final decision in Wilders's trial cannot avoid being 'partial' in the double sense of 'biased' and 'incomplete'. This chapter is tentative. It concerns a complicated and controversial question. If my conclusions are true, they have far-reaching consequences for jurisdiction concerning conflicting values and competing rights and aspects of justice. In jurisdiction and penal law it is often tacitly assumed that the accused party is *either* guilty *or* not guilty; or that, in a conflict between two parties, A and B, *either* A is right and B wrong, *or* A is wrong and B right. On the face of it, these 'either/or' assumptions seem valid because, in the relevant cases 'and/and' conclusions seem incoherent. The latter would mean that the accused party may simultaneously be wrong *and* right; guilty *and* not guilty. This seems to violate Aristotle's rule of non-contradiction, which states that the same thing cannot be true and not true at the same time in the same respect. On further consideration it is less evident that the 'either/or' assumption is true. The 'either/or' assumption presupposes that a third possibility (a 'tie judgment') does not exist, while such a possibility does exist in many other fields. A game may end in a draw, a game of chess may result in a stalemate and a voting may tie. And in weighing two values, it is not necessarily the case that one value or principle outweighs the other: they may have equal weight. As we have seen in chapter 1 there is still another possibility: 3NT. Neither side outweighs the other, while they do not have equal weight either. I will argue that it may happen that both sides in a judicial dispute have a legitimate claim neither of which outweighs the other.

THE JUDGE'S MEMBERSHIP OF A POLITICAL PARTY

In the 2010 trial against Wilders his legal adviser Bram Moszkowicz challenged judge Moors twice. The first challenge concerned some of Moors's remarks, which raised the appearance of partiality. The remarks gave Wilders the feeling that he was debating with a member of parliament from the political party D66. The challenge was dismissed: Moors's remarks were not regarded as a sign of partiality. An editorial in the Dutch newspaper *NRC* (9 October 2010) gave the following comment:

> In a democratic constitutional state a party membership is irrelevant; even if each judge would be a member of any party. The power is regulated by justice, which has been democratically determined and in this way prevents arbitrariness and legal insecurity. The judicial interpretation of rules of law has been assigned to independent judges. . . . The particular predilection and persuasion of a judge is not only unimportant, it is irrelevant to her work.

The writer of this editorial supposes that legal interpretations are entirely separated, and separable, from personal political and ethical dispositions and predilections. However, as several legal theorists point out, and as we will discuss in more detail later, the distinction between politics and the formulation and application of legal rules is less strict than it, on the face of it, seems to be.[5] It is true that judges have to neutrally apply the rules laid down in the law, but, as said before, the law is silent about their ranking and about how to take a decision if they conflict. The judge herself has to 'balance' the rules and the values and interests on which the rules are based. In the case under consideration the judge has to weigh the right to freedom of speech against the right to freedom from insult, hate and discrimination.

JUSTITIA'S BLINDFOLD AND TWO KINDS OF IMPARTIALITY

Impartiality is an ambiguous concept. It may refer to at least two distinct kinds of impartiality:

1. Impartiality with respect to the *person(s)*. This requires that the judge passes a judgement 'without distinction of person'.
2. Impartiality with respect to the *case*. This requires that the judge rules out her personal belief or predilection with respect to the case and that she passes an objective or intersubjective, instead of subjective, judgment. This kind of impartiality is usually called 'neutrality'.

Justitia's blindfold protects against partiality towards the *person* but does not guarantee neutrality with respect to the *case*, because it does not rule out the judges' personal beliefs and predilections. Therefore, impartiality in the first sense and second sense are not mutually inclusive: impartiality towards the person does not necessarily include neutrality towards the case, and *vice versa*. This entails that, if judge Moors was impartial towards Wilders as a person, this does not necessarily mean that he was neutral with respect to the case.

THE CASE

With respect to Wilders's trial at least four questions are relevant:

(1) Did Wilders violate article 137c of the Dutch penal code, that is, did he offend a group, in this case, the Muslims?
(2) Did he violate article 137d of the penal code, that is, did he incite to discrimination and hate?
(3) Does the right to free speech cease where it transforms into hate speech and insult? Or does free speech not exclude hate speech?
(4) If free speech does not end where hate speech and insult start, does it outweigh what Waldron calls 'the right to dignity'[6] and the right to be protected against injury, discrimination, stigmatization and psychological oppression?

The answers to the first two questions are, to a large extent, determined by the interpretation of the terms in which these articles are expressed, such as 'offence', 'incitement' and 'discrimination'. These concepts are contestable and poly-interpretable.

LIMITS TO FREEDOM OF EXPRESSION

The nature of the questions (3) and (4) mentioned earlier is fundamentally different from that of the first two questions. They concern evaluative judgments about complicated and controversial philosophical issues. It is implausible that judges are capable of univocally resolving issues about which political philosophers and legal theorists are deeply divided. Some philosophers, for instance, John Stuart Mill, believe that speech can offend but cannot harm.[7] Others concede that it can harm but that this harm does not outweigh the benefits and does not outweigh the harms due to suppression of free speech. Not surprisingly, Salman Rushdie defends the freedom to offend: 'What is freedom of expression? Without the freedom to offend, it ceases to exist.' Michael Dummett, an emeritus Oxford philosopher, criticizes Rushdie for failing to appreciate that people can be deeply insulted and hurt when, what they hold most dear, is mocked and vulgarized. According to Dummett, quoted by Parekh,[8] Rushdie lacks 'the concept of something's being holy' and shared the western intellectual's arrogant assumption that religious believers 'may properly be affronted, indeed deserve to be affronted'. The distinction between 'offensive for' and 'offensive about' a religious group is, with respect to the effects of the relevant speech, largely artificial. This is crucial because it is usually argued (also by Wilders and his lawyer) that only offending persons and not defaming a religion is punishable. If religion is part of one's identity defaming the religion entails offending the religious believers. I will return to this point later in this chapter.

VEIL OF IGNORANCE

As we noticed already, Justitia's blindfold protects against partiality towards the *person* but does not guarantee neutrality with respect to the *case*, because it does not rule out the judges' personal beliefs and predilections. Like other people, judges will have a specific view on world and society, originating from their personal comprehensive beliefs, including their moral and political convictions. Just as it is important that the judge is behind a metaphorical blindfold ('Justitia's blindfold'), which renders her impartial towards the relevant person, so it is important that she is behind a kind of Rawlsian 'veil of ignorance', which renders her 'ignorant' about her personal background belief and makes her neutral towards the case under consideration. However, it is implausible that she, however honest and truthful she may be, is capable of completely detaching herself from her personal convictions, predilections and background beliefs. Besides, if the reasons for either decision do not objectively and determinately outweigh the reasons for the rival decision, and if the law does not determinately guide the decision, the elimination of one's background belief (if possible at all) may render the judge incapable of passing a decisive judgment. See chapter 7 for a more detailed discussion of this problem.

IMPLEMENTATION OF THE LAW

One could reply that judges must merely apply the rules of law. However, as discussed earlier, these rules are sometimes ambiguous and poly-interpretable. More important, indeterminacies in law are not rare.[9] In the case under consideration indeterminateness is caused not only by the contestable and poly-interpretable notions 'discrimination' and 'incitement to hate', but especially by the law's silence or lack of clarity with respect to the comparative importance of the relevant rights and principles and their constraints. If there is no consensus about the right interpretation and balance, then dependence on the judge's discretion seems unavoidable.

The website 'Rechtspraak.nl' of the Dutch Courts discusses the question whether judges are capable of judging impartially in the Wilders trial. The answer on the website is: 'Because of the separation of powers judges are strictly impartial and independent.' In an interview in the Dutch newspaper *de Volkskrant* (13 June 2008) judge Theo de Roos emphasized that political views of judges do not influence their work in any way. However, this is questionable. A large-scale study among judges of the High Court in the United States[10] showed that, in politically sensitive lawsuits, judges appointed by a Republican president systematically differ in their judgments from judges appointed by a Democratic president. 'Democratic' judges have significantly more often a 'liberal' judgment, while 'Republican' judges have significantly more often a conservative judgment. We can see this in table 11.1, which, in addition, shows that the outcome of the trial is influenced by 'group polarisation'.

For instance, a 'Democratic' judge in a panel with two other 'Democratic' judges gives significantly more often a 'liberal' judgment than a 'Democratic' judge in a panel with two 'Republican' judges. The investigators conclude that the outcome of the trial in the relevant cases of ethically and politically sensitive jurisdiction strongly depends on the political colour and comprehensive belief of the judges and on the composition of the panel. The Dutch judicial system differs from the American one, but it is plausible that political predilection of judges may also influence the outcome of trials in politically sensitive issues and about principles of justice that are susceptible to different interpretations and that, in addition, may mutually conflict. If the results of the American study apply to the Wilders trial, there is a real chance that its result at least partly depends on the composition of the court.

Table 11.1. 'Liberal' judgments of individual judges in politically sensitive lawsuits

		Composition of the panel (colleague judges)		
		2 'Republican' judges	1 'Republican' and 1 'Democratic' judge	2 'Democratic' judges
% 'Liberal' judgments	'Republican' judge	31	37	46
	'Democratic' judge	44	52	64

JUSTICE IS CONFLICT

Justice is a multifaceted concept. It concerns not one rule but several. This entails that, under particular circumstances, rights and rules of justice may conflict (see chapter 5). This is also the case in the issue under consideration: the right to free speech may clash with the 'right to dignity' and the right to be protected against discrimination, stigmatization, humiliation and psychological oppression. These rights are symmetrical: neither is significantly more important than the other. According to Stanley Fish, in the present day, the dangers of not considering the harms of hate speech are greater than those that attend the limitations on free-speech doctrine that such regulations may entail. John Rawls regards self-respect as 'perhaps the most important primary good'.[11] That is why he regards promotion and protection of a social basis for self-respect as a fundamental aspect of justice. If this is correct, then violation of the basis for self-respect for a subgroup of citizens is a serious injustice. It cannot be denied that many of Wilders's expressions are deeply humiliating and offensive for a great many Muslims. It is not far-fetched that this may easily violate the social basis of self-respect of Muslims. Gradually a social climate has arisen in which Muslims are systematically treated in such a way that they feel ashamed about their Islamic identity and feel themselves more and more second-class citizens.

However, it is important to stress that although the importance of a social basis of self-respect may mean that Wilders's statements concern a form of injustice towards Muslims, this does not necessarily mean that, all things considered, the right to be protected against violation of self-respect and psychological oppression determinately outweighs the right to free speech. It does mean that rights and competing aspects of justice may clash.

JUSTITIA'S SCALES AND SWORD

If it is true that different aspects of justice may mutually conflict, and if it may occur that neither of two conflicting rights or rules of justice outweighs the other, then it is plausible that Justitia's scales do not always tip in one direction and give an unambiguous answer. If the idea of 'conflicting justices' is sound, it may be the case that in some situations and in some conflicts there is no (single) right answer. In that case neither of the relevant two rival claims tips the scales of justice.

RONALD DWORKIN'S REJECTION OF INDETERMINATENESS

Ronald Dworkin recognizes that application of the law is often a question of weighing principles rather than applying rules. Raymond Wacks summarizes Dworkin's view as follows:

Dworkin claims that, while rules are applicable in all-or-nothing fashion, principles and policies have the dimension of weight or importance. In other words, if a rule applies, and it is a valid rule, a case must be decided in a way dictated by the rule. A principle, on the other hand, provides a reason for deciding the case in a particular way, but it is not a conclusive reason: it will have to be weighed against other principles in the system.[12]

Dworkin believes that the weighing process will virtually always yield a single right answer to every legal question, at least in principle.[13] He rejects the idea of indeterminateness in law. Dworkin agrees that there are hard cases and controversial judgments among judges. But he points out that justice is seriously compromised if the result of hard cases depends on the judge's personal opinion, intuition and discretion. Dworkin emphasizes that disagreement does not demonstrate the non-existence of a single right answer. Instead of indeterminate the answer to the relevant question may be inconclusive, due to the complexity of the issue and the great number of variables involved. Dworkin argues that if we continue our research we may find a (single) right answer. He rejects the idea of indeterminateness because it would mean that in the relevant case there is no determinately right answer, which, according to him, is highly implausible. He argues as follows:

> We claim not just that there is . . . no decisive reason to take one side or the other, and may never have one, but that, no matter how hard we look and think, we will not find any consideration or argument that would make the case on one side even marginally stronger than the case on the other.[14]

Dworkin recognizes the theoretical possibility of a 'tie' judgment: the judgment that neither of the claims is stronger than the other. But he thinks that the probability of such a tie is very small and that it is implausible that all hard cases 'lie at the exact centre of the scale we imagined'.[15] In this reasoning Dworkin supposes that the scale contains a *single point* that represents the equal strength of two rival claims (or the equal goodness or weight of two options). If he is right, this entails, of course, that, starting from this single point, a marginal improvement of one of both sides is sufficient to tip the scale. And because it is highly improbable that a particular case, even a hard case, 'lies at the exact centre of the scale', it will be virtually always true that one claim is stronger than the other. However, Dworkin overlooks the value relation '3NT', which is characterized by the absence of a point of 'equivalence' or 'equal strength' and which entails a large range of indeterminatenss (see chapter 1). Contrary to what Dworkin supposes, a 'tie judgment' does not concern a single *point* but a wide *range*. That is why, contrary to what Dworkin supposes, marginal, and even large, improvements need not tip the scale, due to the large improvement phenomenon. That is also why tie judgments need not be rare.

Chapter 11

DIFFERENT DISCOURSES

In a pluralistic society there are different discourses, such as a liberal and a religious discourse. Often, a particular discourse is dominant.[16] This means that political debates and judicial disputes do not always take place between equals. In the public and political debate on free speech versus freedom from discrimination and in the trial against Wilders the dominant discourse is the 'liberal language'. Different discourses may create misunderstandings between the parties. More importantly, the party who is member of the dominant culture and expresses herself in the dominant discourse has a more favourable point of departure compared to the rival party that belongs to, and speaks the discourse of, a minority culture. This domination may lead to biased jurisdiction, and therefore injustice, if the judges belong to the majority culture, which is usually the case. Parekh discusses the same issue in the context of the debate on the Salmon Rushdie affair in the UK twenty years ago:

> [T]he parties involved in public debates on important issues in a multicultural society often tend to talk past each other, both because each tends to define the issue in its own terms that are often not intelligible to others, and because they have only a limited understanding of each other's history, background and way of life. Most conservative and liberal British writers argued that Muslims were opposed to free speech, whereas the latter were only asking why free speech should include untrue and deeply offensive remarks about religions and religious communities. . . . For their part Muslims, too, systematically misunderstood the grounds of the liberal emphasis on free speech, the difficulties involved in restricting it, the depth of the British commitment to it, and so on.
>
> One of the main reasons for this had to do with the fact that the two groups knew little about each other's way of life and thought. Muslims felt distressed by *The Satanic Verses* for the kind of reasons mentioned earlier. Since these reasons did not form part of the liberal world of thought, liberals had difficulty appreciating their nature, relevance and force. Muslims attempted to articulate their reasons in a liberal language but found it extremely difficult to do so, both because they had few biculturally literate intellectuals and because no such conceptual translation is ever accurate.[17]

Parekh points out that the two discourses are not always entirely and accurately translatable into each other. He continues:

> Free speech is not the only great value, and needs to be balanced against such avoidance of needless hurt, social harmony, protection of the weak, truthfulness in the public realm, and self-respect and dignity of individuals and groups. There is no 'true' way of reconciling them; it all depends on the history, traditions, political circumstances, and so on of a society. . . . No single value trumps

all others, and their relative importance can only be decided in the light of the social and cultural context and the likely consequences.[18]

'LITIGATION' VERSUS 'DIFFEREND'

If it is possible that neither of two conflicting rights or rules of justice determinately outweighs the other, it may occur that the judge is incapable of making an unambiguous and impartial decision. Two rival parties may both have a legitimate claim (expressed in a different discourse), neither of which outweighs the other. Following Jean-François Lyotard we may call this kind of judicial dispute a 'differend'. In such a dispute either decision would wrong one of the parties. Lyotard:

> A *differend* (in contrast to a litigation) is a case of conflict that cannot be equitably resolved for lack of a rule of judgment applicable to both arguments. One side's legitimacy does not imply the other's lack of legitimacy. A single rule would do wrong one of both.[19]

If this argument is valid, it fundamentally changes our view on some kinds of jurisdiction, namely, those kinds that can be subsumed under Lyotard's term 'differend'. This would mean that besides the possibility that one party is right and the other wrong, the judge has to recognize that in some cases there is no (single) right answer and that both parties' claim may be right and legitimate. In another, non-judicial, context Amartya Sen summarizes the problem of making a decision between 3NT options or policies as follows:

> When there are several objects of value, one alternative course of action may be more valued in one respect but less so in another . . . [We may be] faced with an irreducible conflict of compelling principles [and] . . . admit both the superiority of one alternative over the other and the converse . . . [N]eeds of policy do require that something or other must be ultimately done . . . However, it does not follow – and this is the important point to get across – that there must be adequate reason for choosing one course rather than another. Incompleteness . . . in overall judgements might well be a damned nuisance for decisions, but the need for a decision does not, on its own, resolve the conflict. This implies that sometimes even institutional public decisions may have to be taken on the basis of partial justification.[20]

The phrase 'partial justification' may suggest that the justification of the final choice is – although not entirely complete – nevertheless virtually complete. But this is not the case. The reasons for the chosen alternative are not weightier than the reasons for the non-chosen one. This renders the justification of the final choice 'partial' in the double sense of 'incomplete' and 'biased'. In the context of law, justice and jurisdiction this conclusion has special significance. It means that the final decision cannot avoid injustice towards the party whose claim is neither recognized nor honoured, while this claim is not less legitimate than the honoured one.

PARADIGM SHIFT

Insight into conflicts of justice does not resolve these conflicts but may help to see that the legitimacy of one claim does not necessarily exclude the legitimacy of a rival claim. This may help to promote respect for and recognition of other parties' sensitivities and claims. If the argument of this chapter and the previous ones is sound, it suggests the need of a paradigm shift in our thinking about justice, recognizing the possibility that two rival parties may have conflicting but legitimate claims neither of which overrides the other. This recognition avoids the undecidability that is inextricably bound up with the current 'either/or' paradigm, in which one is either right or wrong. In an approach that does not exclude the possibility of 'and/and', one of the outcomes of a trial like that of Wilders may be that the defendant is regarded as being both guilty and not guilty and that he is neither univocally acquitted nor unambiguously sentenced. This seems contradictory and odd, but it may concern a moral paradox similar to the one described in the previous chapter (with respect to the doctrine of restraint, being simultaneously justified and unjustified). If the social basis for self-respect is an important primary good the violation of which is unjust (chapter 7), then Wilders's statements are unjust because they inflict significant damage to the self-respect of Muslims and Moroccans. Besides, the statements may (directly or indirectly and unintentionally) cause hate and discrimination against these minorities. If the right to free speech does not outweigh this damage, Wilders is guilty. But the crucial point under consideration in this chapter is that, if free speech does not outweigh the relevant damage and the rival claim, this need not necessarily mean that, conversely, the latter outweigh the former. It may be the case that neither side outweighs the other. It is not clear what this conclusion would mean for the sentence. Perhaps the judges may express an ambiguous verdict by blaming but not punishing the defendant. This approach would recognize the legitimacy and partial justification of the complaints of Muslims and Moroccans without denying the legitimacy and partial justification of Wilders's use of the right to freedom of expression. I realize that this conclusion is contentious. My thoughts are only tentative. They are meant to stimulate further discussion about the important question whether two conflicting claims may be legitimate while neither outweighs the other. In the light of the incomplete comparability (3NT) thesis defended in this book an affirmative answer to this question seems plausible.

NOTES

1. Jeremy Waldron, *The Harm in Hate Speech* (Cambridge, Mass.: Harvard University Press, 2012), 160.
2. Ibid., 105.
3. John Rawls, *A Theory of Justice*, revised edition (Cambridge, Mass.: Belknap Press of Harvard University Press, 1999), 115–116.
4. Ibid., 37.
5. See, for instance, Richard Posner, *The Problems of Jurisprudence* (Cambridge, Mass.: Harvard University Press, 2000); *The Problematics of Moral and Legal Theory* (Cambridge, Mass.: Belknap Press of Harvard University Press, 2002); and Stanley Fish, *The Trouble with Principle* (Cambridge, Mass.: Harvard University Press, 2001); Larry Alexander, *Is There a Right of Freedom of Expression?* (Cambridge: Cambridge University Press, 2005); John Griffith, *The Politics of the Judiciary* (London: Fontana Press, 1997); and Cass R. Sunstein, David Schkade, Lisa M. Ellman, Andres Sawicki, *Are Judges Political? An Empirical Analysis of the Federal Judiciary* (Washington, D.C.: Brookings Institution Press, 2006).
6. Waldron, *The Harm in Hate Speech*, 105, 138.
7. John Stuart Mill, *On Liberty and Other Writings*, ed. Stefan Collini (Cambridge: Cambridge University Press, 1989), chap. 3.
8. Bhikhu Parekh, *Rethinking Multiculturalism: Cultural Diversity and Political Theory* (New York: Palgrave, 2000), 301.
9. See, for instance, Herbert Hart, *The Concept of Law* (Oxford: Oxford University Press, 1997); Richard Posner, *The Problems of Jurisprudence* and *The Problematics of Moral and Legal Theory*; Stanley Fish, *There Is No Such Thing as Free Speech and It's a Good Thing, Too* (Oxford: Oxford University Press, 1994) and *The Trouble with Principle*; and Alexander, *Is There a Right of Freedom of Expression?*
10. Cass Sunstein et al., *Are Judges Political?*
11. Rawls, *A Theory of Justice*, 386.
12. Raymond Wacks, *Philosophy of Law: A Very Short Introduction* (Oxford: Oxford University Press, 2006), 46.
13. Ronald Dworkin, *Taking Rights Seriously* (Cambridge, Mass.: Harvard University Press, 1978), 279–290; Ronald Dworkin, *A Matter of Principle* (Cambridge, Mass.: Harvard University Press, 1985), 119–145; Ronald Dworkin, 'Do Liberal Values Conflict?', in *The Legacy of Isaiah Berlin*, eds. Ronald Dworkin, Mark Lilla and Robert B. Silvers (New York: NYRB, 2001); and Ronald Dworkin, 'Indeterminacy in Law', in *The Oxford Companion to Philosophy*, ed. Ted Honderich (Oxford: Oxford University Press, 1995), 399.
14. Dworkin, 'Indeterminacy in Law', 399.
15. Dworkin, *Taking Rights Seriously*, 287.

16. See Bhikhu Parekh's interesting discussion in chapter 10 ('Politics, Religion and Free Speech') of his *Rethinking Multiculturalism. Cultural Diversity and Political Theory* (New York: Palgrave, 2000).

17. Parekh, *Rethinking Multiculturalism*, 304–305.

18. Ibid., 320.

19. Jean-François Lyotard, *The Differend: Phrases in Dispute* (Minneapolis: University of Minnesota Press, 1988), xi.

20. Amartya Sen, *On Ethics and Economics* (Oxford: Blackwell Publishers, 2003), 67.

Chapter 12

Autonomy and Recognition

SUMMARY

Incommensurability of values and incomplete comparability of options have not only problematic but also favourable consequences. They create room for autonomous choices, not dictated by reason. Most philosophers who take part in the contemporary philosophical debate on freedom of the will regard, as a necessary condition of an autonomous choice, the presence of more than one rationally eligible option. Incompletely comparable options (3NT options) satisfy this condition. Another positive aspect of the issue of incommensurability is that it makes us aware of a plurality of universally valid and irreducible human values. This awareness helps to promote recognition of different legitimate rankings of these values. In contrast to toleration and value relativism, recognition and value pluralism are positive concepts that generate respect for differences in priorities and weights assigned to human values by different persons, societies and cultures. This may contribute to a peaceful coexistence of people who recognize each other in choosing disparate rankings of universally valid but sometimes conflicting human values.

****

In the previous chapters we have discussed several problematic implications of incommensurability for ethics and justice. In this final chapter I will discuss two fruitful implications: incomplete comparability of options creates room for autonomous choices not dictated by reason, and insight into competing incommensurable values promotes recognition of different possible rankings of options bearing these values.

Chapter 12

AUTONOMOUS CHOICE

There are at least two distinct concepts of autonomy. The original concept comes from Immanuel Kant. Kant's autonomy is based on the *categorical imperative* as contrasted with the *hypothetical imperative*. The latter imperative is conditional: it has the form of 'if . . . then'; *if* I want to achieve x, *then* I have to do y. A hypothetical imperative depends on personal desires and aims. As the adjective 'categorical' indicates, the categorical imperative, by contrast, is unconditional and independent from personal desires and subjective aims. In the case of a conflict between a selfish and a moral option, the categorical imperative gives absolute priority to the latter. In line with the meaning of the Greek words 'autos' (= self) and 'nomos' (= law), Kant's autonomy is a self-enacted moral law – a self-imposed categorical *imperative* – originating from human reason. According to Kant, reason shows what we 'ought to do'. We are free to the extent we obey to the duties our reason imposes on ourselves. Kant's autonomy concerns reason-based principles that are universally valid and the same for all.

The kind of autonomy under consideration in this chapter is different: it concerns 'personal autonomy' in the sense of freedom to make one's personal choices and to choose one's own life.[1] It is an ideal of self-creation of people who control, to some degree, their own destiny by means of successive free and conscious decisions throughout their lives. This conception of autonomous choice requires the availability of several morally and rationally acceptable options. It is related to value pluralism and the possibility to make personal choices between options that bear incommensurable human values. These choices remain within the restraints of – but are not *dictated* by – reason. That is why they depend on personal autonomous *decisions* and are not the same for all rational persons. In the rest of this chapter I use the notion 'autonomy' in this sense. Here follow the conditions of an autonomous choice.

Conditions of an autonomous choice (applied to choosing option *A* instead of option *B*):

1) *Significantly different options*: *A* and *B* represent significantly different human values, so that it makes a significant difference whether the agent chooses *A* instead of *B*.
2) *Freedom to do otherwise*: The agent is as free to choose *B* as to choose *A*.
3) *Rational deliberation*: Before the agent takes a decision, he or she carefully and rationally considers and compares the reasons for choosing *A* and the reasons for choosing *B*.

4) *3NT*: After rational deliberation the agent concludes that (i) *A* is not better than *B*, (ii) *B* is not better than *A* and (iii) *A* and *B* are not (roughly) equally good (see chapter 1).

Condition 4 requires that neither option is better than the other. Where the considerations for and against two alternatives are incompletely comparable, reason is indeterminate with respect to the question which option *should* be chosen. It provides no better case for one alternative than for the other. The agent is in a sense *free to choose* which course to follow.[2] If, by contrast, the agent would conclude that, with respect to what is relevant to his choice, choosing *A* is better than choosing *B* (reasons for choosing *A* outweigh the reasons for choosing B), it would be irrational, or a sign of weak will, to choose *B* instead of *A*. Suppose the agent concludes that *A* is better than *B*. If he chooses *A*, he is rational. But is his choice autonomous? The choice is free in the sense that the agent is not forced to choose *A* and that he has the freedom to do otherwise (to choose *B*). However, if he concludes that *A* is better than *B*, he cannot choose *B* without rendering the choice irrational or a sign of weak will. Condition 4 also requires that, after deliberation, the agent concludes that, with respect to what is relevant to his choice, the options are not (roughly) equally good. Suppose the agent concludes that *A* and *B* are equally good, that is, that they virtually bear the same values in the same amounts. In that case it does not matter whether the agent chooses *A* or *B*, so that condition 1 is not satisfied. Thus, only if 3NT applies, there is freedom to do otherwise (to make a significantly different choice), without violating rationality. Which particular item the agent chooses is up to him. His specific choice makes him a rational agent that differs from other rational agents who make a different choice. In other words, 3NT enables autonomous choices that constitute the agent's personality and identity, within the limits of practical reason. The agent chooses his options because he *decides* to choose them and not because he *ought* to choose them on the balance of reasons.[3] The conclusion is that incommensurability, or more precisely, 3NT, is a condition sine qua non of this kind of rational autonomous choice.

THE FREE WILL DEBATE

We can make a connection with the philosophical debate on free will, especially the approach by Robert Kane – a leading philosopher in the free will debate. Like many other philosophers in the free will debate, Kane adheres to the so-called principle of alternative possibilities, which states that free will exists only if the agent has the freedom to do otherwise. According to this view, there cannot be free choices without alternative possibilities. Kane adds that 'freedom is deficient' if it were always the case that we could only do otherwise by mistake, weakness of will or irrationality. As we have seen, the existence of 3NT value relations creates room for doing otherwise without becoming irrational or doing wrong. It supports the principle of alternative possibilities because it creates alternative possibilities for rational choice. Precisely because reason under-determines the choice, it creates the freedom to choose between options neither of which is less rationally eligible than the other.

SELF-FORMING ACTION

A putative example of a free choice, given by Kane, is the following.

> Consider a businesswoman . . . who is on the way to a meeting important to her career when she observes an assault taking place in an alley. An inner struggle arises between her moral conscience, to stop and call for help, and her career ambitions which tell her she cannot miss this meeting. She has to make an effort of will to overcome the temptation to do the selfish thing and go on to her meeting. If she overcomes this temptation, it will be the result of her effort to do the moral thing; but if she fails, it will be because she did not *allow* her effort to succeed. For while she willed to overcome temptation, she also willed to fail. That is to say, she had strong reasons to will the moral thing, but she had also strong reasons, ambitious reasons, to make the selfish choice that were different from, and incommensurable with, her moral reasons. When agents, like the woman, decide in such circumstances, and the indeterminate efforts they are making become determinate choices, they *make* one set of competing reasons or motives prevail over the others then and there *by deciding*. Their acts of deciding in other words are 'will-setting'. Thus the choice they eventually make, though undetermined, can still be rational (made for reasons) and voluntary (made in accordance with our wills), whichever way we choose.[4]

As Kane points out, if there were no good competing reasons for the other option, then the woman would not be rational if she would choose this option. In that case, she had not really the freedom to do otherwise, without being irrational, because she would have no good reasons to do so. Thus, Kane concludes, by the presence of a competing rational option, 'the indeterminism paradoxically opens up the genuine possibility of . . . choosing or doing otherwise in accordance with, rather than against, our wills (voluntarily) and reasons (rationally)'.[5] The agent is torn between competing motivations and rival visions of what she should do or become. Kane speaks of 'will-setting' or 'self-forming' actions. As he points out, free will is not just about free action. It is about self-formation, about the formation of our 'wills' or how we got to be the kinds of persons we are, with the characters, motives and purposes we now have. The eventual choice makes the agent the kind of person she decides to be. She makes one set of competing reasons or motives prevail over the others, by deciding. Thus the choice is rational (made for reasons) and voluntary (made in accordance with the will), whichever way the agent chooses.[6] The businesswoman had strong reasons to will the moral thing, but she also had strong reasons, ambitious reasons, to make the selfish choice that were different from, and incommensurable with, her moral reasons. As Kane argues, she struggles between her moral conscience and her career ambitions.

However, Kane's example does not necessarily satisfy the fourth condition of autonomous choice (3NT), mentioned earlier. It is true that the relevant reasons – moral reasons and selfish reasons – are incommensurable (as Kane notices), but this need not mean that neither option is better than the other, which is the case if 3NT applies. Incommensurability does not exclude that one option is right and the other wrong. If it is wrong not to help the assaulted person, then doing the other thing is wrong and is a form of what, in Kane's vocabulary, might be called 'deficient freedom'. Autonomy requires the availability of more than one option that is rationally and morally permissible. The example of the woman, by contrast, does not concern a choice between competing moral options, but between a moral and a selfish option. As the free will debate can learn from the incommensurability debate, not all incommensurable options are 3NT options. Some incommensurable options may still be comparable, so that one of them may be definitely better than the other. In chapter 1 we have seen that incommensurability is a central but not sufficient condition of 3NT. Another condition of 3NT (incomplete comparability) is symmetry: neither value is significantly more important than the other. Moral reasons and selfish reasons are not symmetrical; that is, the former generally outweigh the latter with respect to the question of what is the right thing to do if they conflict. Therefore, the options with which the business woman is confronted do not satisfy the fourth condition of autonomous choice. If moral reasons outweigh selfish reasons, the moral option is better than the selfish option, so that 3NT is not satisfied. In that case the agent is not free to do otherwise without doing the wrong thing or showing a weak will. Still Kane's example may be adequate for the freedom of the will debate. The woman's choice may be free, even if she chooses the selfish option, provided that it is not the result of a weak will: then she freely decides to do the wrong thing. But the woman's choice is not autonomous in the sense under consideration, even if she chooses the moral option, because then she does what she morally ought to do, while the relevant autonomy concerns choices that are not morally or rationally required. Kane's example also differs from Kant's autonomous choice which is based on the detachment from personal desires, and on giving the moral option absolute priority. In Kane's conception of free choice, the choice of the self-interested option is as free as the choice of the moral option. Kant would say that the former choice is not really free. 3NT-based autonomy, in turn, differs from Kantian autonomy, in the sense that a 3NT-based autonomous choice is neither dictated by reason, nor by morality, so that there is freedom to do otherwise without acting against a moral law or doing the wrong thing.

RECOGNITION

Let us briefly discuss another positive effect of being aware of characteristics of incommensurable values. In order to understand a pluralistic society and world, it is important to have insight into possible conflicts between incommensurable values. As Bernard Williams rightly notices, ignoring or distorting facts about these possible value conflicts cannot lead to well-considered judgments.[7] Insight into conflicts between options that represent incommensurable values shows that it need not be the case that one option is right, while the other is wrong. This entails that, in value conflicts, choices of people may differ without defect or mistake. The other party need not be wrong if she makes other choices. Insight into value pluralism prevents black-white thinking. It promotes recognition of and respect for unlike rankings of competing values. Respect means seeing powerful and legitimate reasons for what other rational and sincere people believe and do. Moral pluralism significantly differs from moral monism with respect to consequences for people's attitude towards other people. While moral pluralism is compatible with and promotes respect, moral monism is compatible only with tolerance: permitting what is actually regarded as objectionable. Moral pluralism also significantly differs from moral relativism. The latter makes values exclusively dependent on context, perspectives and points of view; the former concerns universally valid human values. Different cultures, different societies and different people realize different goods to different extents. This does not mean that all cultures are equally good or that neither society or person is ethically superior to any other. It means that an adequate moral approach can differ from others in the emphasis it places upon goods that we all recognize. The incommensurability idea supports the view that one side in a disagreement may be, but need not be, less rational or reasonable than the other. It shows the possibility of choosing and recognizing different reasonable ways of life. It can help us to realize that the values of our way of life reflect a series of partly autonomous choices. Moral pluralism is aware that no single morality will be capable of giving full expression to all human values. In this context the following remarks by John Rawls are relevant:

The full range of values is too extensive to fit in any one social world and there is no social world without loss. It is a basic error to believe that values, if they are true, must be compatible. In the realm of values, as opposed to the world of fact, not all truths can fit into one social world.[8]

This awareness can help to liberate us from a monistic view of human values, which allows only a single right ordering. If the good is plural, and we need to choose among the different goods in order to be able to develop a good life, then pluralism offers us the freedom to choose the way of life we want from the set of good options. The pluralistic approach may prevent unjustified exclusion and hostility. It may help to promote peaceful coexistence in diversity and mutual respect. But value pluralism does not mean that all ways of life are equally good or acceptable. They must fall within the range of genuinely human ways of life in which universally valid values and ethical principles receive the recognition and observance they deserve.

NOTES

1. See Joseph Raz, *The Morality of Freedom* (Oxford: Oxford University Press, 1986), chap. 14.
2. Ibid., 333–334.
3. I owe these thoughts to Ruth Chang, *Making Comparisons Count* (New York: Routledge, 2002), 170–172; and Ibid., chaps. 13 and 14.
4. Robert Kane, 'Rethinking Free Will: New Perspectives on an Ancient Problem', in *The Oxford Handbook of Free Will*, 2nd ed., ed. Robert Kane (Oxford: Oxford University Press, 2011), 387; and Robert Kane, *A Contemporary Introduction to Free Will* (Oxford: Oxford University Press, 2005), 136.
5. Kane, *A Contemporary Introduction to Free Will*, 143–144.
6. Ibid., 136.
7. Cf. Bernard Williams, 'Conflicts of Values', in *Moral Luck*, ed. Bernard Williams (Cambridge: Cambridge University Press, 1981), 71.
8. John Rawls, *Political Liberalism* (New York: Columbia University Press, 1996), 197, n. 32.

Glossary

This glossary explains the senses in which I use the relevant terms in this book. The terms marked with an asterisk below are explained elsewhere in the glossary.

- *Ambivalence*

    A third possible attitude towards alternatives for choice, in addition to preference and indifference. Being torn between the options, because neither option is better than the other, while they are not equally good (3NT*).

- *Autonomous/arbitrary choice*

    A choice that is decisively dependent on the agent's personal will. The reasons for choosing one option do not outweigh the reasons for choosing the other option (see chapter 12).

- *Bidirectionality*

    Two contributory values* of a covering value* are 'bidirectionally divided' if one option is better with respect to one contributory value while the other option is better with respect to the other contributory value.

    - *Significant bidirectionality*

        One option contains a significantly larger amount of one contributory value, while the other option contains a significantly larger amount of another contributory value.

- *Cardinal ranking*

    Ranking by amounts of a unit of value.

- *Complete comparability*

    Two options are completely comparable if they have a determinate relative worth compared to each other – that is, if one option is better than, worse than or (roughly) equally good as the other.

- *Complete ordering*

    An ordering of a set of options is complete if each option has a determinate relative worth compared to every other option of the set (i.e., if each option is, compared to every other option of the set, better, worse or equally good).

- *Contributory value*

    A value contributing to a covering value*.

- *Covering value*

    A value with respect to which options are compared. A covering value often contains more than one contributory value*.

- *Definitely better/worse*

    Option A is 'definitely better' than option B if reason shows that it is better to choose A instead of B (so that it is irrational or less rational to choose B rather than A); and A is 'definitely worse' than B if reason shows that it is better to choose B instead of A (so that it is irrational or less rational to choose A rather than B).

- *Difference principle*
    - *John Rawls's difference principle*: According to this principle social and economic inequalities are to be arranged so that they are to the greatest benefit of the least advantaged (worst-off).
    - *Ruth Chang's difference principle*: Chang's claim that a small unidimensional difference in value cannot trigger incomparability where before there was comparability.

- *Equally good*

    'Equally good' is an ambiguous phrase and may mean different things. Options A and B may be 'equally good' in the following two senses: (1) A and B are identical with respect to what is relevant to the choice: they contain the same relevant values in the same amounts; (2) A and B contain disparate relevant values but A's overall amount of value is equal to B's overall amount of value. For the reader it is important to know that I use the phrase 'equally good' in the first sense.

- *Equivalence relation*

  Two values have an equivalence relation if a particular amount of one value is equivalent to a particular amount of the other value.

- *Ethical deficit*

  A decision between two options that represent conflicting ethical principles or values contains an ethical deficit, if the reasons for choosing one option do not outweigh the reasons for choosing the other option, so that there is no overall reason that justifies the choice of one option rather than the other.

- *Failure of transitivity*

  Although A is not worse than B, there is a C that is better than A but not better than B. For a further explanation, see chapter 1.

- *Idealistic belief*

  A belief that generates idealistic, religious or moral commitments and social aims.

- *Impartial and objective*

  Detached from a specific personal belief, intuition or subjective preference.

- *Imprecise/rough equality*

  - In a 'real' sense: an imprecise version of precise equality. Real imprecise equality is due to the imprecise or vague character of values, in the sense that their boundaries cannot be precisely indicated and their amounts cannot be exactly measured.
  - In a misconceived sense: a conflation of imprecise equality in the 'real' sense and a fundamentally different phenomenon: 3NT*. See chapter 3.

- *Improvement phenomenon*

  - *Small* improvement phenomenon: Although A is not worse than B, a small improvement of A does not make A better than B. The small improvement phenomenon applies to cases of imprecise equality* in the 'real' sense.
  - *Large* improvement phenomenon: Although A is not worse than B, a large improvement of A does not make A better than B. The large improvement phenomenon applies to cases of 3NT*.

- *Incommensurability*

  Literal meaning: inability to be compared by a common standard.
  Precise meaning of *incommensurability of values*:

Two values are incommensurable if they have different dimensions that cannot be reduced to one dimension and cannot be measured and compared on a common cardinal* scale of units of value.

(There are different versions of incommensurability, such as 'semantic', 'mathematical' and 'value' incommensurability. When I use the notion 'incommensurability' without further specification, I mean 'incommensurability of values', which is the topic of this book.)

- *Incompatibility*

Incompatible values or options cannot be (optimally) combined or realized simultaneously. Incompatibility is distinct from, and unrelated to, incommensurability*: incompatibles may be commensurable, and incommensurables may be compatible (see chapter 7).

- *Incomplete comparability*

Two options are incompletely comparable if they have no determinate relative worth compared to each other – that is, neither option is better, worse or (roughly) equally good as the other option (3NT).

- *Incomplete ordering*

An ordering of a set of options is incomplete if some options have no determinate relative worth compared to some other options of the set – that is, if some options are, compared to some other options of the set, neither better, nor worse, nor (roughly) equally good.

- *Inconclusiveness*

A value relation between two options is inconclusive if their relative worth is not (yet) clear: it is not (yet) clear which option is better than the other or whether they are equally good.

- *Indeterminateness*

Absence of a determinate relative worth

Unlike inconclusiveness*, indeterminateness does *not* mean that – due to insufficient knowledge or lack of information or other shortcomings or difficulties – we do not *know* the relative worth of the options. Instead, it means that – due to incomplete comparability – such a relative worth does not *exist*. Indeterminateness is due to the fact that it is not true that one option is better than the other, nor true that they are equally good (3NT). I prefer the term 'indeterminateness' to 'indeterminacy' because the latter is often identified with 'vagueness' or 'impreciseness', which is a different phenomenon (see chapter 3).

- *Index-problem*

    An index-problem arises if two or more incommensurable values or goods have to be aggregated in a single measure.

- *Insignificant amount fallacy*

    The mistaken belief that the comparability of a significant option A and a significant option B can be demonstrated by the comparability of a significant option A and an insignificant option B. For a full explanation see chapter 3.

- *Large improvement argument*

    Argument that makes use of the large improvement phenomenon*

- *Large improvement phenomenon*: see improvement phenomenon*
- *Lexical priority*

    One value is lexically prior to another if it has absolute priority to the other (i.e., irrespective of the amounts of the two values; thus, even if the amount of the lexically prior value is very small and the amount of the other value is very large).

- *Negative liberty*

    'Freedom *from*', as distinct from the 'freedom *to*' ('positive liberty'*)
    Isaiah Berlin understands by negative liberty the freedom from interference by others.

- *Non-idealistic belief*

    Belief that does not generate idealistic or moral commitments with respect to society and public domain.

- *Objective*: see 'impartial and objective'
- *Ordinal ranking*

    Ranking on a list in terms of 'more/less value' or 'more/less importance', which do not indicate how much the amounts of value differ in quantities of units of value.

- *Parity*

    'Parity' is Ruth Chang's designation and interpretation of 3NT*. It mistakenly explains 3NT as a fourth positive value relation within the domain of complete comparability (in addition to, and of equal standing as, 'better', 'worse' and 'equally good'). 'Parity' conflates 'real' imprecise equality* with 3NT, which is a fundamentally different phenomenon. See chapter 3 and appendix of chapter 4.

- *Positive liberty*

    'Freedom *to*', as distinct from the 'freedom *from*' ('negative liberty'*).
    Isaiah Berlin understands by positive liberty the freedom of self-mastery and of rational control of one's life, including the freedom to participate in political activities and collective self-government and to be involved in making the laws under which one lives.

- *Practical reason*

    The capacity for resolving – through reflection and deliberation – the question of what is the right, better or more preferable thing to do. When we reason practically, we weigh and compare reasons, evaluate the strengths and weaknesses of alternatives, before coming to an assessment about what we should do or want to do.

- *Prima facie/pro tanto duty*

    Duty that has to be satisfied only if it does not clash with a weightier value, duty or requirement.

- *Public/private split*

    Separation of public rules of basic justice from ideas about justice that are based on private comprehensive beliefs or conceptions of the good.
    The public/private split should be distinguished from the separation between religious and political authority – the separation of 'Church and State'. The recognition of the separation of 'Church and State' need not entail the recognition of the public/private split. See chapter 7.

- *QALY*

    Quality adjusted life year
    QALY combines length of life and quality of life. 'QALYs added' or 'QALYs gained' is a measure of health benefit from medical treatment. Examples:

    - 1 QALY may be one life year with a complete (100%) quality of life; or two life years with a 50% quality of life, or four life years with a 25% quality of life, et cetera.
    - One life year with a quality of 30% is 0.3 QALY.
    - If a medical treatment adds three life years with a quality 50%, the health benefit is 1.5 QALYs.

Glossary

- *Rationality of a choice*
  - *Rational* choice

    Choice guided by practical reason*
  - *Irrational* choice

    Choice of an option that is worse than its alternative
  - *Completely rationally justified* choice

    Choice of an option that is at least as good as its alternative
  - *Incompletely (or partially) rationally justified* choice

    Choice of an option that is neither worse than, nor better than, nor equally good* as its alternative
  - *Rationally permissible* choice: see *incompletely rationally justified* choice
  - Rationally *required* choice

    Choice of an option that is better than its alternative.
- *Rational undecidability*

  Inability to decide between significant options on the basis of an overall ('all things considered') reason that justifies the choice of one option *rather than* another while the options are not (roughly) equally good* with respect to what is relevant for the choice (see chapter 4).
- *Revealed preference theory*

  This theory is based on the assumption that, with respect to two options, the agent's attitude is always one of preference or indifference. The theory states that a choice between options reveals the agent's preference. However, apart from preference and indifference, there is the possibility of ambivalence*, namely, if it concerns two options that have a 3NT* relation. Therefore, a choice between options need not be a sign of preference for the chosen option: the choice may be made radically and autonomously* from an attitude of ambivalence.
- *Rough equality*: see imprecise equality
- *Significant bidirectionality*: see under *bidirectionality*
- *Small improvement argument*

  Argument that makes use of the small improvement phenomenon*
- *Small improvement phenomenon*: see improvement phenomenon*

- *Symmetrical*

  Two values are symmetrical if neither value is significantly more important than the other.

- *3NT*

  There is a 3NT ('triply not true') relation between options A and B if it is (1) not true that A is better than B, *and* (2) not true that A is worse than B, *and* (3) not true that A is (roughly) equally good as B.

- *Trichotomy thesis*

  The thesis that there are not more than three positive value-relations: 'better', 'worse' and 'equally good'.

Bibliography

Alexander, Larry. *Is There a Right of Freedom of Expression?* Cambridge: Cambridge University Press, 2005.
Allingham, Michael. *Choice Theory. A Very Short Introduction*. Oxford: Oxford University Press, 2002.
Anderson, Elizabeth. 'Practical Reason and Incommensurable Goods'. In *Incommensurability, Incomparability, and Practical Reason*, edited by Ruth Chang. Cambridge, Mass.: Harvard University Press, 1997.
Aristotle. *Ethics*. Penguin Books, 1978 [ISBN 0 14 044.055 0].
Arneson, Richard J. 'Rawls versus Utilitarianism in the Light of Political Liberalism'. In *The Idea of a Political Liberalism: Essays on Rawls*, edited by Victoria Davion and Clark Wolf. Lanham, Md: Rowman and Littlefield, 2000.
Arrow, Kenneth Joseph. *Social Choice and Individual Values*. New Haven and London: Yale University Press, 1963.
Audi, Robert, and Nicholas Wolterstorff. *Religion in the Public Square: The Place of Religious Convictions in the Political Debate*. London: Rowman & Littlefield, 1997.
Barry, Brian. *Justice as Impartiality*. Oxford: Clarendon Press, 1999.
Benhabib, Seyla. 'Deliberative Rationality and Models of Democratic Legitimacy'. *Constellations: An International Journal of Critical and Democratic Theory* 1 (1994): 26–52.
Berlin, Isaiah. *Four Essays on Liberty*. Oxford: Oxford University Press, 1969.
Berlin, Isaiah. 'Two Concepts of Liberty'. In *Four Essays on Liberty*, edited by Isaiah Berlin. Oxford: Oxford University Press, 1969.
Berlin, Isaiah. 'The Pursuit of the Ideal'. In *The Crooked Timber of Humanity*, edited by Henry Hardy. Princeton, N.J.: Princeton University Press, 1990.
Berlin, Isaiah. 'The Pursuit of the Ideal'. In *The Proper Study of Mankind*, edited by Henry Hardy and Roger Hausheer. London: Pimlico, 1998.
Bird, Alexander. *Thomas Kuhn*. Princeton, N.J.: Princeton University Press, 2001.

Blackburn, Simon. *Ruling Passions: A Theory of Practical Reasoning*. Oxford: Oxford University Press, 1998.
Boot, Martijn. 'Parity, Incomparability and Rationally Justified Choice'. *Philosophical Studies* 146 (2009): 75–92.
Boot, Martijn. 'The Aim of a Theory of Justice'. *Ethical Theory and Moral Practice* 15 (2012): 7–21.
Boot, Martijn. 'The Right Balance', *The Journal of Value Inquiry* 51 (2017): 13–32.
Boot, Martijn. 'Problems of Incommensurability', *Social Theory and Practice* 43 (2017): 313–342.
Brand, R. B. 'Utilitarianism and the Rules of War'. *Philosophy & Public Affairs* 1 (1971): 145–165.
Brock, Dan. 'Ethical Issues in the Use of Cost Effectiveness Analysis for the Prioritisation of Health Care Resources'. In *Public Health, Ethics, and Equity*, edited by Sudhir Anand, Fabienne Peter and Amartya Sen. Oxford: Oxford University Press, 2006.
Broome, John. *Weighing Goods: Equality, Uncertainty and Time*. Oxford: Blackwell Publishers, 1995.
Broome, John. 'Is Incommensurability Vagueness?' In *Incommensurability, Incomparability, and Practical Reason*, edited by Ruth Chang. Cambridge, Mass.: Harvard University Press, 1997.
Broome, John. *Ethics out of Economics*. Cambridge: Cambridge University Press, 1999.
Broome, John. *Weighing Lives*. Oxford: Oxford University Press, 2004.
Calabresi, Guido, and Philip Bobbitt. *Tragic Choices: The Conflicts Society Confronts in the Allocation of Tragically Scarce Resources*. New York, London: W.W. Norton, 1978.
Carens, Joseph. 1996. 'Realistic and Idealistic Approaches to the Ethics of Migration'. *International Migration Review* 30 (1996): 156–170.
Chang, Ruth. 'Introduction'. In *Incommensurability, Incomparability, and Practical Reason*, edited by Ruth Chang, 1–34. Cambridge, Mass.: Harvard University Press, 1997.
Chang, Ruth. *Making Comparisons Count*. New York: Routledge, 2002.
Chang, Ruth. 'The Possibility of Parity'. *Ethics* 112 (2002): 659–688.
Chang, Ruth. 'Parity, Interval Value, and Choice'. *Ethics* 115 (2005): 331–350.
Chang, Ruth. 'Voluntarist Reasons and the Sources of Normativity'. In *Reasons for Action*, edited by David Sobel and Steven Wall, 243–271. Cambridge: Cambridge University Press, 2009.
Clapham, Andrew. *Human Rights: A Very Short Introduction*. Oxford: Oxford University Press, 2007.
Cohen, Gerald. 'On the Currency of Egalitarian Justice'. *Ethics* 99 (1989): 906–944.
Cohen, Gerald. 'Rescuing Conservatism: A Defence of Existing Value', unpublished manuscript; lecture presented at the Centre for Ethics at the University of Toronto, 16 October 2008.
Cohen, Gerald. *Rescuing Justice and Equality*. Cambridge, Mass.: Harvard University Press, 2008.

Constant, Benjamin. 'Liberty of the Ancients Compared with That of the Moderns'. In *Political Writings*, edited by Benjamin Constant. Cambridge: Cambridge University Press, 1988.
D'Agostino, Fred. *Incommensurability and Commensuration: The Common Denominator*. Burlington, Verm.: Ashgate, 2003.
Daniels, Norman. 'Democratic Equality: Rawls's Complex Egalitarianism'. In *The Cambridge Companion to Rawls*, edited by Samuel Freeman. Cambridge: Cambridge University Press, 2003.
Daniels, Norman. *Just Health: Meeting Health Needs Fairly*. Cambridge: Cambridge University Press, 2008.
Daniels, Norman, and James Sabin. 'Limits to Health Care: Fair Procedures, Democratic Deliberation, and the Legitimacy Problem for Insurers'. *Philosophy & Public Affairs* 26 (1997): 303–350.
Derrida, Jacques. 'Force of Law: The Mystical Foundation of Authority'. In *Deconstruction and the Possibility of Justice*, edited by Drucilla Cornell, Michel Rosenfeld, David Gray Carlson, New York/London: Routledge, 1992.
Dworkin, Ronald. *Taking Rights Seriously*. Cambridge, Mass.: Harvard University Press, 1978.
Dworkin, Ronald. *A Matter of Principle*. Cambridge, Mass.: Harvard University Press, 1985.
Dworkin, Ronald. 'Indeterminacy in Law'. In *The Oxford Companion to Philosophy*, edited by Ted Honderich. Oxford: Oxford University Press, 1995.
Dworkin, Ronald. 'Do Liberal Values Conflict?' In *The Legacy of Isaiah Berlin*, edited by Ronald Dworkin, Mark Lilla and Robert B. Silvers. New York: NYRB, 2001.
Eberle, Christopher J. *Religious Conviction in Liberal Politics*. Cambridge: Cambridge University Press, 2002.
Feldman, Fred. 'Adjusting Utility for Justice: A Consequentialist Reply to the Objection from Justice'. *Philosophy and Phenomenological Research* 60 (1995): 567–585.
Finlayson, James Gordon. *Habermas: A Very Short Introduction*. Oxford: Oxford University Press, 2005.
Finnis, John. 'Abortion, Natural Law, and Public Reason'. In *Natural Law and Public Reason*, edited by Robert P. George and Christopher Wolfe, 75–105. Washington, D.C.: Georgetown University Press, 2000.
Fish, Stanley. *The Trouble with Principle*. Cambridge, Mass.: Harvard University Press, 2001.
Fish, Stanley. *There Is No Such Thing as Free Speech and It's a Good Thing, Too*. Oxford: Oxford University Press, 1994.
Galston, William A. *Liberal Pluralism: The Implications of Value Pluralism for Political Theory and Practice*. Cambridge: Cambridge University Press, 2002.
Gaus, Gerald. *Justificatory Liberalism*. Oxford: Oxford University Press, 1996.
George, Robert P., and Christopher Wolfe. 'Introduction'. In *Natural Law and Public Reason*, edited by Robert P. George and Christopher Wolfe, 1–9. Washington, D.C.: Georgetown University Press, 2000.

Gray, John. *Isaiah Berlin*. Princeton, N.J.: Princeton University Press, 1997.
Gray, John. *Two Faces of Liberalism*. Cambridge/Oxford: Polity Press, 2000.
Greenawalt, Kent. *Religious Convictions and Political Choice*. Oxford: Oxford University Press, 1988.
Griffin, James. 'Incommensurability: What's the Problem?', In *Incommensurability, Incomparability, and Practical Reason*, edited by Ruth Chang, Cambridge, Mass.: Harvard University Press, 1997.
Griffin, James. *Well-Being*. Oxford: Clarendon Press, 2002.
Griffin, James. *On Human Rights*. Oxford: Oxford University Press, 2008.
Griffith, John. *The Politics of the Judiciary*. London: Fontana Press, 1997.
Habermas, Jürgen. *The Inclusion of the Other: Studies in Political Theory*, edited by Ciaran Cronin and Pablo De Greiff. Cambridge, Mass.: MIT Press, 1998.
Hampshire, Stuart. *Morality and Conflict*. Cambridge, Mass.: Harvard University Press, 1983.
Hampshire, Stuart. *Justice Is Conflict*. Princeton/Oxford: Princeton University Press, 2000.
Hardin, Russell. *Indeterminacy and Society*. Princeton/Oxford: Princeton University Press, 2003.
Hare, R. M. 'Rules of War and Moral Reasoning'. *Philosophy & Public Affairs* 1 (1971): 166–181.
Hargreaves Heap, Shaun, and Martin Hollis, Bruce Lyons, Robert Sugden, Albert Weale. *The Theory of Choice*. Oxford: Blackwell Publishers, 1992.
Hart, Herbert. *The Concept of Law*. Oxford: Oxford University Press, 1997.
Hart, Herbert. 'Rawls on Liberty and Its Priority'. *University of Chicago Law Review* 40 (1973).
Hope, Tony. *Medical Ethics: A Very Short Introduction*. Oxford: Oxford University Press, 2004.
Hsieh, Nien-hê. 'Is Incomparability a Problem for Anyone?' *Economics and Philosophy* 23 (2007): 65–80.
Hurley, Susan. *Natural Reasons, Personality and Polity*. Oxford: Oxford University Press, 1989.
John Simmons, A. 'Ideal and Nonideal Theory'. *Philosophy & Public Affairs* 38 (2010): 5–36.
Kamm, Frances M. 'Deciding Whom to Help, Health-Adjusted Life Years and Disabilities'. In *Public Health, Ethics, and Equity*, edited by Sudhir Anand, Fabienne Peter and Amartya Sen. Oxford: Oxford University Press, 2006.
Kornhauser, Lewis A. 'No Best Answer?' *University of Pennsylvania Law Review* 146 (1998): 1599–1637.
Kornhauser, Lewis A., and Lawrence Sager. 'The Many as One: Integrity and Group Choice in Paradoxical Cases'. *Philosophy & Public Affairs* 249 (2004): 249–276.
Kuhn, Thomas. *The Structure of Scientific Revolutions*, 2nd ed. Chicago: University of Chicago Press, 1970.
Kuhn, Thomas. 'Reflections on My Critics'. In *Criticism and the Growth of Knowledge*, edited by Imre Lakatos and Alan Musgrave. Cambridge: Cambridge University Press, 1999.

Larmore, Charles. *Patterns of Moral Complexity*. Cambridge: Cambridge University Press, 1988.
Levi, Isaac. *Hard Choices: Decision Making under Unresolved Conflict*. Cambridge: Cambridge University Press, 1999.
Lockwood, Michael. 'Quality of Life and Resource Allocation'. In *Bioethics: an Anthology*, edited by Helga Kuhse and Peter Singer. Oxford: Blackwell Publishers Ltd, 2006.
Lukes, Steven. 'Comparing the Incomparable: Trade-Offs and Sacrifices'. In *Incommensurability, Incomparability, and Practical Reason*, edited by Ruth Chang. Cambridge, Mass.: Harvard University Press, 1997.
Lyotard, Jean-François. *The Differend: Phrases in Dispute*. Minneapolis: University of Minnesota Press, 1988.
Macedo, Stephen. 'In Defense of Liberal Public Reason: Are Slavery and Abortion Hard Cases?' In *Natural Law and Public Reason*, edited by Robert P. George and Christopher Wolfe, 11–50. Washington, D.C.: Georgetown University Press, 2000.
MacIntyre, Alasdair. *After Virtue*, 2nd ed. Notre Dame, Ind.: University of Notre Dame Press, 1984.
MacIntyre, Alasdair. *Whose Justice? Which Rationality?* Notre Dame: University of Notre Dame Press, 1988.
McKirahan, Richard D. Jr. *Philosophy before Socrates*. Indianapolis/Cambridge: Hackett Publishing Company, 1994.
Mill, John Stuart. *A System of Logic*. London: Longmans, 1949.
Mill, John Stuart. *On Liberty and Other Writings*, edited by Stefan Collini. Cambridge: Cambridge University Press, 1989.
Mill, John Stuart. *Utilitarianism*, edited by Roger Crisp. Oxford: Oxford University Press, 2002.
Miller, David. *Political Philosophy: A Very Short Introduction*. Oxford: Oxford University Press, 2003.
Morton, Adam. *Disasters and Dilemma: Strategies for Real-Life Decision Making*. Oxford: Basil Blackwell, 1991.
Mulhall, Stephen, and Adam Swift. *Liberals and Communitarians*, 2nd ed. Oxford: Blackwell, 1997.
Nagel, Thomas. 'War and Massacre'. *Philosophy & Public Affairs* 1 (1971): 145–165.
Nagel, Thomas. *Mortal Questions*. Cambridge: Cambridge University Press, 1979.
Nagel, Thomas. 'Moral Conflict and Political Legitimacy'. *Philosophy & Public Affairs* 16 (1987): 215–240.
Nagel, Thomas. 'Pluralism and Coherence'. In *The Legacy of Isaiah Berlin*, edited by Ronald Dworkin, Mark Lilla and Robert B. Silvers. New York: NYRB, 2001.
Neal, Patrick. 'Political Liberalism, Public Reason, and the Citizen of Faith'. In *Natural Law and Public Reason*, edited by Robert P. George and Christopher Wolfe. Washington, D.C.: Georgetown University Press, 2000.
Nord, Erik. 'The Trade-Off between Severity of Illness and Treatment Effect in Cost-Value Analysis of Health Care'. *Health Policy* 24 (1993): 227–238.
Nozick, Robert. *Anarchy, State, and Utopia*. New York: Basic Books, 1974.
Nozick, Robert. *Invariances: The Structure of the Objective World*. Cambridge, Mass.: Belknap Press of Harvard University Press, 2001.

Nussbaum, Martha. *The Fragility of Goodness: Luck and Ethics in Greek Tragedy and Philosophy*. Cambridge: Cambridge University Press, 2001.
Nussbaum, Martha. 'Political Objectivity'. *New Literary History* 32 (2001): 883–906.
Nussbaum, Martha. *Frontiers of Justice: Disability, Nationality, Species Membership*. Cambridge, Mass.: Belknap Press of Harvard University Press, 2006.
Parekh, Bhikhu. *Rethinking Multiculturalism: Cultural Diversity and Political Theory*. New York: Palgrave, 2000.
Parfit, Derek. *Reasons and Persons*. Oxford: Clarendon Press, 1984.
Parfit, Derek. 'Equality and Priority'. *Ratio* 10 (1997): 202–221.
Parfit, Derek. *On What Matters*. Oxford: Oxford University Press, 2011.
Parijs, Philippe van. 'Difference Principles'. In *The Cambridge Companion to Rawls*, edited by Samuel Freeman. Cambridge: Cambridge University Press, 2003.
Posner, Richard. *The Problems of Jurisprudence*. Cambridge, Mass.: Harvard University Press, 2000.
Posner, Richard. *The Problematics of Moral and Legal Theory*. Cambridge, Mass.: The Belknap Press of Harvard University Press, 2002.
Powers, Madison, and Ruth Faden. *Social Justice: The Moral Foundations of Public Health and Health Policy*. Oxford: Oxford University Press, 2006.
Quine, Willard Van Orman. *The Ways of Paradoxes and Other Essays*. Cambridge, Mass.: Harvard University Press, 1976.
Raphael, David Daiches. *Concepts of Justice*. Oxford: Oxford University Press, 2001.
Rawls, John. 'Social Unity and Primary Goods'. In *Utilitarianism and Beyond*, edited by Amartya Sen and Bernard Williams. Cambridge: Cambridge University Press, 1982.
Rawls, John. *Political Liberalism*. New York: Columbia University Press, 1996.
Rawls, John. *A Theory of Justice*, rev. ed. Cambridge, Mass.: Belknap Press of Harvard University Press, 1999.
Rawls, John. *Justice as Fairness: A Restatement*. Cambridge, Mass.: Belknap Press of Harvard University Press, 2001.
Raz, Joseph. *The Morality of Freedom*. Oxford: Oxford University Press, 1986.
Raz, Joseph. 'Incommensurability and Agency'. In *Incommensurability, Incomparability, and Practical Reason*, edited by Ruth Chang. Cambridge, Mass.: Harvard University Press, 1997.
Reidy, David. 'Rawls's Wide View of Public Reason: Not Wide Enough'. *Res Publica* 6 (2000): 49–72.
Richardson, Henry S. *Practical Reasoning about Final Ends*. Cambridge: Cambridge University Press, 1997.
Richardson, Henry S. 'Gradations of Researchers' Obligation to Provide Ancillary Care for HIV/AIDS in Developing Countries'. *American Journal of Public Health* 97 (2007): 1956–1961.
Robeyns, Ingrid. 'Ideal Theory in Theory and Practice'. *Social Theory and Practice* 34 (2008): 341–362.
Ross, William David. *The Right and the Good*. Oxford: Oxford University Press, 1930.
Sandel, Michael J. *Liberalism and the Limits of Justice*, 2nd ed. Cambridge: Cambridge University Press, 1998.

Scanlon, Thomas. 'Contractualism and Utilitarianism'. In *Utilitarianism and Beyond*, edited by Amartya Sen and Bernard Williams. Cambridge: Cambridge University Press, 1982.
Scanlon, Thomas. *What We Owe to Each Other*. Cambridge, Mass.: Belknap Press of Harvard University Press, 1998.
Sen, Amartya. *Inequality Re-examined*. Cambridge, Mass.: Harvard University Press, 1992.
Sen, Amartya. *On Ethics and Economics*. Oxford: Blackwell Publishers, 2003.
Sen, Amartya. 'Incompleteness and Reasoned Choice'. *Synthese* 140 (2004): 43–59.
Sen, Amartya. 'What Do We Want from a Theory of Justice'. *Journal of Philosophy* 103 (2006): 215–238.
Sen, Amartya. *The Idea of Justice*. London: Penguin Books, 2009.
Seung, T. K., and Daniel Bonevac. 'Plural Values and Indeterminate Rankings'. *Ethics* 102 (1992): 799–813.
Sidgwick, Henry. *The Methods of Ethics*. Indianapolis/Cambridge: Hackett Publishing Company, 1981.
Sinnott-Armstrong, Walter. 'Moral Dilemmas and Incomparability'. *American Philosophical Quarterly* 22 (1985): 321–329.
Smilansky, Saul. *Ten Moral Paradoxes*. Oxford: Blackwell Publishing, 2007.
Stemplowska, Zofia. 'What Is Ideal about Ideal Theory?' *Social Theory and Practice* 34 (2008): 319–340.
Stocker, Michael. *Plural and Conflicting Values*. Oxford: Oxford University Press, 1999.
Sunstein, Cass R. *Legal Reasoning and Political Conflict*. Oxford: Oxford University Press, 1996.
Sunstein, Cass R. 'Incommensurability and Kinds of Valuation: Some Applications in Law'. In *Incommensurability, Incomparability, and Practical Reason*, edited by Ruth Chang. Cambridge, Mass.: Harvard University Press, 1997.
Sunstein, Cass R. and David Schkade, Lisa M. Ellman, Andres Sawicki. *Are Judges Political? An Empirical Analysis of the Federal Judiciary*. Washington, D.C.: Brookings Institution Press, 2006.
Swift, Adam. 'The Value of Philosophy in Nonideal Circumstances'. *Social Theory and Practice* 34 (2008): 363–387.
Wacks, Raymond. *Philosophy of Law: A Very Short Introduction*. Oxford: Oxford University Press, 2006.
Waldron, Jeremy. *The Harm in Hate Speech*. Cambridge, Mass.: Harvard University Press, 2012.
Walzer, Michael. 'Political Action: The Problem of Dirty Hands'. *Philosophy & Public Affairs* 2 (1973): 160–180.
Williams, Bernard. *Moral Luck*. Cambridge: Cambridge University Press, 1981.
Williams, Bernard. *Problems of the Self*. Cambridge: Cambridge University Press, 1999.
Wolff, R. P. *In Defense of Anarchism*. Berkeley: University of California Press, 1998.
Wolterstorff, Nicholas. 'The Role of Religion in Decision and Discussion of Political issues'. In *Religion in the Public Square: The Place of Religious Convictions in Political Debate*, edited by Robert Audi and Nicholas Wolterstorff. Lanham, MD: Rowman and Littlefield, 1997.

Index

ambivalence: in addition to indifference and preference, 54
amount/importance distinction, 33–35
Anderson, Elizabeth: about incommensurability and rational choice, 34; defending Rawls against the author's criticism, 101, 114, 116, 123, 141, 183
Aristotle: his statement 'without commensurability, no equality', 22; about logical contradiction, 191, 199
Arrow, Kenneth: his impossibility theorem, 99, 161
autonomous choice: incomplete comparability as condition of, 64, 122–23, 211–16

basic liberties. *See* liberty
Berlin, Isaiah: about conflicting liberties, 137–39; about positive and negative liberty, 136–38, 223–24
bidirectionality: as one of the conditions of incomplete comparability, 12
Brock, Dan: about a wide range of indeterminateness, 23, 28n21, 170
Broome, John: about lexical priority, 87n43; his standard-configuration, 17, 21

burdens of judgement: as sources of reasonable disagreement, 109–10
Buridan's ass, 55

Calabresi, Guido, 172
chaining argument: for the existence of 'parity', 44–47, 52
Chang, Ruth: about a fourth value relation (*see* parity)
Cohen, G. A.: his belief that justice may conflict with other human interests, 72; his criticism on my idea of incomplete comparability, 32–35; his criticism on my thesis that integrity and legitimacy may irresolvably conflict, 178, 190; about relative weight assignment to incommensurable values, 57
comparability: as condition of rational justification of the choice, 60–61
comparison: as a bipartite procedure, 16; nominal/notable, 45–51; of rival theories of justice, 90, 93; standards in justice, 150–57
Condorcet, 137, 161
consensus, 99–100, 109–13, 140–42

235

236

Index

Daniels, Norman, 24, 83, 170–71
difference principle: John Rawls, 98–99, 102–4, 106–7, 220; Ruth Chang, 44–52, 220
differend. *See* Lyotard, François
Dworkin, Ronald: his belief in a single correct answer to every legal question, 78, 205; his doubt about conflicting values, 80–81; his rejection of indeterminateness, 78, 187, 204–5; about weighing principles, 73

Eberle, Christopher, 131, 180, 193n4
efficiency: versus fairness/justice, 3, 21–23, 57, 151, 153, 163, 167–71
equivalence relation, 23–24, 142–43, 221
ethical deficit, 60, 71, 73, 84–85, 221

failure of transitivity, 22, 221
free speech, 104–6, 198–208
free will, 213–17

Gaus, Gerald, 186–88
George, Robert, P., 114, 118, 180
Gray, John: about conflicting liberties, 139
Greenawalt, Kent, 184, 195nn43–44
Griffin, James, 73

Habermas, Jürgen, 115, 124
Hampshire, Stuart, 91
Hart, H. L. A., 72, 106, 143, 181, 185–86
Heraclitus, 72, 74, 91

impartial reasons, 41, 42, 159
impartial spectator, 163
imprecise equality, 11, 17, 23, 25, 37, 221, 223; as distinct from incomplete comparability, 37–38
improvement argument/phenomenon: large, 17–19, 23, 39–42, 205, 221, 223; small, 24, 38, 39–41, 221, 225
incommensurability, 7–8, 221–22; as distinct from incomparability, 7–9; as distinct from incompatibility, 136–37; as necessary but not sufficient condition of incomplete comparability, 12
incomparability. *See* incomplete comparability
incompatibility: as distinct from incommensurability, 136–37
incomplete comparability: conditions of, 11–12; as condition of autonomous choice, 64, 122–23, 211–16; as distinct from incommensurability, 7–9; versus imprecise equality and parity, 37–38, 43–52, 60–66, 223; instead of 'incomparability', 20
incomplete ordering/ranking, 15, 53, 56, 222; and majority rule, 84, 99, 162
inconclusiveness: as distinct from indeterminateness, 185–89, 222
indeterminateness: as distinct from inconclusiveness, 185–89, 222; internal and external indeterminateness of Rawls's theory of justice, 101–43; range of, 19–20, 40–41, 77–78
indifference: as distinct from ambivalence, 54–56, 225
indifference curve, 54
insignificant amount fallacy, 32, 41, 48–49, 223
integrity, 117, 127, 132, 175–79; versus legitimacy, 175–79; moral, 179

justice: aspects of, 72, 91, 97, 143–44, 160, 171, 197–99, 204; comparative, 155–56; conceptions of, 110–11; versus efficiency, 21–23, 151–53, 163–71; is conflict, 72, 204; partial, 197–209; theories of, 2, 89–94
justification of the choice: incomplete rational, 58–60

Kamm, Frances: on weighing values, 56–57, 169
Kane, Robert: on free choice, 213–15

Index

Kant, Immanuel, 100, 212, 215–16
Kuhn, Thomas, 93

large improvement phenomenon. *See* improvement argument/phenomenon
legitimacy: liberal principle of, 112, 124, 126, 135, 192; versus integrity, 175–80
lexical priority, 26–27
liberty: basic, 98–107; negative, 125, 136–38, 180, 223; positive, 124, 136–38, 180–81, 224
Lyotard, François: his 'differend' in contrast to litigation, 187, 207

MacIntyre, Alasdair, 90, 113
majority rule: and incomplete ranking, 84, 99, 162
Mill, John Stuart: on conflicting aspects of justice, 72–73, 79–80, 90–92, 157, 201
Miller, David, 151

Nagel, Thomas, 60, 81, 124
Neal, Patrick: his criticism on Rawls's original position, 132–34
negative liberty. *See* liberty
neutrality, 113–14, 200–202
nominal-notable comparison/test. *See* comparison
Nord, Erik: about equity versus efficiency in health, 169–71
Nozick, Robert, 74, 93–94
Nussbaum, Martha, 92, 95n.13, 108, 109, 143

original position, 114–17, 181–83
overlapping consensus. *See* consensus

paradigm shift, 197, 208
paradox: of absent equivalence, 24–25; moral, 175–80, 190–92, 208; for voters, 99, 161, 163
Parekh, Bhikhu: on free speech, 105, 202, 206; his two secular theses, 184; on integrity, 131, 179, 185; on weighing incommensurable values, 188
Parfit, Derek : on imprecise equality, 11, 23, 38, 41, 42
Parijs, Philippe van, 108
parity, 43–52, 60–66, 220, 223
partial ordering. *See* incomplete ordering/ranking
Plato, 91–92, 137
pluralism: fact of reasonable, 114, 116–19, 129–30, 141, 184; moral, 216; value, 211–12, 216–17
positive liberty. *See* liberty
preference: as distinct from ambivalence, 54–56, 219, 225
principle of alternative possibilities: and freedom of choice, 213–14
public justification, 124–26, 176–77, 188–89; public/private split as condition of (*see* public/private split)
public/private split: as condition of public justification, 125–28, 135–36; in distinction to separation of 'Church and State', 136, 183–84
public reason: incompleteness of, 119–23, 135, 182; publicly accessible reasons, 115, 122–23; scope (narrow and wide version) of, 114–16, 118–19, 139

QALY (quality adjusted life years), 21–22, 168, 224

ranking: cardinal versus ordinal, 8, 219, 223; incomplete, 15–16, 94–95, 141–43; of justice, 83–84, 99–101, 120–21, 141–43, 161–62
rationality: rational justification of the choice, 58–60; rationally eligibility/permissibility, 33–34, 58–59, 61–64, 225; rationally requirement, 33–34, 61–62, 225; rational undecidability, 55–60, 225; rational under-determination of the choice, 24, 50–51, 53, 172

Rawls, John: criticism on his restricted public reason, 114–26; his liberal principle of legitimacy, 124; about incommensurability, 97; indeterminateness (internal and external) of his theory (*see* indeterminateness)

Raz, Joseph, 4n2, 11, 22, 24, 44, 45, 61, 62, 64, 65

reasonable disagreement, 109–13, 129–30; sources of (*see* burdens of judgement)

reasonableness, 128–35

reasonable pluralism, 117–19

reciprocity, 102, 114–17, 121, 131

Regan, Donald, 23

rough equality. *See* imprecise equality

Sandel, Michael, 114, 118, 119, 121, 180

Scanlon, T. M., 124

Sen, Amartya: his denial of significant problems of incommensurability, 9, 57; his denial of the need of a theory of perfect justice, 149–64; his view on incomplete/partial justification of public decisions, 207; his view on incomplete rankings of justice, 83–84, 113, 143, 188, 207

separation of 'Church and State', 126–27, 136, 183–84, 224; in distinction to public/private split, 136, 183–84, 224

Sidgwick, Henry: on conflicting aspects of justice, 41–42, 72–73, 80, 92

significant bidirectionality. *See* bidirectionality

small improvement phenomenon. *See* improvement argument/phenomenon

Sunstein, Cass, 87n27

Swift, Adam: defending Rawls against the author's criticism, 101, 185

symmetry: as one of the conditions of incomplete comparability, 12

theorem: Arrow's, 99, 161

vagueness, 11, 19, 38–42, 65, 222

value pluralism. *See* pluralism

value pump, 62–65

veil of ignorance, 112–15, 119–21

voters' paradox. *See* paradox

Wilders, Geert, 197–99

Wolfe, Christophor, 114, 118, 180

About the Author

Martijn Boot is an Assistant Professor at University College Groningen, the University of Groningen, the Netherlands.